THE HEROIN TRIANGLE

THE HEROIN TRIANGLE

MARSEILLES...
MONTREAL...
NEW YORK

THE CONFESSIONS OF MICHEL MASTANTUONO
AS TOLD TO MICHEL AUGER

Translated by Gaynor Fitzpatrick

 METHUEN

Toronto   New York   London   Sydney

Copyright © 1976 Les Éditions de l'Homme Ltée.
English translation copyright © 1978 Methuen, Inc.

Originally published in French under the title *Mastantuono*

Translation of Mastantuono.
ISBN 0-458-92520-9

Mastantuono, Michel, 1943-

1. Mastantuono, Michel, 1943-   2. Narcotics,
Control of — Biography. I. Auger, Michel, 1944-
II. Title.

HV5805.M37A3513 364.1'57'0924[B]   C77-001773-8

Methuen, Inc.
777 Third Avenue
New York, NY 10017

Methuen Publications
2330 Midland Avenue
Agincourt, Ontario
M1S 1P7

Printed and bound
in the United States of America

1 2 3 4 5   1   0   9   8

6/79
9/03

CONTENTS

INTRODUCTION

The seizing of large quantities of heroin by police always attracts a lot of publicity because of the enormous resale value of the drugs involved. But rarely does an event of this type go beyond the reporting of the story, and if it does, we are usually treated to revelations which will allow us to find out the "real" truth behind the inner workings of a supposedly sophisticated network of well-organized criminals.

Michel Mastantuono, the young Marseilles-born barman, was closely associated with the most recent French connection. He was caught in Montreal and then convicted in New York for his part in smuggling to the United States 200 kilos of pure, white heroin. But he was just a small part in a big machine which supplied more than a ton of drugs to U.S. addicts. The quantity he personally smuggled was just enough to satisfy the junkies of New York for almost an entire year. He finally decided to tell his story to the U.S. court and thereby help to dismantle an organization of almost one hundred people — Americans, Frenchmen and a few Canadians.

He was not the only one to talk but his testimony was the key to the apprehension and convictions of many "Mr. Bigs" in the network. There is still a price on his head, but he is now a free man living quietly in a small American town.

I first met Michel Mastantuono after I had written a series of articles on drug trafficking which involved a group of Quebec artists and entertainers. Michel was still in jail at the time. When I talked to him he struck me as frank, and unlike other convicts who just wanted to "explain" to reporters their involvement in order to appear in better light, he asked me to help him write this book.

Soon after his release we began taping lengthy interviews. He told me everything and I, like many other people who had believed that drug trafficking was a job done by sophisticated professionals, became more and more disenchanted. I soon discovered that the actual "French Connection" worked quite differently from the fictional accounts we had seen on the screen or had read about in books. In reality, it was, a surprisingly disorganized group of people who had access to the laboratory in southern France where raw opium was transformed into 96% pure heroin. The French Mafia-type organization was behind everything, but the leaders used "stringers" like Mastantuono to carry out the riskiest part of the smuggling operations. Sometimes, it was the least important cog in the wheels of the big machine that broke down and then the whole thing would collapse. That was what happened after Michel Mastantuono was picked up in Montreal.

But even if all heroin supplies in the Marseilles-Montreal-New York triangle had been annihilated after the arrests of Mastantuono and his bosses, it does not mean that the ring will never start again. In fact, police in France, Canada and the United States suspect and have strong indications that a similar triangle will soon be in operation again. Detectives met recently in Montreal, and a new conference has been scheduled for Spring, 1978 in Paris to try to prevent the resurrection of that trade.

Who knows, there may be another Mastantuono at work right now. As one RCMP drug specialist told me recently, "There will always be some drug trafficking in the France-Canada-U.S. triangle because too much money is at stake. Despite the arrests that have been made, a lot of people who unwittingly get into this business, don't think they are taking great risks."

I would like to leave it to the reader to decide what really prompted Michel Mastantuono to take these great risks and play for such high stakes. I know opinions will vary but I feel that before you pass judgment, his story is well worth listening to for he has a lot to say.

Michel Auger
January, 1978

1/
THE QUARTIER DU PANIER

Marseilles, including its port and the quartier du Panier, has always been a major smuggling center. I was born there on July 2, 1943, the youngest in a family of four boys and four girls. I don't remember the war. My earliest memory, when I was three, was of my father dying of cancer. My mother had taken me to see him at the Municipal Hospital, where he lay near death, no longer able to eat and hardly able to speak. On the night table were some hard biscuits we called *cagouesses* in the south. He handed them to me, I looked at him and ate them. That is the last picture I have of my father. Three months later he was dead.

We lived in a house in the country, outside Marseilles, where I spent my days running through the fields with my brother Felix, who was two years older than I, and Simone, the youngest of my sisters. My mother had a job in town, ten kilometers from home, cleaning offices. She didn't earn much money and had to struggle to make ends meet. Some of my brothers and sisters also went to work, and every evening around seven Felix, my little sister Simone and I waited for everyone to return home. Looking through the one window that faced the street we could see the bus coming. My mother, carrying groceries for supper, was always the last to arrive. It was a happy existence; everyone spoiled me — not only because I had never known my father, but because I was the baby — they called me Michou. I suppose we were a close-knit and wonderful family although, like most children, I didn't really know why.

When I was seven years old one of my sisters said it was time for me to go to school. I made a terrible scene as I was being registered. I thought I would be locked up, and never see my family again. I couldn't bear the idea of being separated from them, especially from Simone. Why couldn't I just go on playing, as before?

At first I was a good student, but there was trouble later on when we had to move away from the country. My mother found the daily trip into town too tiring. Besides, she could not get used to the idea of leaving Felix, Simone and me alone so much. She was away all day, returning only at nine in the evening and leaving again at six o'clock in the morning. Well, we were alone, and absolutely refused to eat in the school cafeteria. It wasn't because the food was bad, but we were used to eating together as a family, and would rather walk the three kilometers to home. It was then that my sixteen-year-old sister also wanted to go to work to earn her own living. One of my brothers was finishing school and had one year to go before getting his *Certificat d'Etudes**.

So my mother looked for an apartment in Marseilles and finally found one, in the downtown area of the city, with two rooms and a kitchen. The four of us moved in, and my mother enrolled me at montee Saint-Esprit School in the center of the quartier du Panier. The change upset me. The district was overrun by thieves and I couldn't move about freely because my sisters thought I would be beaten up. The school stifled me and I started hanging around the streets with young hoods who stole. Having more freedom than I, they knew their way about town and the large stores. Me, I was just a peasant boy. I tried to keep up with them and often witnessed little things that weren't particularly honest. They would steal at Prisunic**, but although I went along, I was much too afraid to ever take anything myself.

That's how I began life in the city. I no longer applied myself to school work, which proved to be disastrous for me.

At that time, the Panier was a very small section of Marseilles, resembling a medina, the Arab quarters of North African towns, a maze of narrow, dirty streets which reeked of garlic and rosemary.

---

* Primary school graduating certificate.
** A low-price chain store.

During the war, the Germans had considered blowing it up. All the cellars of the houses were connected and it was possible to enter one underground passage and emerge ten or twenty passages further along. Pursuit was almost impossible. It was in the Panier that I met Jean-Pierre Kella, Fiocconi and others who later got mixed up with trafficking. They were my companions, my little school friends.

Marseilles' great attraction, however, was the sea. We used to swim in the coves of the old port among the boats that were tied up in front of the houses. The water was thick with grime and oil, but we didn't care. We spent all summer long there, and I was happy enjoying the sun and the friendly, sociable atmosphere.

When they left school, all my friends became young hooligans. They had money, began to dress well, and spent their evenings at night clubs. I felt I was not as sophisticated as they were and even developed a few complexes about it. Theirs was a lifestyle I was not accustomed to.

At fourteen then, I too had enough of school and dreamt about going to work to earn my own living. I became a plumber, my first job, earning seven thousand old francs, about fourteen dollars a week. My mother let me keep all of my pay and even gave me more money when things were going well. Yet, I didn't keep up with the others, as deep down, I suppose, I didn't really want to. I watched them and admired them, but they also frightened me. Seeing some of them end up in jail or from time to time in correctional institutions scared me. All around us, and especially in the Panier, there wasn't a family where either a brother, a cousin, or a father hadn't become a crook or a gangster; everyone knew someone who was either in prison or had been killed settling a score.

Between fourteen and eighteen I did what everyone else does in Marseilles: I worked on the docks unloading cargo vessels. As I had developed more than a passing fancy for everything to do with shipping, I got involved with smuggling cigarettes and liquor, and stealing crates of tomatoes that came from Algeria, and clumps of bananas brought in from Africa. It wasn't just for the hell of it; we knew it was illegal, but we felt since we were stealing from a company rather than from an individual, it was O.K. It was just petty larceny, not to be taken seriously.

Unloading boats was heavy physical labor, and I was making up to twenty dollars a day. Once I remember working on a boat which had a cargo of sugar on board. Each sack weighed close to 46 kilos and I weighed only about 70 kilos. I perspired heavily and the sugar stuck to my skin. Albert, the supervisor, was a friend of mine who knew I was a hard worker who could look after myself. If a boat was due during the night he would often ask me to stay around. We earned double pay at night, and it was easier to do a bit of trafficking when it was dark. We would finish at five o'clock in the morning, before the Customs' people arrived and during that time we could almost come and go as we pleased. I usually accepted his offer because I could earn extra pocket money, some of which I saved. I bought new clothes and tried to live like the others.

I quit the docks, drove a truck for a time, took a few other jobs, and finally went into the restaurant business with my brother Felix. We took over the management of a small place we called Chez Michel et Felix, located in the rue de la Prison, which seems ironic when I look back. One of my cousins, a wine distributor, had offered me a job driving a van and I arranged with my brother and sister, who helped in the restaurant, that I would work there from 11:30 A.M. to 1:00 or 1:30 P.M., then drive for my cousin till six o'clock in the evening, when I would return to the restaurant for supper. In this way I managed to have two jobs.

I was eighteen years old and everything was going O.K. for me as I was well-paid and lived at home with my mother. That was when I met my first wife. We began to go out together and a romance developed. Her parents were against our marriage because I came from the Panier and had an Italian name. Although my fiancée became pregnant her parents still wouldn't consent; they arranged for an abortion and sent her away to Strasbourg.

But we were unhappy living apart and when she decided to come back to Marseilles she told her parents that she wanted to live with me. We were both very young, both eighteen, when she got pregnant again and we got married straight away. My family helped pay for our wedding and even bought my wife's wedding dress; her parents didn't even attend the ceremony. We moved in with my mother.

I decided to return to the docks and began earning a lot of money, and meeting people. They were crooks and gangsters, highly respected in the Milieu, the underworld community. They made deals, got involved with robberies, and had girls working for them. In fact, several of them had risen high in the ranks of Marseilles "society." They spent their time in and out of jail. I didn't want to have anything to do with that kind of life. Although I envied them their money, fear prevented me from doing what they did. So I worked hard, and by the end of the first year my wife and I got established and thought about buying a house.

One day I unwittingly got mixed up in some big business. People, whose names I won't mention, told me that a boat was due that very evening, but that the job was a bit awkward to handle because it had to be done that night. It involved a shipment of pants from the Middle East. There would be problem — a Customs' officer was in on the deal.

I said "O.K. I'll take my cousin's van and come along." They offered me two thousand francs — about four hundred dollars — which I thought was a lot of money, underestimating the risk of that type of job. In the dark we tied up the Customs' launch alongside a white boat. Out of the portholes, from the half deck, people were throwing huge sacks into the launch, about twenty or thirty of them, close to a ton of merchandise. When the loading was completed, we returned to port and transferred the lot to the van. A Customs' officer climbed in next to the driver's seat and we drove off to deliver the jeans, at least that's what I believed they were. When we got to the bridge leading into town, the port exit was blocked by a barrier. The Customs' man beside me said, "Rush it." I got very frightened.

"We're only carrying jeans — why the Customs' barrier? What's going on?" Instinctively I had slowed down, but as the Customs' men at the gate approached us I stepped on the gas. They followed, firing at us and riddled the van with bullets. Then the Customs' officer beside me told me to slow down so he could jump off. "Stay put, trust me — I'm a good driver," I told him. "We'll give them the slip. Hang on!"

They chased us all over the port of Marseilles. Finally — and very abruptly — the manhunt ended. Throughout the chase, a Renault 4L had tried to overtake us. Meanwhile, we were frantically throwing bags out of the side door of the van. Whenever our pursuers tried to pass us on the left I would squeeze them against the wall. This maneuver so unnerved them that they gave up. I parked the van on a side street and headed for home.

My mother was very upset when I told her, if anyone later inquired, that I'd been home since midnight. "But Michel . . ."

"Mother, trust me — you know nothing — please do as I say."

And to my wife: "We went to the movies. O.K.?"

The Customs' officers showed up at our door an hour later. They had located the van and traced my cousin through the license plates. He told them he had lent me the van. When they asked me to come along with them to police headquarters, I protested. What did they want with me?

"We have a few questions for you."

In France you have no choice. I went with them.

First they hit me. I was terrified and confused. When they accused me of trafficking I denied everything.

"Where were you last night?"

"Last night? At the movies."

"What did you see?" I told them about a film my wife and I had seen. "But I don't understand! What do you want with me?"

"What did you do after the movies?"

"I went home to bed."

They continued to rough me up, hoping to make me talk.

"This is stupid." I told them. "My van was stolen and you bring me here and beat me up. That's crazy!" For saying "crazy," they hit me again.

Then I was taken into another room. In a corner were the sacks we had tossed out of the van. Suddenly I realized that they contained poppy heads and opium. That was when I got really scared, but told myself if I cracked they would give me five years. It *was* only five years in those days. I continued to deny everything and repeated over and over again, "It wasn't me; it wasn't me." They must have finally realized they didn't have a case and handed me a report to read. Glancing through it I understood why the police had stopped chasing us. They had run out of ammunition, after emptying four revolvers without ever puncturing the tires of the van! A little later my family started to worry about me and tried to get in touch with some lawyers. I was released because everything tied in: I had gone to the movies with my wife, my alibi was tight, and they couldn't find anything wrong with it. But for months and months after that they pestered me with questions.

Subsequently I learned that they had taken about two tons of opium from the van. When I met the Customs' man who had suggested the whole thing, I didn't pass up the opportunity to tell him off. "You bastard, first you don't tell me what I'm carrying — I thought it was jeans — and then it turns out there were drugs in the bags. And besides, I hardly made anything on the deal."

"Don't worry, Michel," he said, "we'll take care of you. You did O.K. Here's your share." With that he handed me about twenty thousand francs.

After that scare I didn't want to have anything more to do with the port and smuggling. I left to do my military service at Carpianne, which is approximately midway between Marseilles and Cassis. About thirty of my boyhood chums from Marseilles were also stationed there.

On my first leave I had an argument with my wife. We agreed that we had married too young, that we didn't really love each other and had only been attracted to each other physically. We decided that she should go and live with her parents while I was in the service. I became a motorcyclist in the military police and was posted to Germany and Algeria and sometimes even escorted convoys into the port of Marseilles. When I got out of the army I was twenty years old and didn't feel like going back to live with my wife. When we got divorced she was given custody of our child, and I went back to work in the family restaurant.

I was crazy about cars and started collecting some. I went to nightclubs and ran after girls. But then I fell in love with Monique, who came from Corsica, and got married. We bought a restaurant in La Ciotat with the family's help but then agreed to give it up and return to Marseilles. I went back into the family business with my brother and sister.

However, in the meantime I had got to know all of the Cannes underworld and again was bored with family life. In the early sixties Marseilles was known as "little Chicago," a violent town with at least one murder a day. It was ruled by the powerful Guérini family. Mémé Guérini is in prison now, but he and his brother and all the gangsters who supported him reigned in the city for almost thirty years. Throughout the south of France they had political and police contacts, rigged the elections, and during the war had worked with the Resistance. After the war they controlled the Secret Service. The Guérini legend still lives on in Marseilles. Gangland slayings became almost standard practice — a sort of local custom. One saw so many that no one even paused at the sound of gunfire. I well remember the first one I witnessed. I was coming out of our restaurant after a long conversation with one of my partners about a cigarette deal. We were walking quietly through the Panier when I suddenly drew away from my friend, instinctively. I heard the screech of car brakes and saw a hail of machine gun bullets. My friend was hit and collapsed in a stairway. I felt myself all over to make sure I hadn't been hit too. By the time I realized that he had been murdered, the car had sped away. The sight of him lying in a pool of blood petrified me. People anxiously gathered around us. The police arrived almost immediately, and it was obvious that they would take me away for questioning. I told them I had seen absolutely nothing — it would have been suicidal to tell the truth. They interrogated me all night and even tortured me. At dawn, when they found out I wouldn't talk, they let me go.

I remember another incident during the time I managed a small bar in Marseilles. One morning shortly after opening up, Jules Matti, the first customer, came in. While he was drinking his coffee and we were talking, a car suddenly stopped outside. This character got out, and walked into the bar carrying a revolver. I was panic-stricken and asked "What's happening? I haven't done anything." I thought he had come for me, but he pointed the gun at Jules and shot him dead on the spot. I just stood there, waiting my turn — I was a witness. But my reputation, my past if you like, were sufficient proof that I wouldn't talk. He told me to keep my mouth shut, I'd seen nothing. The police closed the bar for six months and during the investigation they concluded that I had been forced to keep quiet because I had contradicted myself, one time telling them that I was at the coffee machine during the shooting and another time that I was serving. They decided I must have seen the person who had fired the shots because of the mirrors on the wall. So they took me to the police station, and then to Marseilles Jail where I was roughed up. When they saw I wouldn't talk they let me go. As I had lost my livelihood, I decided to go for big stakes and went to see the man who had shot Matti.

"Listen," I told him, "what the hell goes on! I don't give a damn about Matti — he's dead now and no one can do anything for him, but you could have waited until he had left the bar before hitting him. You've really screwed me."

"I know, Michel," he said, "but we'd been trying to get him for days. We knew he had coffee in your bar nearly every morning. We had no choice."

"O.K., but the police have closed me down and I'm losing three hundred francs, (about sixty dollars) a day."

"Don't worry — we'll take care of you," he assured me.

He called back the same evening to tell me everything had been arranged. I was paid the four thousand francs — about eight hundred dollars — which I had advanced for the six months' franchise on the bar. Subsequently he gave me another six thousand dollars, and told me to take a holiday.

In the Panier killings were even more prevalent than elsewhere and we had a blasé attitude toward the underworld. One day, when I was on my way out, I realized that the quartier was surrounded by the army, or rather the CRS, the anti-riot squad, which had been tipped off that Salvati, one of the most notorious Marseilles gangsters, was in the area. They were trying to catch him, but the local population always sided with the crooks so they were unsuccessful.

I remember a TV program where the camera was concealed on one of the avenues of Paris, possibly on the Champs-Elysées, shooting a man running down the street wearing a pair of handcuffs. He stopped several passers-by, pointing to the keys in his pocket and asked them to unlock his handcuffs. You could see the surprise and shock on people's faces as they scattered in all directions. When a similar film was made in Marseilles everyone in the street collaborated with the criminal, asked him for the keys, and unlocked his handcuffs. This will give you an idea of the social climate of a city, which has always been a major narcotics trading center, especially in the early sixties.

Because Marseilles was a large port city it had a sizeable colony of Arabs who lived in a kind of ghetto. The citizens of Marseilles were very racist and if an Arab tried to move to another district his children couldn't attend school without getting beaten up and the grocer refused to sell to him. They got the message fast and went back to their own neighborhood. Nor were they allowed to be pimps or smugglers. When I saw the movie *The French Connection* I was surprised to find the action taking place in laboratories inside the Arab quarter. That was unthinkable and pure fiction.

I had known the people reputed to be traffickers for a long time. Yet I was so naive I never knew exactly what heroin was or how it was processed. I would read in the newspapers that a laboratory had been discovered near Aix-en-Provence or near Marseilles and that people had been arrested, etcetera, but I wondered what exactly they had been arrested for.

I continued making the rounds of nightclubs and slowly made my way into the underworld. But I soon ran into serious problems with some of the hoodlums, who were also my pals. The proprietress of one of the clubs was a friend of mine. One day I noticed a girl talking to her. They were whispering and I could tell it had something to do with me. The lady introduced us and the girl started playing up to me. I acted cool until the proprietress leaned over and breathed softly in my ear, "There's a lot in this for you, Michel." I looked at the girl a little more seriously and turned on the charm. We started going out together and soon fell in love. Every evening we spent together and, inevitably, she became my mistress. But then things started to go wrong.

There was a crook in Marseilles by the name of "Petit Jo," who, together with a dozen of his friends had formed a syndicate which organized burglaries and holdups and were involved in prostitution. One day the notorious Petit Jo, whose real name I never knew, approached me on the way to the club.

"Michel," he said, "that girl you are going out with works for me. Best for your health if you drop her."

I was astonished. "She never told me that she worked for you," I said. "She meets me, we go to bed, and then she leaves, that's all. We see each other for a few hours and then I go home — remember, I'm a married man."

Evidently, I did't sound convincing. As he was leaving he mumbled to himself that we would "sort things out."

The next day I was walking along the waterfront when a car pulled up beside me. It was Petit Jo with four of his cronies.

"Get in, Michel."

"Don't be crazy. There's no way I'm getting into your car." Luckily for me there were several people hanging about who knew me — they couldn't kill me in front of witnesses.

"O.K. my friend, it's up to you, but we'll be seeing each other." With that they drove off and I knew I was in a fix. I phoned the girl to ask her about Petit Jo.

"I told him that I loved you and was ready to work for you," she said.

"Don't you realize that I'm a married man and he's trying to kill me?" I shouted.

"Oh, Michel, if he kills you, I'll kill myself too! Please be careful — something terrible could happen."

That evening I phoned a friend who suggested I go to see Petit Jo and try to reason with him. If he refused to listen, I had no choice but to get him first. I borrowed a gun from a friend, and he volunteered to come with me. We drove to the Bowling Club in the rue Venture, where I knew I would find Petit Jo. He was sitting in an armchair when I walked in. I pointed the revolver at him, and said, "Come with me, Jo." He followed me outside and looked scared when I made him get into my car. Frankly I didn't have the guts to kill him, but tried to make him understand that although I wasn't in love with the girl, she loved me, and wanted to stay with me. "It's either you or me," I said.

He panicked and screamed, "You can keep her, Michel!"

"What? Keep her, with you shadowing me all the time?"

"O.K. Michel, let's shake hands and be friends." He really believed I intended to kill him.

Because of this incident a whole legend grew up around me. I, Michel Mastantuono, had scared Petit Jo.

I told the girl the case was closed; there was no need to worry about Petit Jo. She could carry on as usual if she needed the money. That's how I became a pimp, and since I knew other girls I ended up with two, and then three of them working for me.

At that time I was also quite a violent guy and often got into fights. People would be on their guard when they saw me coming. I had the reputation of being dangerous and always ready for a fight, especially over women.

When you went dancing at a nightclub in Marseilles, a girl who refused you was not allowed to dance with anyone else. The guy she had rejected would say, "You turned me down. You gave me the brush-off, who do you think I am?" and he would force her to sit down with him again. Once at the Spoutnik Club I remember dancing with a girl who had just turned down another guy because, she said I was "cuter" than he was. I told her to stay with me and we'd see what would happen. The boy came up to us as we were dancing, separated us and hit the girl. Then he stepped back to punch me but he was out of luck; I got him first. That was enough to start a free-for-all.

I sometimes went to Paris and during one of my visits I got mixed up with something which convinced me to give up this line of business. A friend of mine had taken a girl who had been working for someone who then swore to kill him. I was sitting in a Paris bar one afternoon when I heard gunfire; I got hit in the arm, the girl who was with me was wounded in the leg, my friend was killed, and some innocent bystanders also suffered injuries. The police arrived and took me to the hospital to have my wound dressed, and then to the police station where I was roughed up so much that I had to go back to the hospital for a week. They had beaten me all night long, I had to stand up the whole time, and then they had hit me again and bashed in my teeth. Police officers in each corner of the room had bounced me back and forth like a punch ball. They had almost killed me, but had to let me go in the morning because they couldn't pin a thing on me.

I didn't particularly like Paris. I felt embarrassed like most Marseillais feel when they get there. As soon as Parisians hear our distinctive Marseilles accent they immediately think we are bandits, before they find out anything about us. Also, I had been involved with the police each time I had visited Paris. As my identity card described me as a waiter, living at 1 Montée des Accoudes, Marseilles, I was a suspect because of the reputation of my Panier address. Parisian girls, on the other hand, liked me and my accent, which gave me a chance to have lots of mistresses. I was a likeable enough fellow who easily got involved with women, letting them dominate me and make me do stupid things.

When I arrived home from Paris my family was frightened. I explained to my wife that I was through living this way and that we should make a new start. I had a hard time trying to work again quietly in the restaurant. Quietly! That's a joke, seeing that what I was doing did not bring me much money.

I was twenty-two when a friend offered me a job in the market unloading vegetable crates and arranging them for sale in the stalls. This was one way I could supplement my income. For six or seven months I again worked in the restaurant during the day and unloaded vegetables, sometimes until three in the morning or even longer, at night. It was hard labor. Some of my other friends offered me a different kind of work. When they had a job to do they asked me to come along, mostly because I had the reputation of being a good driver. They would tell me that I could earn more with them in one hour than I could with the other jobs in a whole year. Some of these offers were very tempting, but I turned them down.

On the other hand, things were going badly with my second wife. She got fed up and I convinced myself that although I had tried to earn an honest living, I was still in a mess. I had kept my nose clean for more than a year avoiding any contacts with the underworld. But they were always after me, pestering me to do small jobs for them. It didn't do any good to tell them that there was nothing doing and that I wasn't interested. At that time, the big names in the Marseilles underworld were Mémé Guérini, Robert Lenoir, Tani Zampa and Petit Jo. He and all my other childhood friends had become expert thieves. But I preferred to "live on dry bread" rather than end up behind bars. I knew that with my connections and talents I could have risen to great heights in the underworld. In many ways I was more capable than these guys. I wasn't extravagant, put money aside, and didn't try to cheat people. I always had steady work and kept my promises.

I began to read a lot, particularly books on astrology. I wanted to learn things because I felt handicapped, not because I lacked brains — I was alert, quick and had a good memory — but because I hardly knew how to write; everything was in my head. For example, at the restaurant, I would serve about sixty people, without ever writing anything down. Whenever a customer would ask me for the bill I would show him the menu with the prices, and say, "You had three steaks — that's fifteen francs." I wouldn't write the word "steaks," just the price of whatever had been ordered. If people wanted a bill I would call my sister and ask her to write it out for me. Our customers were fascinated. I usually told them when they asked me how I did it, "Oh, it's just practice."

Our restaurant, which was located in an old stable, had been built in Napoleonic times; Napoleon himself had slept in the rooms upstairs. The building had been declared a historic site and although we had rebuilt the entrance and restored the dilapidated interior, we weren't allowed to touch the windows or the front of the building. Our food was very good and we had a large clientele. The specialities of the house were pizza, spaghetti and filet mignon, as well as bouillabaisse, of course.

My life was beginning to bore me and I sensed, though not very clearly, that if I stayed in Marseilles, I would eventually get mixed up in some serious crime and risk ending up in jail. My family liked being there, although it was hard for them to earn a living. I didn't have the Marseilles mentality, as did my married brothers who, after a day's work, would sit in a bar with an aperitif, go home for supper, and then to bed. On Saturdays they would play a game of boules. Their lives seemed boring to me and I could see no future in Marseilles.

I was twenty-four years old when I suggested to my wife that we do something to change our lives completely. I had heard fantastic things about Canada, a young country, and told her I could go into the restaurant business and she could practice her hairdressing profession. At worst, she could become a waitress. We could forget the past and start afresh. But she was scared to leave Marseilles — Canada was too far away and she would miss her family. I agreed with her, but told her that if things went well we could have them come over to visit us once or twice a year. I was really anxious to get away from Marseilles; if I stayed I might get sucked back into the underworld. The French police were beginning to know me. Although I had never been convicted of a crime, I'd been arrested on several occasions. One policeman went so far as to tell me he had his eye on me — one mistake and he'd have me in the "freezer" for a long time. I'd been interrogated several times in connection with killings and I was fed up with being harangued. Also, I felt our families were smothering us.

At last Monique agreed to emigrate. I filled out all the forms, indicating that I was a plumber by profession, but knew the restaurant business. I had x-rays and blood tests taken, underwent a series of medical examinations and finally obtained my Canadian immigration visa.

My wife went through the same procedure, but backed out at the last minute. She just couldn't leave her family and, although she wouldn't talk about it, I knew she was frightened about us being alone in Canada. We had just come through a sad experience — our little son had lived only eight days. She kept asking me to wait — first for one week, and then for another month. Finally, I gave her an ultimatum: whatever she decided, I was buying my plane ticket.

Besides all the frustration caused by Monique's indecision, my family was also hassling me. I was unreasonable, I had a restaurant, a job, a normal family life, and that there was no reason for me to feel sorry for myself. What was the matter with me? I couldn't very well tell them they were a burden to me. A new life, a new start in a young country would be the answer. Although I had traveled a lot, had spent holidays in Italy, Spain and elsewhere in Europe, Canada fascinated me. I would go.

Marseilles had always struck me as a city completely different from others. During the riots in May, '68, Paris was shaken by waves of unrest, but Marseilles was hardly touched. Such disturbances didn't affect the power of Mayor Gaston Deferre and his sidekicks, who were well acquainted with the underworld. The elections continued to be fixed; gangsters often controlled the distribution of election placards and publicity posters and tried to intimidate Gaston Deferre's Communist opponents from appearing during the campaign. Marseilles became a battlefield. Every night you could hear the noise of machine-gun fire. At certain times people stayed indoors — too frightened to go out in the streets.

Yet, I still love Marseilles, its port, the Canebière, the chateau d'If, the scent of rosemary and thyme. It's a wonderful town which has everything to thrill the tourist. The people are friendly and full of life, exuberant and love to exaggerate, just as Pagnol, the great French dramatist has described them in his plays. Marseillais all think they are Napoleons, especially those who come from Corsica — they have to shine. But this doesn't detract from their other good qualities and their sunny dispositions. I still love them and am proud of them.

2/
THE QUIET IMMIGRANT

In Paris I boarded the plane that was to take me to Canada.

From the airport I had telephoned my mother to tell her that I was on my way to Montreal. During our conversation, I suddenly was gripped by fear at the thought of leaving her and my family behind, and hung up as soon as I heard the announcement, "Flight 031, now leaving for Montreal." Panic-stricken, I said to myself over and over again, I cannot go, I must return home. I had a one-way ticket and only two hundred dollars in my pocket. I didn't know a soul in Canada. Would people there understand me? Would I find a job?

I had absolutely no idea what I would find. Based on the romantic stories I had heard in France, Canada to me was log cabins and Indians. I was sure, however, that emigrating would mean fortune, adventure and a new way of life for me.

I arrived in Montreal on April 29, 1969 and had no difficulties at the airport. My visa was in order and the immigration authorities, who spoke French, were very kind and I could understand them. When I got outside the airport I had a terrible shock; the huge cars I saw told me I was in a huge country, where everything would be on a different scale than in France. It was overwhelming, yet fascinating, and I felt a little like a child in front of a Christmas tree.

It was about two o'clock in the afternoon when I left the airport; the air was cool — quite different from Marseilles at that

17

time of the year. I took the bus into town, and had to pay in French francs because I had not thought of changing them into Canadian dollars at the airport. The ride cost me the equivalent of four dollars which shook me a bit.

Despite my apprehensions, my impressions were favorable. It was comforting to see that all the street signs, or nearly all of them, were in French, and that when I found a hotel room in the rue Saint-Denis downtown, the two Frenchmen who ran it were friendly when they found out I came from Marseilles.

"Are you on holiday?" one of them asked.

"No, I'm an immigrant." I said.

"It's a good country to work in," the other one told me. "Don't worry. Everything will be all right."

My room was nondescript and I again felt downhearted. I went to bed and woke up at five in the morning. Later, walking down the street I asked a passer-by where I could get some cigarettes. He told me to go across the road to the drugstore.

"That's it," I thought. "They don't understand me any more." Confused, I wandered around. Finally, I went back to the drugstore and after looking at the displays of pharmaceuticals I found the cigarette counter and the place where I could also buy a cup of coffee. Cigarettes in a drugstore? I must be dreaming, I thought. I can't remember whether I asked for Gitanes, Gauloises or some other brand, but I ordered a coffee which I didn't touch.

In Marseilles I had been given an address by a man who told me to see his friend, Henri, who worked at the Castel du Roy on Drummond Street, twenty blocks away. As I walked along the street I looked at the cars and the people. I was overawed. I hadn't imagined Canada like this at all. The prices of goods in the windows seemed exorbitantly high, and when I translated their dollar value into francs I decided one would have to become a millionaire to live here. When I reached the Castel du Roy, Henri wasn't there. I left a message for him to get in touch with me when he returned.

The next morning I met a young man who had been on the plane with me. Although we hadn't spoken to each other during the flight I guessed he was French by the way he looked and dressed. We recognized each other and started talking.

"What are you doing up and around so early? Can't sleep?" he asked.

"I still have jet-lag," I said, "but what are you doing here?"

"I'm waiting to meet a friend in front of this bar, when it opens. He works in a restaurant."

We decided to have a coffee. I could tell the young man also felt a little lost in the city and his first impressions were the same as mine. When we later went back to the bar, which was open for business by then, the bartender spotted my Marseilles accent and I told him I was looking for work.

"Upstairs at the Club des Moustaches they're hiring waiters, French only," he said.

I hung around the bar for a while and then strolled around town. The next day I went to apply for the job. My references confirmed that I knew my trade and I was hired.

The Club des Moustaches in the rue de Montague reminded me of France: the small tables, the chairs and the tiled floor. I was happy to have a job which brought me a hundred and fifty to two hundred a week — an enormous sum, I thought.

I changed hotels and took a small room on Drummond Street for sixteen dollars a week. The bed linen was changed once a week and, although it wasn't paradise, it was O.K.

I started to get settled, meet people and make friends including some girls, and began to live well. It was a happy life and very different to the one I had been used to in France.

My family and I kept in touch, writing letters back and forth. Sometimes I telephoned them, and my mother cried when she heard my voice. She would beg me to come home, but I had decided to draw a curtain over my past and there was nothing she could do to stop me. I felt free at last.

A few days later, Henri came to see me. A friend of his had a nightclub and was looking for a barman. Was I interested?

But I no longer needed Henri. Why change jobs? I thought. I was content and felt secure. But then I wasn't so sure; why not check it out? It couldn't hurt and wouldn't commit me to anything.

Chez Clairette was a cabaret and restaurant owned by a lady from Marseilles who had been living in Canada for years and was by then a naturalized citizen. She directed the artists herself and also had her own singing spot in the show. Clairette was a woman of about forty-five, very nice, very lively and gentle at the same time. Her accent was similar to that of the exuberant and jolly women in the south of France. She treated me almost as if I were her son; in fact, she reminded me a lot of my mother. I left my other job to become her barman, but did all sorts of other chores at the same time. I immediately felt at home with her. The clientele at the club was mixed — stage artists, doctors, lawyers, businessmen and politicians. The atmosphere was relaxed and friendly with none of the apparent social distinctions prevalent in France. All the patrons and performers talked to me and I was suddenly reminded of Marseilles.

I didn't need to look for odd jobs now to pay my way, and was determined to work and succeed honestly with a view to owning my own restaurant one day. I finished at about three or four in the morning and then simply went home to bed. A friend now shared a small studio apartment on the rue Durocher with me. The building had a swimming pool, a sauna and a snack bar, where I worked at midday making lunches in return for a free meal. I only had my rent to pay and was able to put money aside. Five months after arriving in Canada I bought a used car, a Parisienne, for seven hundred dollars. I never had such an easy time financially and, although I didn't live like a millionaire, I wasn't short of anything. At the end of six months I had even managed to save seven or eight hundred dollars.

Most important of all, I didn't feel alone; I had met interesting people I liked. One in particular was André A...*, the manager of Chez Babette at that time, who also came from the south of France and whose accent was similar to mine. André was twenty-four, a big fellow, with square shoulders and a nice face. He was jolly and full of life, but always complaining about Canada's cold climate. I had met him at Clairette's, along with Michèle Cardon, the club cashier, and her husband, Jean, the accordion player from Chez Babette. Jean usually came to pick up his wife after work and, as we

---

* For reasons he prefers not to disclose the author will not reveal the true identity of André A...

all got on well together, we sometimes went to play boules in La Fontaine Park, and then on to a restaurant for something to eat. André and I soon became close friends. Clairette asked him to be the manager of her club; the whole staff became one happy family. Clairette was like a mother to us, though she sometimes annoyed me by fussing over me as if I were a child. I felt I was back in Marseilles with my family. But that was Clairette through and through, doing things out of kindness. She is one of the most wonderful women I have ever met.

I was happy with my job and my nice apartment and thought I had everything I wanted in life. I often thought of all the people back home who lived in hovels, and who would have to earn as much as Brigitte Bardot to be able to afford the things I could afford.

I also had several affairs with girls, who became my mistresses for a day or for an evening. It wasn't too much for a boy from Marseilles! My first Canadian "experience" left me cold and disappointed. And the girl I had taken to bed with me wasn't even Canadian!

One evening I met Edmond Taillet at the club. A small, nervous fellow, he seemed to have known Clairette for some time. She introduced us and when he heard my accent he casually asked if I was from Marseilles.

Then he continued talking to Clairette — they seemed to be having a good time drinking together. As far as I was concerned he was just another Marseillais. He spent money with the greatest of ease.

Clairette told me she was hiring Edmond as a performer. "He's a good storyteller," she said. But I wasn't dumb enough to believe that he was just another act in her show, although at one time he had participated in the children's programs produced by Jean Nohain.* They used to call him Captain Latortue, and I had seen him on French television. He was a good musician who had worked with Charles Aznavour, Leo Ferre and several other famous singers. At the club he was fashionably dressed and flamboyant, buying champagne and whisky for everyone. After we discovered that we

---

* French animator, well-known on radio and television

had a lot of mutual friends in Marseilles, he was consistently friendly towards me, buying me drinks, etc. We talked about Mémé Guérini, Robert Lenoir, Tani Zampa and, of course, the whole quartier du Panier. During these conversations I imagined myself back in Marseilles until I realized that he knew all the underworld "society," the important traffickers and the prominent gangsters. I also discovered that he was involved in shady business dealings and it became clear to me how he was able to spend money so lavishly.

Edmond Taillet stayed in Montreal for about two weeks, and I saw him almost every day at Chez Clairette's. Several times he dropped in at my place to take advantage of the sauna and the swimming pool. When I remarked that he seemed to know Montreal as well as I knew Marseilles, he told me that he had been in Canada several times to negotiate artists' contracts. I looked at him and he knew that I knew. "Contracts . . .?" I asked.

Big names like Aznavour or Brel earned a lot in those days, but small fry like Taillet weren't highly paid in Canada — his reputation didn't match the money he spent. He explained to me that he was also a pimp and had three or four girls working for him in Paris.

One evening when our crowd was having supper together, Taillet asked Cardon if he knew of a girl who owned a car and would be willing to take a trip with him.

The next day Taillet invited himself and me to the Cardon's home for a spaghetti supper. Sitting at the table he suddenly said, "Jean, you know I only have two weeks left to find a girl with a car to go to France." I wondered what it was all about.

The next day while Taillet was at my place Cardon dropped in to tell him that he had found the girl he was looking for. "I don't know if she'll be interested," Cardon added, "but there's nothing like asking."

So we all went to a restaurant in Old Montreal to meet Noella, the barmaid, a nice Canadian girl. Taillet started explaining the world of show business to her, told her he was a night club performer and so on and so on. He then put a bundle of bills on the table and invited her to have a drink. I could see she was impressed with Taillet's dazzling stories when he dropped names such as "Aznavour" and "Bécaud" here and there. The sight of all that money and the attention she was getting was having the desired effect.

"You know," he added casually, "I'm on holiday and I don't know the city. You have a car. Why don't you show me around?"

"I would, but I don't have a driver's license."

Taillet suggested he could do the driving and made a date with her for that same evening. They arrived later at Chez Clairette's, behaving as if they were lovers. I'd never seen anyone so downright dishonest with a girl. What was he up to? Although he was a pimp in Paris, I knew he couldn't have her working for him in Montreal without running into difficulties with certain Mafia gentlemen who were trying to control the entire prostitution racket. Maybe he was in another business such as trafficking women for white slavery. But the car angle kept coming back to my mind.

A few days later I asked Taillet how things were going with Noella.

"She's O.K." he said casually.

"But the whole thing doesn't make sense, Taillet."

By way of an explanation he promised to tell me about it later, and cut me in.

"Cut me in? I don't understand. You mean I'd get part of the profit from the girl? I'm not interested; she's not my type."

"No. It's not that, Michel."

We left it at that and several days later Noella came to the restaurant to talk to me about Taillet. She thought he was my childhood friend. "Edmond is fantastic; he's taking me to France. We're engaged. We're taking my car and we're going to Marseilles."

I was stunned.

Even though I suspected something illegal was going on I decided to send greetings to my family. At that time I had absolutely no idea what proportions this adventure would take. If I had, I would have kept quiet.

In 1969 it cost about five hundred dollars to ship a car from Canada to France. Noella left with Taillet and I completely forgot about them until the day Noella returned, alone.

"Did you have a good holiday?" I asked.

"Just great."

She had visited Marseilles, Paris and Aix-en-Provence and in

Marseilles she had been to a club where "all the bums hang out." At Aix they had had an accident. The car broke down and she had to leave it there for ten days.

At that moment it hit me. Everyone in Marseilles knows that the laboratories for processing heroin from its morphine base are located in Aix-en-Provence.

Then Noella showed me photos of my family's restaurant in Marseilles, and she told me she had met my mother and my sisters and I said I was pleased to have news of them. I didn't let on that I suspected anything. Noella was neither naive nor childish. She was an intelligent woman who had chosen to be a barmaid. Yet Taillet had managed to lead her on. She evidently knew nothing and sounded happy.

"I've got some news for you, Michel," she concluded.

I expected her to announce, "I'm in the heroin business," but she said: "I'm going to get married."

"Married! That's great. To whom?"

"Taillet, of course."

"Taillet?"

"I'm starting to save already."

We went to supper. I felt sorry for her and became increasingly anxious, frightened and then disgusted. How could I say anything? She was happy, in love . . . How could I warn her, even indirectly. I was convinced that Taillet was part of the underworld and this knowledge terrified me.

In the Marseilles underworld there is an unwritten "law of silence." If you break that silence, reprisals are swift and brutal. I thought about my family — could I risk putting them in danger? I knew that whole families had been wiped out to prevent them from talking. Even though I had been brought up with the idea that we all must help one another — after all, what was this girl to me? I hardly knew her. I had to protect myself and my family. I would say nothing.

I carried on with my work at Chez Clairette. Two weeks after Noella's visit Taillet arrived at the club. I now looked at him in a different light. I saw him as a disgusting person, but didn't dare let on. He had struck me as someone who knew what he was doing. In

The old port in Marseilles.

A street in the quartier du Panier in Marseilles.

Jacques Bec.   Joseph Mari, a well-
                                known figure in the
                                Marseilles underworld
                                and boss of the Bec-Taillet
                                team.

The car interior was in a pitiful state once the heroin
sachets had been removed.

Edmond Taillet.

Danielle Ouimet and Michel Girouard at Chez Clairette on the night Michel Mastantuono first met Danielle Ouimet.

Danielle and
Michel.

Danielle Ouimet in her apartment
on rue Saint Mathieu in Montreal.

Film star Danielle Ouimet relaxing in her Montreal apartment.

Suitcases with false bottoms were used extensively to smuggle large quantities of heroin through Customs. Individual sachets, below, each containing 500 grams of heroin are worth millions of dollars once the powder has been diluted and is offered for sale on the black market.

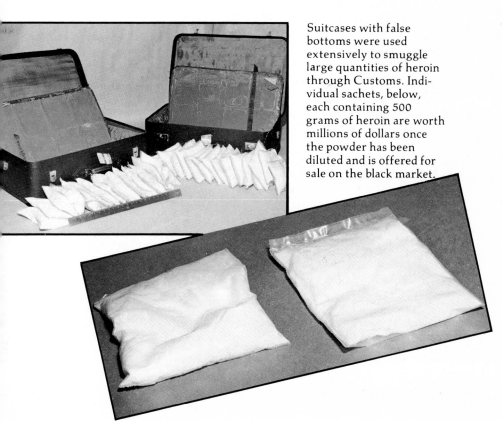

Danielle descending the steps of a landing stage after one of her many transatlantic flights.

Felix Rosso.

Joseph Signoli, one of
Mastantuono's collabora-
tors in the drug ring.

Mastantuono's boat under
construction at a Montreal
dock. Robert Gauthier
and he planned to use it
for heroin smuggling runs
across the Atlantic.

Mastantuono's Corvette.

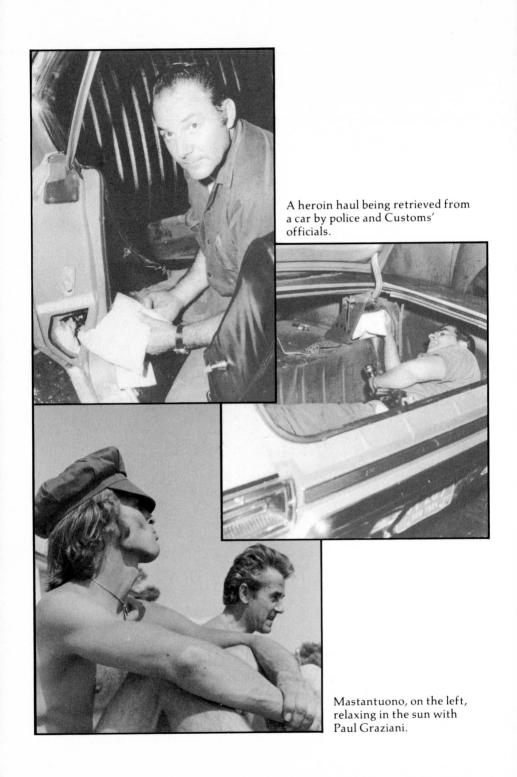

A heroin haul being retrieved from a car by police and Customs' officials.

Mastantuono, on the left, relaxing in the sun with Paul Graziani.

a way I admired him, or rather I respected him in the same way as
you would respect an expert craftsman.

"I'm going to give Noella a call," he said casually.

"Everything O.K. with her?" I asked.

"Couldn't be better. Fantastic."

That evening he introduced me to a Jacques Bec, a newcomer. I
immediately saw the difference between the two men. Bec was a
Parisian, educated and impressive. His distinguished appearance
and confident manner made me feel inferior. People like him knew
how to express themselves with ease — a trait that I did not
possess. They could cross America as casually as I would go for a
drive in the Laurentians. I wanted to be more impressive, and
personal attractiveness and external signs of wealth mattered to
me. When I met people like Bec, I was reminded of my modest life
style. They lived extravagantly and I envied them. Taillet told me
Bec was the "manager of the Charlots, Idelman's partner."

I was flabbergasted that Bec had such important contacts as
the Charlots, who were a well-known group.

Then Noella arrived. She and Taillet still seemed to be having a
grand love affair. I realized that Noella must have met Bec in Paris.
At the end of a very amusing evening Taillet mentioned that I had
an apartment downtown with a pool and a sauna. Bec was mad
about saunas. "Could I come over tomorrow if it's convenient?" he
asked eagerly.

"Of course," I said.

He and Taillet arrived at about eleven the next morning for a
swim and a sauna. Taillet asked me if he could phone Cardon and I
heard him say, "We want to see you. We've got something to ask
you when there aren't any customers, O.K.? I'll call you back later."

Then Bec turned to Taillet and said, "Well, there's Michel. We
could send him."

"What's that?" I said.

"Listen, Michel, Noella's car is arriving from France next week.
Could you pick it up at the dock?"

"Why can't Noella go?"

"She doesn't have a driver's license."

"What's in the car?"

"Heroin."

Just like that. I was astounded even though I had suspected it. "You're crazy. Forget it."

"We'll give you three thousand dollars."

"Not interested. I don't want trouble with the government. I'm French and from Marseilles — it's too risky. And besides, I'm not interested."

"We'll see you later."

"If I can help you with anything else, gladly, but not this, definitely not."

I didn't want to have anything to do with it. Morever, I was frightened. Any involvement with heroin or marijuana could land you in prison for a long stretch.

To this day I don't know why I told them I might be able to help them later. I suppose I was a bit fascinated by all the drama, the mystery surrounding dope. It excited my curiosity, and I wanted them to think I was a tough guy. Morally, I already felt like an accomplice, seduced by their money, although I didn't really know where I stood with them. At that point I wasn't ready to participate directly in heroin trafficking. Deep down I did it mostly out of pride, so I wouldn't look like a fool. I wanted to be on their level and the fact that they confided in me was sufficient proof that they almost considered me to be one of them.

Two weeks later Taillet and Bec telephoned Cardon from my place and told him they would wait for him there. "When you've got the car, call us here."

While Taillet appeared calm, I felt very nervous. Bec didn't stop moving around; he went to the sauna, came back, went downstairs again, got dressed, made a phone call. He couldn't keep still.

I asked Taillet if Cardon had agreed to get the car for them. "Yes. He's earning three thousand dollars for the job."

Early in the afternoon Taillet heard from Cardon. "I just got back," he said, "everything is fine and I've got the package."

Taillet went down to the sauna to tell Bec about it. They celebrated and went wild.

I didn't want to appear like a fool or a peasant so I didn't dare ask the questions that were running through my head. How many kilos? How much money? Where and to whom were they going to sell the stuff?

A few days later, Taillet and Bec again arrived at my place to work out the details. Bec said: "It's easy. Ask Noella for supper this evening and I'll simply tell her that I want to go to New York. I'll say I've heard the trip from Montreal to New York is beautiful and ask her if we can go in her car. We'll pay for her time off work, for the trip, the hotels and all her other expenses. Since you'll also be in New York, I'll tell her she can stay there with you for two or three days."

When Bec suggested the New York trip to Noella that evening, she said, "I'd love to go, but I don't have a license, I can't cross the border. A friend of mine could probably drive us. I'll call him."

When she came back from the phone, she told them her friend would drive. I never found out who it was.

The next day Noella, Bec and the driver, who didn't have any idea of what was going on, left for New York. Taillet was to follow by plane later to avoid the risk of both of them being caught. Once Bec had crossed the border he phoned Taillet at my place to say that the package had safely arrived in the U.S.

Taillet mentioned that he was looking for a way to dump Noella. "I've had enough of her, but I'm not sure how to do it."

"You'll hurt her a lot. She's really in love with you." I said.

Noella had told me that she had slept with a man in Paris after she had met Taillet. I still don't know why I provided him with a reason for breaking up with the girl. I bitterly regretted it later. When I told him about it, he said, "You know this man?"

"Yes, I know him."

The matter rested there.

Several days later he came to my place to call Marseilles; I think it was the Bar de l'aviron. He asked for someone called Badi and said: "I'm sending the little one to a holiday camp," which meant he was sending the car across the border.

I went back to my quiet life at the Chez Clairette, but I thought about them often and the big money they were earning smuggling heroin. I was becoming intrigued.

When Noella came back from New York a week later she came

to see me at the club. Bec had left for France from New York.

Noella was in tears. "He's left me." she cried.

"How come? You were supposed to get married."

"We were! But he found out about that guy I slept with in Paris. God! Why was I so stupid! I didn't even enjoy it! Anyway, Edmond is using it as an excuse to get rid of me. It's so unfair. I love him! Michel, will you try to explain if you see him?" Her eyes filled with tears. "We were going to get married. He even bought me a diamond ring when we were in New York." I was ashamed as I listened to Noella because I knew that Taillet had paid only five dollars for the ring, the hypocrite. "He came to the restaurant where I work and gave me hell." Noella went on. "First he hit me, then he told me I was a tart because I'd cheated on him. He told me that in France they kill girls for that. Then he threw the ring out of the window."

I tried to comfort her. "Never mind, there are other men in the world, Noella."

Taillet arrived an hour later after she had left.

"Edmond, what you did was sickening," I told him. "You could have broken off more gently, at least you could have left her the ring."

"I don't care, she got in my way in Marseilles," he explained.

I became more friendly towards him, and asked, "Everything went O.K.?"

"Yes."

Taillet always stayed at the Lasalle Hotel in Montreal. A few days later he invited me over and showed me ninety thousand dollars folded up in a piece of paper. It was his share for delivering twenty-seven kilos of heroin to a New York group of Puerto Ricans controlled by Antonio Florès.

Shortly after, he returned to Paris and I continued to see Noella occasionally. We drove up to the Laurentians to spend a few days together and I did my best to cheer her up. But I wasn't at ease with her. I felt ashamed for not being honest. She was still very upset and insisted Taillet would come back to her. She went so far as to phone him in Paris and he called her once — to protect himself — he was warned she might have caught on and might tell what she knew. Two months after the break she told me one evening that Taillet had really duped her. "What do you think he had in the car?"

I pretended I didn't know. .

The same evening I called Taillet to tell him that Noella suspected something. But I didn't hear from him again for some time. I was reasonably certain that he was still trafficking. I carried on with my work at Chez Clairette, living quietly and seeing the same friends.

In November 1969 Taillet came back to Montreal. I can remember the scene perfectly. He arrived with Bec and two French girls, Ginette and Anne-Marie, who were working as waitresses at Chez Clairette. The four of them used the pool at my place and then we all went out to eat. The two men behaved as if they were in love with the girls.

One day Ginette told me she was going to Paris on holiday with Taillet. I already knew the story well; it was the same as Noella's, except that Ginette didn't mention a car.

A month and a half later I saw Taillet and Bec again.

"We're waiting for the car," Taillet said.

"Who's car?"

"Ginette's."

"You've loaded it?"

"Yes. It's arriving next week."

A few days later he asked me if I could do a job for him. "Ginette is bringing her car back from New York. The body needs fixing. Could you do it for me? I'll pay your costs."

"O.K." I had offered my services out of friendship, not expecting to get paid.

Ginette brought a Ford Falcon around to the club and asked me whether it was true that I had promised Edmond to work on it. I said I would look after it and she drove it to my house. There were holes in it and traces of white powder all over the trunk. I tasted some and was certain it was heroin. That was pure guesswork, of course, as I'd never tasted it before. Afterwards I had a headache for about an hour. I recognized the risk I was taking and, as it was impossible to repair the mess, I let the matter drop. Ginette asked me to sell the car for her but I told her it was unsellable. She had become aware of the role she had played and knew she had been tricked. "I carried marijuana in the car," she said, "and I've had enough trouble with Taillet. He's a pig and he's used me like a child. It's cost me a lot of money and I've lost my job."

He had, however, given her six thousand dollars for taking her car across the border — she hadn't suspected that she had actually been carrying heroin.

A few days later Anne-Marie, the other girl, came to see me with a similar tale. She had sent her car to France and was supposed to go over and bring it back, but neither Taillet nor Bec had called her and both had disappeared.

I told her the same thing I had told Ginette. "I don't know these guys any better than you do. It's none of my business. So sort it out with them — it's nothing to do with me."

3/
A DIFFERENT KIND OF MISTRESS

I was getting used to Montreal and felt comfortable with my Canadian life. I was still in contact with my family but had no news of my wife. Then things began to happen which completely changed my life.

One evening everyone got particularly excited at Chez Clairette. Danielle Ouimet, the Canadian movie star and sex symbol, had been booked as a singer. The place was in a frenzy.

Who was this girl?

I didn't know Danielle Ouimet and didn't give a damn about her but I had heard her name mentioned around Montreal. I had also seen her on publicity posters announcing her film *Valerie*. She was pretty, very pretty indeed, with long blonde hair, a sort of Canadian Brigitte Bardot, I suppose.

During the afternoon André A..., who was now manager of Chez Clairette, called me at home to ask if I was coming to the club in the evening. I told him I would be down at six o'clock, as usual.

He had become very friendly with me during the past few months and we had discussed Bec and Taillet and their various business dealings. "Those guys are moving heroin," I had told him. "They earn a bundle and it looks pretty easy." He agreed there was a fortune to be made and told me it would be good to get in on it. After all, if Noella, Ginette and Anne-Marie could bring in cars for Taillet, why not? Taillet had impressed André enormously, even more than he had impressed me.

As soon as I arrived at the club that evening, André rushed over to me. "If you could just see her, Michel, that girl . . ."

"What girl?"

"Danielle Ouimet."

"What's so great about her?"

"She's fantastic — really great."

"O.K. If she's that great, I'll have her."

"You'll have her? You're kidding!"

"Not at all. If she's O.K., I'll have her!"

It was almost a dare. I'd slept with a fair number of girls who had performed at Chez Clairette, so why not with Danielle Ouimet? I had nothing else in mind beyond a one-night stand. "You're acting as if she were some kind of madonna, André. Would you care to make a small wager? Say a bottle of Scotch?"

André thought I was mad. "I bet you don't even get to take her out."

We lit the chandeliers and got the club ready. Towards eight o'clock Clairette arrived and the three of us stood talking around the cashier's desk. Then we saw a blonde girl come in wearing a black vinyl coat. Her outfit was ordinary enough but what struck me was her extraordinarily beautiful hair which fell below her waist. Her clear blue eyes and sexy bearing impressed me.

"Well," said André. "What do you say now?"

"Oh, she's quite something. But the bet still stands."

Later I heard a warm, sensual, almost indiscernible "hello" just behind me. I turned around. She was now wearing a long dress made from a light fabric that clung to her body; she was naked underneath. I found myself staring at her and probably looked very lecherous. She seemed embarrassed. I was already imagining her in my bed. I saw a woman, The Woman, reclining and remembered the posters where I'd seen her draped across the body of her screen lover.

I was working in the kitchen that evening. For her first songs she had chosen Ferland and Brel. From time to time I came out to watch her but I didn't take much notice of her singing. She was stunning. The club was packed and the hundred or so people in the room applauded her when she finished.

Following her first set, Michel Girouard, the journalist, sang duets with her and after the show he came to see me in the kitchen. He was a regular visitor at the club and had frequently worked as a soloist in the past. Girouard was a homosexual who had a bit of a crush on me, but I didn't take much notice of it. He asked me for some coffee and I mentioned that I wanted to go out with Danielle. I knew he was a good friend of hers.

"Ask her. She'll accept," he said as he was leaving.

I didn't think that it would be all that easy to make a date with her, but obviously Michel had already given me some advance publicity. Five minutes later Danielle appeared in the kitchen and asked for coffee. I became very nervous — she was giving me the once over. I should have been flattered but I was afraid. Normally, women don't make me nervous — far from it — but she wasn't just another woman, she was a sex symbol. My hand shook when I handed her the cup. I didn't dare look at her, I felt as if I'd had an electric shock. When I saw Michel later I asked, "Did you talk to her, Girouard?"

"No. Do you want me to?"

"Absolutely not, I'll talk to her myself, later."

"Try. She'll accept, you'll see."

I was restless all evening long, going to the bar, returning to the kitchen to make coffee and going back to the bar again. Before the second show Girouard came to ask for another coffee; then Danielle wanted more coffee. Now I was more at ease. She looked at me as if to say, "Will you ask me or won't you." So, I blurted out, "Would you like to have dinner with me?"

"If you like," she replied casually, taking out her notebook. "When? I don't have any TV shows tomorrow, so I'll be free. Come round to my place."

I asked for her address.

"Rue Saint-Mathieu."

"Let me have your telephone number — I'll call you before I come."

Now Clairette called me to bring *her* some coffee. She asked whether I was trying to make out with the girl.

"Me? Of course not. Never!"

"Oh come on — you Marseillais learned how to screw before you could walk."

André overheard Clairette's remark, looked at me and smiled.

"You owe me a bottle of Scotch," I said smugly.

When the show was over a man wearing a wolf-skin coat sat down at the bar. Danielle changed her clothes and as she was leaving the club with him she turned to me, "O.K., Michel, I'll expect you tomorrow."

I was happy as a king.

I found out much later that her escort had been Robert Gauthier who was crazy about boats and, in fact, was a real sailor.

The next day I called Danielle and we arranged to meet at her apartment. On my way there I got cold feet and didn't know whether to go through with the date or drop the whole thing. I figured André would make fun of me if I backed out now. Going up in the elevator I became nervous again and wished I hadn't started this silly game. But I reminded myself once more of André and the others and how they would kid me. Strangely enough, their opinion was more important than my date with Danielle. I didn't consider myself good enough for this glamorous star. What on earth was the barman from Chez Clairette doing in the apartment of someone as famous as Mlle. Ouimet? Yet I was proud, although the thought of being alone with her scared me to death. I didn't see the woman in her, only the "movie star" who had probably slept with dozens of men and had remained a celebrity even in bed. I was no novice when it came to girls, but I felt I was out of my depth.

She offered me coffee once I was inside her apartment and said she knew of a little restaurant in the Laurentians. We took my car. She was relaxed, laughed a good deal, chatted to me about my work, and continued to make small talk as we drove out of the city. I didn't quite know what to say to her. Eventually, I started to talk about Canadians in what I thought was a flattering manner. She intimidated me a little, and I felt embarrassed just because I didn't know how to behave towards her. I hadn't been educated in her ways and though I knew how to approach certain subjects, I realized my limitations. By the time we'd finished our meal I had run out of things to say and started to worry about the check — I didn't have too much money with me. I should have been myself rather than play games, but I couldn't get through to her. Yet the fact that she had accepted my dinner invitation proved to me that she found me attractive; but why would someone like her want to go out with *me?* Then again, I thought, "I'm dreaming." I was that naive. Perhaps this was what had attracted her? Suddenly I had a silly idea and suggested we go to visit a friend of mine who worked at a ski resort nearby. She agreed. On the way there I started telling her about my life — that I had been married, divorced, had remarried and had had a child. That seemed to impress her.

When she told me that she also had a child, by a Frenchman, I knew I hadn't made it. She was twenty-three and considered single, having always concealed the existence of her child. And to think I had tried to impress her with my son and my wives!

The afternoon was awful. Following coffee at the ski lodge we decided to drive back to Montreal. Both of us said very little in the car. From time to time I took her hand and caressed it. When we reached the city I asked her to come back to my place for some coffee; she accepted. Sitting down on my bed, which was the only comfortable place in my sparsely furnished apartment, she looked at my books as I hurried to the kitchen. I came back, walked over to her and kissed her. She responded remarkably quickly. We kissed again and I stopped being nervous. Our physical contact had brought her down from her pedestal. Now I could think of her as an ordinary woman and forget all the stuff I had read about her. My fears were gone and I felt at ease. Towards evening I took her back to her place and then went down to the club. As I came through the door, André winked at me and asked how things had gone.

"Perfectly. I have a date with her this evening."

Clairette knew instantly there was something between me and Danielle. Although I was deliriously happy, I felt awkward and embarrassed because everyone was looking at me.

When I was getting ready to leave the club with Danielle, two men offered to take her home. I knew they were plainclothes cops because she had told me she had received threatening letters after her film had been released; some people had found it too daring. "Don't bother to come with me tonight," she told them, "I'm going home with Michel." For a moment everyone in the club who had heard her remark froze. Clairette looked at me, André looked at me, the policemen looked at me and they all seemed astonished. I felt very proud and said in a loud voice: "Well, shall we go then?"

She had an attractively furnished penthouse apartment in the rue Saint-Mathieu. The pictures on the wall, painted by her, were quite good, mainly abstracts in many different styles. There were also a lot of dolls she had designed herself. The living room was not the star's room I had imagined. However, the bedroom had a canopy bed, a white carpet, a black bedspread and black and white curtains with a design showing nude women and men intertwined in sexual acts. I felt comfortable in these sensual surroundings.

After pouring me some coffee she disappeared. I heard the water run in the bathroom and wanted to take off my own clothes and join her in the shower, but I didn't feel suave enough to carry it off. Again, I started to worry whether I was doing the right thing just being there. So I waited in the living room, visualizing her nude body under the shower, getting ready for me! I wondered whether, after having had the audacity to shower within earshot, she would come out dressed or undressed. I hadn't previously experienced this kind of freedom by a woman; I was a bit shocked.

When she entered the room dressed in a short transparent negligee, she casually asked, "Would you like more coffee?"

"Yes, please."

Now she became very matter-of-fact. "I'm going to bed. I suppose you are going to stay?" Seeing her so free and easy frightened me even more.

"Yes, of course."

I took a shower, thinking all the while, it's not true, it's too quick, she has propositioned me. Finally I joined her in the bedroom. In contrast to her previous behavior Danielle put out the lights before undressing and we slid under the covers. I felt her nude body pass over mine as she changed to the other side of the bed. I liked the feel of her soft skin. We made love, and continued to make love for three hours. The "sex symbol" quickly vanished, as she was not what I had expected — I had slept with more sensual women. Perhaps it was better to see her nude body in a movie or dream about her rather than be in bed with her. Frankly, I was disappointed.

The telephone woke us at noon. It was Michel Girouard.

"Yes. It was marvellous, fantastic," she cried.

They were obviously closer friends than I had imagined.

I then left her apartment to go to work.

André was waiting for me. "Did you make out?" he asked.

"Yes, but it's no big deal. Not worth the effort." After our first night together I'd come down to earth with a thud.

I intended to avoid her after that, but somehow a fairly regular arrangement evolved between us and during the five nights she sang at Chez Clairette she would wait for me almost every evening. I was proud to think that I was having an affair with Danielle Ouimet, but also knew I wasn't the only man she slept with. She was the kind of woman that men fell for, and she had to have several at the same time. I was the one who attracted her sexually, I thought.

"Why do you want me," I once asked her, "when you can have so many other men?"

"I don't know. You're kind and gentle and loving and affectionate; you're a new kind of experience for me."

I guess I was different from the others; I was neither an artist nor a homosexual nor a businessman.

We went almost everywhere together and people began to take it for granted that I was her lover. She had a car that the Ford Motor Company had put at her disposal to publicize *Valerie*. I drove her everywhere and everyone stared at us as we went by. We didn't attend many cocktail parties, however, and would often stay at home or go to ordinary restaurants or dancing, although I could hardly even afford these outings. I didn't give her expensive gifts — in fact, I didn't even send her flowers. But I still managed to go through all my savings and every penny I earned.

Suddenly, I had financial problems, which made me start to think about Bec and Taillet and the money they were earning on the heroin market. I knew they were in France but had lost contact with them.

One evening Clairette told me it was impossible for me to continue seeing Danielle because I was no longer doing my work properly. I thought her criticism was unwarranted and I became so incensed that I walked out. A day or two later Jacques Bec called me. He had caught me at the right moment psychologically; I was ready to go into business with him.

4/
HEROIN
AND THE DS

Edmond Taillet had got into dope peddling through Joseph Mari, a well-known figure in the Marseilles underworld. They had met in one of the local bars, owned by Antoine Guérini, the big Corsican boss, and Mari had asked Taillet to deliver a shipment of drugs to Puerto Rican traffickers in New York City.

Taillet had approached his friend Jacques Bec, the musician, who at the time was in financial difficulties after several of his attempts to put on shows in Paris had failed. Bec was small, fair, thickset and athletic and looked like a businessman, all in all an impressive character. He had many contacts in show business and it was easy for him to approach Johnny Halliday, a well-known French rock star of the sixties, and ask his secretary to help out Edmond Taillet, a fellow musician, whose baggage would be over the weight limit on his next trip to Canada. Could Taillet's two amplifiers be shipped together with those belonging to Halliday's group who had been booked to perform in Sherbrooke, Quebec? Bec's request was granted and the amplifiers, stuffed with twenty-three kilos of heroin, were put aboard a plane. They were supposed to have been picked up at Montreal's Dorval Airport by Edouard Rimbaud*, a French writer of detective stories. However, Rimbaud

---

* Edouard Rimbaud was also known in France under the pen name of Louis Salinas. He wrote a novel entitled "Les Pourvoyeurs" (The Providers), published by *Les Presses de la Cité*, in which he described the workings of Puerto Rican drug rings in New York City. Some of the action takes place in Montreal and certain scenes are set at a local night club. Rimbaud was a frequent guest at *Chez Clairette*. His other associates were Émile Alonzo, Jean-Claude Kella and Laurent Fiocconi, otherwise known as "Big Charlie."

had been arrested before leaving New York City and subsequently received thirty years for his part in the operation.

As the amplifiers landed in Sherbrooke, together with Halliday's instruments, a taxi driver was sent to pick them up and in Rimbaud's absence Guido Rendel, one of his associates, took delivery of them in Montreal.

As this transaction had gone through without a hitch, the Taillet-Bec partnership continued and they moved another two carloads of drugs across the Canada-U.S. border.

Eventually, they had disagreements and broke up. It was Taillet who had all the connections with the Marseilles underworld. Bec had by this time joined Jo Signoli* and contacted me in Montreal early in May 1970. He asked if I had a car — he would like to work with me. I had no car at my disposal at the time, but when he suggested I come to Paris, I agreed, providing he paid my expenses.

He said he would and I promised to leave the next day. It all fitted in very nicely as Danielle had asked me to join her at the Cannes Film Festival and I could combine business and pleasure. I went to see André the same evening to ask him if he would lend me the money for the fare, because Bec wanted me to bring a carload of heroin from Paris to America. André got very excited. "If you like, we could be partners and share everything, expenses and profits, fifty-fifty." That was fine with me.

Bec was waiting for me at Orly Airport. He had to attend a funeral that day and suggested I go with him so that we could discuss our business. He was the manager of the Charlots group at the time and the wife of one of its members had died. The whole of the Parisian show business crowd was there. He introduced me to his fiancée, Marie-France, and took me to La Villa des Fleurs, a hotel in the rue de Liège. Everything — his car, the people, the hotel and his money — impressed me very much.

As soon as we were alone Bec explained what I would have to

---

* Jo Signoli, the boss of Le Consul, a Paris bar, was a Marseillais and old-time friend of Joseph Orsini, a well-known underworld figure. Both these men had collaborated with the Gestapo during World War II.

do. He said it was easy and not at all dangerous. I was to buy a car, load it with heroin, have it sent to Canada, then drive it to New York. In return, I would get one thousand dollars per kilo plus expenses. A gold mine — better than any lottery!

Bec also explained he had dropped Taillet because he had robbed him by taking a few kilos without paying. I already knew that Taillet hadn't paid Noella and I didn't like the idea of people cheating and stealing from each other. Bec suggested I become his partner, explaining he had made his contact in Marseilles and wanted to get his own team together.

I didn't want to appear overanxious. I told him that I was going to the Cannes Film Festival the next day to meet my fiancée, although I had already decided to go into the trafficking business.

Meanwhile, Bec had repaid me my fare money and I felt some moral obligation toward him.

I found Danielle in Cannes surrounded by well-known artists and felt a bit lost and ill-at-ease in their company. We met a photographer who wanted to take pictures of both of us and who also asked Danielle to pose in the nude for him. She refused, saying, "That was O.K. last year, but not now." Apparently the year before she had undressed on the beach.

Everything was going well. We stayed at the Hotel Negresco in Nice on the Promenade des Anglais. One evening, just as I was about to go to bed, Bec telephoned and I informed him officially that I had made my decision.

Although I had been disgusted by the methods Taillet had used with Noella and the other girls, I thought at first I would pull a similar stunt using Danielle. I would offer to buy a car for her in France, as a gift for an adored mistress. Something had evidently rubbed off on me.

We then took a day's holiday to visit my family in Marseilles, and I met Bec and explained my plan to him. It was simple. We would buy a car and have it shipped to Canada. I neglected to tell him, however, that the car would be registered in Danielle's name. He promised to contact me in one or two hours after he had seen the bosses. That's how I knew that the bigshots were from Marseilles as I had suspected. He called me at my mother's house and we met at midnight in his hotel room. We arranged to meet again in Paris in a week's time.

Danielle and I were happy in Cannes — going to nightclubs and lying on the beach. Then Bec called to tell me he had reserved a room at the Hôtel du Colisée in Paris. "I'll be there registered under the name of Ouimet," I told him.

The next day we flew to Paris and as soon as I arrived, Bec arranged to meet me at the Citroën showroom to look at a car in the window; it was a DS 21 Palace. Bec explained how it could be fitted out, what optional equipment would have to be bought and showed me where the drugs would be cached. He said the car would have to be driven to Biarritz to be loaded up. He gave me five thousand francs for a down payment, and the next day Danielle and I moved to another hotel in the rue Balzac. After lunch, we took a stroll down the Champs Elysées and looked in the window of the Citroën showroom. She admired the DS 21 and I offered to buy it for her and have it sent to Montreal, suggesting it be registered in her name so she wouldn't have to pay duty on it. The idea didn't strike her as unusual and we walked into the Citroën agency to find out the price. I think they quoted us seven thousand dollars and Danielle didn't bat an eyelash. Although I was only a barman she didn't seem at all astonished that I had that kind of dough. She knew I had a share in our restaurant in Marseilles and that my family was fairly well off. That evening we talked about the car.

"It's beautiful and you'll be lucky to find a similar one in Canada; besides, they're far more expensive over there." I told her.

She suddenly seemed reluctant to accept my generous gift and I had to work hard to persuade her that we ought to order it the next day. When Bec found that I had registered it in Danielle's name, he was furious. I explained to him that as a barman and Marseillais I would hardly be in a position to own a seven thousand dollar car, pay five hundred dollars to ship it to Canada and pay duty on it without attracting attention. But Danielle, who was a big-time singer with money and a glamorous lifestyle, would pass unnoticed.

"What happens if you split up? She's a star and if she leaves you you'll be in a mess," he warned.

"I'll take care of that," I assured him.

While waiting to take delivery of the car Danielle and I decided to visit her son who was living with his paternal grandparents in Strasbourg.

On the train I told her frankly that the car would be used to smuggle heroin — I didn't have the guts to lie to her any longer. Although I was more or less committed, I was still willing to pull out of the deal if she refused to go along with me. When she heard what I had to say she didn't reply for some time and I thought I saw tears in her eyes. She finally said in a quiet voice, "That's not very considerate of you, Michel."

We didn't talk about the car any more during the trip but she kept looking at me and, finally, I had to tell her not to worry, I was convinced nothing would go wrong. "I'm giving you the car and you'll get forty thousand dollars and all your expenses paid." At last she agreed and I explained why I was doing all this and how much money it would bring us. Her mood brightened. She felt sure she could clear the car through Customs without being questioned. She didn't see the danger, nor did I.

After the train pulled into the Strasbourg station, I went to a hotel and she was off to see her son. At midnight she called to say she was coming to me. At that time we had known each other for six weeks and I was getting more and more attached to her. Obviously I was flattered by the prestige of having an affair with Danielle Ouimet and the part she could play in helping me in a promising trafficking operation was sheer luck. I began to realize that I was in love with her and if I didn't live according to her style, I'd lose her. I had to make money fast. Yet it struck me as paradoxical that although I was in love with the woman, I was using her to pull a job where *she* ran the risk of landing in jail for twenty years.

We stayed in Strasbourg for two days and then went on to Belgium where she wanted to look over the script of her forthcoming movie. Then we returned to Paris to board our plane for Montreal.

When we got back it was apparent that our relationship had cooled. One evening, when I dropped in at her apartment she said, "Michel, I think it's time we split up."

"What are you talking about? Are you crazy? What about the car?"

"Nothing has changed as far as that is concerned. I'll bring it back to Montreal with the drugs."

She then told me she had fallen in love with an impresario from Montreal whom she had gone out with even before she'd met me, and she had again become his mistress. "It's all over between us, Michel. This is the real thing."

Meanwhile, my partner André had deposited part of the money to buy the car in Danielle's bank account. She signed the check and I returned to Paris with it. The car wasn't to be delivered until a month and a half later, and Danielle and I arranged to meet in Belgium the following month where she'd be filming *Daughters of Darkness*.

I didn't tell Bec what had happened between Danielle and me, and when I tried to call her I could never reach her. We finally met in Brussels and although we embraced and made love, I could sense her feelings toward me had changed. She was cold and obviously in love with someone else. When she asked me to leave her alone while she was making her film I felt dejected, and went to Paris to await delivery of the notorious Citroën DS, returning to Belgium a few times to see her.

Then I was notified that the car would be delivered from the factory. Danielle had, meanwhile, joined me in Paris and we decided to break it in. Danielle loved the car. We spent two glorious days together without a care. She wanted to keep the car, but I had to explain to her that it would have to be taken to Marseilles to be loaded. We could pick it up together and then have it shipped to Montreal. She appeared reconciled and returned to Belgium while I checked in at Villa des Fleurs in Paris, where I met Bec. He was distraught when I told him that Danielle knew everything.

"You never know what a woman will do, Michel. If you want to keep her informed, that's your business; she's your girlfriend. But I don't want to see her or have anything to do with her." Then he added, "I don't suppose you know, Michel, that your fiancée was seen in Paris last week."

"That's impossible; how do you know that?"

"I recognized her from her photos and someone else saw her on the Champs Elysées."

"Ridiculous! Who was she with?"

"A small, slim man with dark hair and glasses."

I immediately realized it must have been the impresario, her other lover. I tried to phone her in Belgium but didn't get through until three o'clock in the morning.

"What's happening?" she asked.

"Is it true that you were in Paris last week?"

"Yes, I had to get some contracts signed and stayed there for a couple of days."

"Why didn't you call me?"

"I'll explain later. It's very complicated. Don't come here Michel, I'm working."

"I understand you were with a man."

"I was with friends from Canada. The man is my manager; you've met him; he looks after my contracts."

I felt a little relieved although I knew she had been lying. My pride was hurt. I preferred to accept her version rather than know the whole truth. I told her I'd see her soon. Bec called me right after I arrived in Belgium. "I have to see you in Paris this evening."

"Can't it wait a couple of days? I only just got here."

He insisted, so I returned to Paris the same day. He asked me to stick around because he thought it wouldn't be long before we had to go to Biarritz. But nothing was ready and I went back to Belgium. An hour after I arrived, Bec wanted me back again, this time to deliver the car to the mechanic who would install the caches to hide the stuff. But I refused to come and, luckily, I had left the car with him and he was the one who took it to Biarritz.

Danielle finished making the movie and we decided to take a holiday until Bec gave me the go ahead to pick up the car in Biarritz. On our way to Paris, Danielle told me that she was pregnant. As if the car wasn't enough of a worry, now this! I was almost sure that the child was mine.

Soon Bec called to say the Citroën was ready. While he and I went to Biarritz, Danielle stayed behind in Paris.

We waited in a bar for an hour until the car stopped in front of the door. Bec left, then returned an hour and a half later. "They've only got ten kilos. The Marseillais haven't managed to bring it all so we'll have to wait for a few more days."

I told him that I would go back to Paris, and with the couple of thousand dollars he had given me before I went on holiday with Danielle, we spent two glorious weeks on the coast.

The car was finally ready. Leaving Danielle in Marseilles this time, Bec and I took the train from there to Biarritz. During the entire eleven hour journey we had to stand or sit in the corridor in front of the toilets as the train was full to capacity. It was a terrible night. Again I waited at a bar for the car to be brought to a parking lot. About an hour and a half later, Bec came to tell me that everything was ready, and we said goodbye.

"See you again in Paris or Montreal."

Danielle had, meanwhile, joined me in Biarritz and together we walked to the car. As soon as she got in she started to cry. The interior smelt of glue and it was obvious that the floor had been raised.

"You'll never get this car across the border," she sobbed.

"The smell of glue will go away," I assured her, "Don't worry about it."

She tried to pull herself together. "Michel, do you really think we can do it without getting caught?"

"I've told you the smell will go. I promise. Everything will be O.K."

We drove off and stopped at an inn for a good lunch and even picked up two hitchhikers on their way to Paris. We left the car with a transport company who undertook to move it to Le Havre. "You'll have your car in Montreal two to three weeks from now and can pay your bill there. Have a good journey home," the man told us as we left his office.

In Montreal I moved in with Danielle and still had between a thousand and fifteen hundred dollars left. But the whole thing was starting to get to Danielle. Not only was she worried about being pregnant, but she was also scared silly about getting the car through Customs. One day she told me that she didn't want to keep the child.

"Don't panic. We've got time," I told her.

"Time! Can't you see it's beginning to show!"

A few days later we went to New York and when we got back, Danielle was no longer pregnant.

Toward the end of September 1970, we were advised that the car was about to arrive. As arranged, I called Bec to ask him to meet us. He said he couldn't come at once but would be in Montreal in a week, and to sort things out for myself.

"How in hell can I do that? Everything has to be paid for and I need money."

I went back to see my friend André who gave me some cash, and I told Danielle to go down to the port to pick up the car. "When you've cleared it through Customs, call me at André's place. If I don't hear from you in one hour or at most an hour and a half, I'll take off. Give me another hour, then call the police. Tell them the car belongs to me and that you don't know where I am or anything about it. That'll give me enough time to disappear." We kissed and she left.

The date was September 29, 1970. I went to André's. We waited for an hour and then another half hour and I began to worry seriously. I knew that Danielle would be all right because she could always blame everything on me. I was pacing up and down the apartment when the doorbell rang. André and I turned white. It was Danielle.

"What happened?"

"Nothing. I've got the car downstairs."

Tense with emotion, I screamed, "How did you get it here? Couldn't you have called me?" It wasn't bad as surprises go. She was very calm. I asked her what had happened.

"I had an argument with one of the Customs' officers." She must be completely out of her mind, I thought. "They'd scratched the car. I raised hell and had to file a complaint to get some compensation." It couldn't be true.

"Why did you do that, Danielle?"

"It's better this way, Michel. If you ever have any trouble I can always say that I obviously didn't know anything about the heroin."

"You're crazy," I said.

Either she was very brave or she truly loved me. The three of us then did something completely stupid; we took the car out for a spin around Montreal. We were absolutely mad. What's worse, we did the same thing again that very evening and took the car to the other end of the city to visit Danielle's parents. It never occurred to us that we might have an accident and the heroin could be spilled all over the road. We did even less thinking when we took Danielle's parents for a spin.

That night we parked in Danielle's garage in the rue Saint Mathieu.

A week later Bec flew in to Montreal looking like Sherlock Holmes in a black jacket, gray pants and spectacles. I took him to our place. As he and Danielle had not met before, I introduced him to her as the manager of Les Charlots and my business partner. He didn't want to go out much because Ginette and Anne-Marie were still looking for him everywhere. Then I learned that the car would have to be delivered to New York by the end of the week. A meeting had been arranged for Saturday, September 27, 1970 in the snack bar of the Taft Hotel. Danielle was to take the car across the border alone — I thought it would be simpler because she was so well-known. She left and I stayed in Montreal with André. As soon as she called me from Plattsburg in New York State, André, his wife and son and I left in a car driven by his friend Longpré, who knew absolutely nothing of what was going on. At the border we told the immigration men we were out for a pleasure drive. They asked us for our papers and André and his family and I showed them our French passports, but Longpré didn't have his on him and couldn't cross. I didn't know what to do on the spur of the moment. Danielle was waiting for us and so I suggested Longpré stay at the border on the Canadian side while we looked at Plattsburg, New York. "We'll pick you up in an hour or two after we've seen the town," I said. It was another stupid thing to do. If the border people had been the least bit suspicious, we would have been in the soup. We had lunch with Danielle and André and his family and friend returned to Montreal. I drove to New York with Danielle to rendezvous with Bec.

I parked the car near the Abbey Victoria Hotel. Delivery was

to be made at four o'clock the next morning. All these arrangements with Bec were discussed in front of Danielle. We checked in
at the hotel, but didn't get much sleep that night.

It was early Tuesday morning and the streets of Manhattan
were deserted. Bec and I drove to the appointed spot. We waited.
We drove around the block three times. Still no one was there. I
couldn't believe the operation could be run in such a slipshod
fashion. How could these people take everything so lightly? The
tension was growing unbearable. Someone was sure to notice us.
Finally a man arrived, handsome and slim, with dark hair.

"Our man's car is here now," Bec told me.

Later I found out that his full name was André Andréani. I
could tell he was from Marseilles from his accent. "It's not ready
yet. Let's go and have a coffee," he suggested.

We went into a bar, but Andréani told us not to talk because
our accents might draw attention. He went to look around outside
and came back to tell us everything was O.K..

Bec and I got into the D.S., Andréani had a red Dodge. I noticed
that four other cars parked along the curb were starting up at the
same time as we were; these were the back-up vehicles, all Cadillacs,
one green, one black, one white and one blue. I knew that the
American buyers were Mafiosi and marvelled at the precautions
that were being taken by these well-organized professionals. We
were both impressed and scared at the same time. Here we were in
America, in a city we hardly knew, driving a car loaded with forty
kilos of heroin which, in the event of trouble, could get us a long
prison sentence. We cruised around Manhattan for an hour and
then crossed a bridge which I think was the Williamsburg Bridge.
For three-quarters of an hour we drove down a three-lane high-
way and ended up in a village where the road came to an end. We
stopped, probably because things weren't quite ready yet, and had
something to eat. Then André Andréani arrived and told us to
follow his car. Two miles beyond the restaurant we met up with
one of the back-up cars, the blue Cadillac. There were two Mafiosi
with Andréani, one of them wearing spectacles. I followed the
Cadillac into a small town where again we drove around for at least
an hour. Finally they signalled to me to take a narrow path through

the open gates leading to a villa. Bec got nervous because we had trouble maneuvering the car into the garage. He closed the doors and Andréani came in to help us dismantle the car. He had a plan which showed where the stuff was hidden and handed us the necessary tools to take the car apart. The caches were planted under the front carpet, under the seats and in the chassis. Forty sachets in all of pure heroin.*

We passed the packages to Andréani who sorted and counted them and resealed those that had torn open in transit. He then divided the forty kilos into four parts and repacked them into four suitcases.

I reassembled the car with only a screwdriver and some glue. Fifteen minutes later the man with the glasses, who I learned later was one of the famous Stassi brothers, arrived with the proper tools.

The Americans spoke Italian and Andréani did the translating. They asked us not to make too much noise; there were children asleep in the room adjoining the garage. When we were through Bec and I drove back to New York in the DS. The others went their own ways. I asked Bec, "What about the money. Who'se got that?"

"Andréani will bring it tomorrow," he replied.

The next afternoon Andréani arrived at our hotel room with fifty thousand dollars. I took twenty thousand for myself to share with André in Montreal. Bec wanted to keep the DS and send it back to France. I told him that was unreasonable and quite out of the question. "I bought the car for Danielle," I argued. "She's shown it to everyone and everyone knows she bought it in France. It would look strange if it suddenly weren't here."

"But I paid for it," he replied.

"O.K. Then lets go fifty-fifty. I'll give you two thousand dollars and we'll call it quits."

He flew to Montreal and I took the DS back to Danielle.

When I arrived at the hotel I felt exhausted, but content. I'd succeeded in one operation. It was no longer merely a dream.

---

* In 1971 a kilo of heroin was worth eleven thousand dollars wholesale. The retail value was one million dollars. In 1977 the same quantity was worth five times as much.

Suddenly I felt powerful — I was on the road to fortune! Looking back, the whole thing didn't seem at all complicated; it seemed easy.

Danielle wasn't at the hotel. She had gone to do some shopping just as if nothing had happened. When she got back she calmly asked, "Is it all finished?"

"Yes. And your car is back in the garage." It seems unbelievable now, but at that time neither of us thought there was much danger in trafficking. When we got in the car she commented, "It doesn't show, does it? It's absolutely as it was before."

Shortly before we got to the Canada-U.S. line, I stopped at a restaurant and hid the fifty thousand dollars in the spare tire. The border authorities waved us through.

A few days later Bec came to ask me if I could move another car for him. I told him I would rather wait. When I gave André his money I asked him how he felt about another car. He was delighted as he wanted to get more involved and possibly bring one in himself, he said. Since he had never had anything to do with any known traffickers, he felt there was little chance that he would be spotted.

I hadn't told Bec about my agreement with André but did mention to him that he and I would first have to come across with money for a suitable car for André as *he* did not know about my partnership with Bec. Bec put down one half — one thousand dollars — towards the purchase of a red Ford Galaxie. I paid the other half.

At that time Danielle's career was going from bad to worse. She was working less and less — without this new source of income she would have been in poor financial shape. The film she had made in Belgium hadn't been released yet and the only work she had lined up were a few radio commercials. But she was always hungry for publicity. In fact, she was prepared to do almost anything to get written up in the press. What mattered most to her was to preserve the star image she had projected to the public in the past.

Our love affair continued as before despite some infidelities, committed by both of us. However, our activities had drawn us closer together and we were now the Bonnie and Clyde of the heroin ring. She hadn't done much to develop her skills as a lover and, although I took what she had to offer, I looked elsewhere from time to time. Danielle was intelligent and cultured; that frightened me a little. I was shocked that she could sometimes be completely callous. The people around her were only there to help her; she didn't really care for or about any of them. But with me she was always gentle and kind. She rarely talked about her son, Jean-François whom she called "Snoopy," who now lived with her ex-fiancé in Montreal, and whom she sometimes saw on Sundays. When I suggested she should have Snoopy with her she said it was better to leave things as they were. She had absolutely no maternal instincts.

5/
THE
GOOD LIFE

Danielle and I were enjoying a good, even frivolous, time. We lived extravagantly, travelled, ate at the best restaurants and generally went short of nothing.

As her lover I too had a public role to play. I increased my wardrobe and we moved to a larger and more attractive place, a very chic penthouse suite at Habitat in Montreal at three hundred dollars a month, which at that time was a lot of money for an apartment. But it was worth it, the view was spectacular; we overlooked the St. Lawrence River and the site of Expo 67. Danielle and I were again very much in love and I was pleased with my business success, even if my rewards weren't as great as those of some others. The first trafficking operation had gone so well. I began to fantasize — why not one or even two cars a month, which would bring in about ten or twelve thousand dollars. There were absolutely no obstacles in my way, a few small problems maybe which I could easily overcome.

Morally, it didn't bother me that I was dealing in heroin. I had no idea of its selling price in New York, nor of the damage it did to young people. I was happy and felt I was doing a conscientious job; the rest didn't interest me. I wasn't any different from any of the others in the drug ring. We had no pangs of conscience about smuggling dope; it didn't seem any worse to us than smuggling household appliances.

One day Bec told me he had twenty-eight thousand dollars in Canada. "It's a delicate operation for me, if I'm asked where the money came from I may have problems explaining it to the authorities in Paris," he said.

"Why not ask Danielle to take it?" I suggested.

When he told her about it, offering to pay her plane fare to Paris plus a thousand dollars, she agreed to leave any time. I decided to accompany her and combine the "business" trip with a holiday.

All I wanted was a few days to arrange for André's car to be shipped to Paris before boarding our plane in Montreal. Danielle carried Bec's money in her purse without taking any special precautions. If we were stopped she would simply say that she was a well-known singer and needed the money in France.

It was October 1970 and the FLQ kidnappings in Quebec dominated the headlines. We assumed that police had more important things to do than think about the drug scene.

While we were waiting for André and the car to arrive in Paris, Danielle and I decided to spend a short holiday in Spain. Everything was ready. Bec had told me to leave André's car in a lot in Place Saint-Augustin with the parking ticket stuck under the sun visor. He also had a set of keys and said he would drive the car to Biarritz himself. A week later, when André arrived in Paris, I showed him where he was to leave the car which was due to arrive in two weeks. I told him I would phone his parents' house in Cannes to let him know when the car was ready. "All you have to do, André, is go to the station in Biarritz, pick up the car in the parking lot, drive it to Le Havre and have it shipped to Canada." As far as we were concerned it was just a routine operation.

All along, my only contact with the network had been through Bec. I still didn't know who was behind our operations and who the suppliers were. Bec always tried to create the impression that he was a bigshot in the outfit, whereas he was only an intermediary. He once bragged to me, "Understand, we do things differently than Taillet; we don't steal and we're always there when the cars are loaded. We count the packages and we know exactly what is being carried." He also tried to tell me that "others" below him in the hierarchy were not as tough as he was. "They don't know how to talk. I'm not just one of the gang — I've got a good head on my shoulders." Until then I had always considered the drug world as somewhat mysterious, a sort of secret society which was impossible to penetrate. The small-time crooks I had known used to talk in low voices, just like secret agents do in the movies. They would show their magnaminity in restaurants by offering to pay for each other. "This is on me," they would say, and grab the check.

Therefore, I was surprised to find "respectable" people like Bec and Taillet arguing about trifling matters such as a mere thousand dollars, more or less. I had also thought that trafficking was a clearly defined business, with a boss at the top and a well-structured organization to serve him. So it amazed me when I saw how the underworld allied itself with these so-called honest folks and show business people such as Danielle Ouimet and persons of Bec's and Taillet's caliber. How easily people from similar walks of life, the respectable, the respected and the envied in high positions could succomb to crime by the inducement and temptation of easy money!

All that hypocrisy left a bitter taste in my mouth and I told myself that everyone was corrupt, and if that was the case, why not me? Why not indeed? People like Bec must have been making three or four thousand francs a week, about six hundred dollars.

When I had first met them, I was dazzled by their elegance, their confidence, their manners and their nonchalance. When I was with them I lost my inferiority complex and became as self-assured as they were. Now I, too, was important. I rubbed shoulders with the entertainment crowd in Montreal, my photograph appeared in the papers and I went to important film premieres. Only when I saw my former idols in their true light did I become disenchanted. In time I even felt superior to them. The fact that I had succeeded on my first run had also improved my status in Danielle's eyes. Whereas previously she would buy this or that without consulting me, now she would ask for my opinion. I was in business, I was no longer a mere barman; I bought her expensive jewelry; I took her on holidays. I lavishly furnished our apartment; I had no money problems. She could draw checks on all my Canadian bank accounts. With the little money at her disposal, she bought me gold chains, a love medallion, a camera and a pair of skis. All in all, she was quite generous toward me. My goal was to save enough money to have my own business in Canada or elsewhere, although I had no specific ambitions. The sword of Damocles dangled above my head; that's why I sometimes did crazy things. For example, one weekend Danielle and I flew to Paris just to buy a pair of pants for me. It was madness, a thousand dollars in air fares just for one pair of pants!

Pleasing myself was most important to me in those days. As long as no one was being killed under my nose and as long as I wasn't killing anyone, I didn't think I was doing anything wrong. If anyone had told me that heroin could kill, I would have been flabbergasted. In France, as in Canada at the time, the drug problem was not as acute as it was in the United States. From books I had read and films I had seen I knew about heroin and how it was being moved through Marseilles. But I had never met a dope addict or a junky. I looked upon the United States as the country which dropped bombs on Vietnam. Every day in the newspapers there were pictures showing children who had suffered napalm burns. Compared to that I didn't think I was doing any great harm.

I consider myself a fairly humane person and if anyone had told me that people could be killed by taking heroin, I would probably have said to them that I wasn't forcing them to take it — if they wanted it, that was their business. I don't drink and no one has ever made me drink, nor have I ever smoked against my will. I have never taken marijuana or hashish. When I'm offered a joint I always turn it down. It was none of my business if Americans wanted to dope themselves up. I also found out much later that the drug problem was political and social in nature. As long as heroin was only being pushed in black ghettos, no one did much about it. Who cared if the blacks drugged themselves senselessly? The United States government only started to take action when the problem reached the white population. The public tends to look upon a trafficker as a depraved and scheming scoundrel without realizing that everyone is capable of becoming one. People in this business come from many different backgrounds — the only thing they have in common is the urge to make a fast buck. A good-looking little broad could find herself on the way to France with a handsome man and then accept a gift of a car. As far as I was concerned, once I had started in this business there was no going back, working for pitiful wages as a barman or a waiter in a restaurant, now that I was earning big money and was accustomed to the good life. I thought in this vein in those days. Once Danielle even suggested I give up what I was doing, but a couple of hours later she forgot all about it. We were in love, we lived well, and nothing else was important to us. That period in our lives was our "Thousand and One Nights" and we even deluded ourselves that it would last forever!

While the second operation was slowly getting off the ground, Danielle and I decided to take a three week holiday at a luxury hotel in the Canary Islands.

We had picked up Snoopy, Danielle's son, in Strasbourg where he was now living with his paternal grandmother. He was three years old, handsome, intelligent and very appealing. A real little prince. He reminded me a little of my own son. Every morning, Snoopy would tiptoe into our bedroom and wake me. "Are you coming, Michel?"

"No. Why don't you wake up your mother today?" I would say. But he knew she would get mad if he did. So I would get dressed and go downstairs with him. We would have breakfast together by the pool, swim all morning and at noon we would wake Danielle. I was the one who looked after Snoopy.

In the evenings we stayed close to the hotel because I didn't want to leave Snoopy alone. Often we took him to the port and spent hours looking at the fishing boats.

While we were there we read in a Canadian newspaper that there had been a second FLQ kidnapping, of the Quebec labor minister Pierre Laporte who was subsequently murdered. We also learned that a state of emergency had been declared in the Province of Quebec and that the army had been called out in Montreal. Danielle was worried and wanted to get back to Canada as soon as possible, but I persuaded her to stay. Although the holiday had cost me more than two thousand dollars I'll never forget those three weeks. We didn't speak of heroin or cars or trafficking. I was with the girl I loved in elegant and luxurious surroundings. It was like a dream!

When we got back to Paris the three of us were Bec's guests at La Villa des Fleurs, actually a second-rate hotel. The rooms were comfortable although we could hear every word the neighbors were saying and especially what they were doing. Most of the guests were transients and a number of them were prostitutes. But Snoopy and I had a good time. I bought him treats and little toy cars which cost me two to three dollars apiece. He loved them so much that he even played with them in the bathtub.

André's Ford was not yet ready for pick-up in Biarritz; there had been a delay in the delivery of the heroin.

I went back to Montreal and left Bec to phone André as planned, when it was time to pick up the car in Biarritz. Meanwhile I continued to live it up. I skied a lot and went for walks and drives. Financially everything was all right — Bec was still supplying me with money.

On December 20, I had an irate call from him. The car had been in the parking lot in Biarritz for a week and no one had collected it. I desperately tried to get in touch with André but no one knew where he was. Then Bec called again; he was even more furious.

"Michel, we have commitments! I've got problems here; my friends want to get rid of the car and your friend has disappeared."

"Don't worry. I'll find him."

Bec had refused to pick up the car himself. It was O.K. for me to stick out my neck but the bastard didn't want to take any risks himself. One morning I received a call from, of all people, André. Surprise! He had returned to Canada without picking up the car at Biarritz! I gave him hell and we had a terrible row. There was a car loaded with at least eighty kilos of heroin sitting right in the middle of a Biarritz parking lot! He told me the police had stopped him as he was about to board the plane from Cannes to Biarritz.

"Why?" I asked.

"Because there were some counterfeit dollar bills among those you gave me for the first shipment, and we hadn't noticed."

"How did the police get on to that?"

"I wanted to buy a car, Michel."

"Why?"

"Because I wanted to take a holiday in France."

I told him he was insane and that we had to pick up the car. "It can't stay there and they're holding me responsible," I explained.

"How can we do anything? It's Christmas."

I swore at him and hung up. Then I called Bec and told him André was in Montreal. He told me we would both have to go back to France. When I argued that the whole deal wasn't worth my while and, anyway, the kitty was empty, he promised to take care of all the expenses. He said he'd meet us at Orly Airport and then I was to come to see him alone.

When I told André that we had to return to France he refused at first, but when I assured him that we would be back in Montreal to spend Christmas with our families, he finally agreed. The journey, first class, cost us each eight hundred dollars and by the time we arrived in Paris, Bec was a nervous wreck and bawled out André for being so stupid. I told him to stop worrying.

As our train rolled into the railroad station of the seaside town on the Bay of Biscay, we could see the car in the parking lot.

"It's there. Everything is O.K.," I whispered with relief.

Just as we were leaving the station, a police car pulled in. André went as white as a sheet so we went into the coffee shop to pull ourselves together. When he was calmer I told him to get the car while I walked to the street corner.

"I'll meet you there," I said. Everything went well but we hadn't driven five hundred metres when I realized that André didn't have a clue how to drive!

"Stop! I'll take the wheel," I yelled. He insisted that he could drive but his night vision was lousy.

"So, you're scared, that's O.K. Let's change places and I'll drive. But one thing's for sure, André: if the police stop us, or if there's a road block, we're finished. With you from Cannes and me from Marseilles driving a car registered in Canada, we've had it."

"It's worse than that, Michel. I haven't any papers for the car."

"What!" I shouted.

"No, not a single one. I left them in Montreal." What an idiot! We were a fine team of smugglers. With a gold mine of eighty kilos in our car we were at the mercy of a simple police check.

It was a terrible journey. André was dying of fright and every time he saw a red light he imagined the cops were waving us down. Getting through Paris was catastrophic. I told André to take away the car and have it shipped from wherever he wanted to ship it and that I would meet him at Orly Airport in time for our return flight to Canada. Fortunately, the agent of Parking de France who had brought in the car remembered André and didn't question his story that he was going back to America and his papers were in Cannes. We left the car with the agent and boarded our plane for Montreal.

As soon as I arrived home, Danielle and I went for a two week skiing holiday in the Laurentians. We took her sister and brother and her parents along. Everything went O.K.

All I now had to do was wait for the Ford to arrive from France. But suddenly things weren't going as smoothly as we had anticipated. Bec phoned to suggest that I shouldn't stick around Montreal when the car was being delivered. "We can't count on André — it's too dangerous. With his history, he risks going to prison," he warned. I agreed to leave Montreal after the Christmas holidays and told André I had some business in Paris and he was to call me at the Villa des Fleurs as soon as the car was off the boat in Montreal.

"Send me a simple message: All is O.K. I have received the cases."

I again took off for Paris and stayed for a few days, spending some time with my family in Marseilles. About twelve days later André phoned to inform me of a new disaster.

"The car is still at Parking de France and has never left Paris."

Had something gone wrong with the boat or had there been a strike? Far worse than that, the car wouldn't start! They had telephoned André in Montreal to ask if he was prepared to pay a mechanic to move it to a repair shop! I told him to hold everything and that I would get back to him.

When Bec heard the news, he couldn't believe it. "I knew it was too risky to let a mechanic near the car. Anyone will see straight away that the doors are too heavy, that there's a double roof and a double floor and that you can practically touch the roof with your head." Bec wanted to go to the Parking de France and fix it himself. I was surprised about his willingness to get involved — he probably wanted to impress me and show me who was boss. I told him he was crazy. Personally, I wouldn't have gone with him for all the tea in China. It was careless and foolish. I wanted André to come back to Paris but Bec didn't think it was necessary. He insisted on going himself and soon discovered the problem was minor. "The starter cable is badly connected and I don't know how to change it. Have André phone the shipping agent and ask him to replace the cable. It can be done without looking inside the car."

Everything went as planned. The car was loaded on a Russian boat, the *Alexander Pushkin,* headed for Montreal. It was mid-January 1971 when André called to tell me: "I've received the cases.All is well."

I immediately returned to Montreal. But the Russian boat was blocked by ice in the St. Lawrence River and would dock ten days later.

Bec had arrived in Montreal and had taken a fabulous suite at the Bonaventure Hotel with his fiancée Marie-France. One morning I received a frantic call from Danielle at Robert Gauthier's house. Would I rush over to the hotel. Bec had apparently tried to commit suicide by taking an overdose of sleeping pills. I found him lying on the bed. A doctor had given him some medication which made him vomit. The toilet was blocked and had overflowed and the room was flooded. He shouted at me at the top of his voice and I tried to calm him down, not only for his sake but also because Danielle and I were known in Montreal; our presence in Bec's suite could be embarrassing. I got out of there as soon as I could — I didn't want to be involved in a front-page scandal.

It was a relief when the car finally arrived and André could retrieve it without difficulty. I had telephoned Marie-France every hour to inquire about Bec's state of health and was told he was doing fine, especially when he heard that the car had been cleared through Customs. He was soon feeling well enough to leave for New York to inform the American buyers and I helped André get the car ready for the border crossing.

At that time André was going out with an actress friend of Danielle's. I had an inspiration. "Your girlfriend is Canadian," I told him. "If you say you're Canadian too and don't show them your French passport, you won't have any difficulty. She doesn't know what's in the car so she'll act natural. It will be a breeze."

He was to check in at the Holiday Inn on Fifty-seventh Street in New York and register under his fiancée's name, then he was to wait for me. I arranged my own trip with Danielle's old friend Robert Gauthier, and gave him a thousand dollars to drive me across the border. Once in Manhattan, I met Bec at the Taft Hotel where he introduced me to Jo Signoli, one of his bosses. Jo was a badly shaven, conspicuous looking character; he in turn introduced me to Richard Berdin. Since I couldn't speak English, Richard accompanied me to the phone booth and called André for me to ask him to park the car in front of the Holiday Inn and leave the keys inside. Bec and I, with Richard following, then headed for Fifty-seventh Street in a Ford Galaxie to pick up the car. With Richard at the wheel of the loaded car, we drove around for about twenty minutes to make sure no one was following us. At Second Avenue I saw Jo Signoli sitting in a parked car next to the driver; all the lights were out. When Richard swung in behind them they started up immediately and we headed for New Jersey. About half an hour later we arrived in front of a villa; the front door and garage doors had been left open. We drove the car in. I can remember it as if it were yesterday. We had to go through a road block on the way and our nerves were in bad shape. After we dismantled the panels we checked, assembled and counted a hundred kilos of pure heroin which took us several hours. Nothing was missing. Jo Signoli informed the buyers' men who were stationed around the villa keeping a lookout.

It was dawn by the time we finished; we were exhausted and covered with grease. After a wash, John Astuto, the buyer's assistant, took us to a cab stand where we separated; Richard went with Jo Signoli and Bec and I returned to the hotel. André and his girlfriend had to fly back to Canada because the car was completely demolished. I gave him an advance of two thousand dollars before they left. Bec and I waited in the hotel room for the money to be delivered. He was nervous and frightened, in fact, he was completely distraught. There had been a lot of incidents involving drugs lately and several couriers had been killed in New York. The tension was too much for him and he decided to go and have a drink. I waited. Soon Richard Berdin arrived with the money in a blue KLM airline bag, which I have kept as a souvenir. We sat down to count it — ninety thousand dollars in all. I think Bec must have been on the lookout for him from the hotel bar because he appeared as soon as Berdin had entered the room. That was the only time he and I met during my trafficking days. I was working on the level of a courier while he was responsible for the delivery of the drugs to the New York Mafia.

Later the same day Robert Gauthier and I drove back to Montreal with the money bag hidden in the spare tire of his Renault 16. It was about four o'clock in the morning when he dropped me at my place. Danielle was waiting for me and in a state of nerves. "I thought you'd never come! What happened? Why didn't you call me?"

I tried to calm her down and, despite the fact that I was so tired, we had a restless night.

The next day I met Bec in his hotel room and we divided the money. I had paid Gauthier one thousand dollars and André had received the balance of his share of twenty thousand. As agreed, I got twenty thousand. The operation had been successfully completed and Bec returned to Paris. It was then that I began to realize that Bec was taking advantage of me. I was thinking of shafting him, getting money against the next run so that I would get what I thought he really owed me.

In February 1971 he was back in Montreal. He came to tell me that he needed to ship more money to France. I suggested he use his girlfriend, Marie-France.

"I can't," he said. "If she gets busted I'll still be in big trouble."

That's when I decided to send Danielle. Bec paid her plane fare and gave her fifteen hundred dollars.

When she returned two days later, she said, "Michel, your colleagues are crazy."

"Which ones?"

"Bec and Marie-France."

Apparently she'd witnessed a terrible family quarrel between the girl and her mother which had nothing to do with the heroin business. Bec had sided with the mother and both of them had insulted Marie-France to the point where he even hit her. The fracas got so bad that the police arrived, at which time Danielle took off in a hurry.

6/
A MICKEY MOUSE OUTFIT

A firm friendship had developed between Robert Gauthier and myself. Things were going so well that we decided to try for a grand slam: we'd get a boat, a sailboat, in which we could hide hundreds of kilos of heroin. We envisioned a hollow keel and a hull which could conceal at least a ton of the stuff.

I suggested that I would pay for the boat and as he had always wanted to sail the Atlantic, he was delighted. "When it's ready, you can go to London and on to Marseilles and we'll load it there together," I told him.

We had made plans and calculations, and in February 1971 I advanced Gauthier thirty-five thousand dollars to start construction in Montreal of the *Jusan*. Gauthier knew something about boatbuilding and had found a "shipyard" for himself.

In addition to Robert Gauthier I decided to take in Michel Maillet* as my partner. Maillet was a freelance journalist I had met at a party three or four months previously. He had been trafficking in diamonds and tried to interest me in some deals, but I turned him down because there wasn't much money in it.

He also told me he had something that was even better than moving heroin. Certain people had offered him a million dollar contract to overthrow the government of Haiti. He never told me

---

* Maillet is a pseudonym chosen by the author to protect the identity of this person.

who the people were who could make this kind of a proposition, but I believe he was in touch with certain secret service agencies.

Later Richard Berdin talked to me about a similar deal he had been offered — a contract to overthrow "Papa Doc" Duvalier, under the protection of the French and American secret services. The man who had approached Berdin was André Labay, one of his partners in the drug business, a freelance spy who had been in the French secret service, and had been chief of the secret police for Moise Tshombe, the former president of Katanga in Africa. Labay had asked Berdin to recruit mercenaries and arrange for arms to be transported to Haiti. However, the project fell through.

In our own operation Maillet was to accompany Gauthier on the transatlantic crossing. I found out later that Maillet was a crook and, although he had not invested any money with us, the bastard had tried to double-cross me by offering to sell some information about me to the police during the time I was preparing the boat.

Danielle and I went to France to check the editing of the film she had just made, and when I met Jacques Bec during the same trip, he asked me for new ideas on the next shipment. I felt that traveling from Paris to Montreal four or five times a month would arouse suspicion and I therefore suggested it was time he took a few risks himself and dealt with the couriers on the French side; I had enough problems at the Canadian end. Bec was interested in the boat venture and offered to give me ten thousand dollars towards its construction.

Danielle and I returned to Montreal.

One evening she asked me to help out Daniel Guérard, a not too successful singer who at one time had appeared at Chez Clairette. I was reluctant but Danielle insisted that the guy was flat broke and could see we were rolling in money. I suggested he could bring in cars, but was worried that he might talk if ever the police got hold of him. But Danielle assured me he was reliable and that I wouldn't have any trouble with him. She arranged for us to meet at Chez Bourgetel.

After a lot of hesitation I decided to buy a car for him which he could take to France and bring back for me. I offered to pay all his expenses and give him ten thousand dollars on top of that. "O.K.

I'm in," Guérard said, "but I want to know exactly what I'll be smuggling." I hardly ever lied and told him it was heroin.

The following day we went to all the garages in Montreal to look for a car. We found a metallic gray Corvette for me which cost seven thousand dollars and a beautiful second-hand red Barracuda for Guérard. I gave him twenty-five hundred dollars to buy the car and he registered it in his own name. I made a hotel reservation for him at Les Arromanches near the Champs Elysées in Paris and notified Bec to look after him and give him some money — he'd only got a thousand in cash from me and his plane fare.

My other business venture consisted of a partnership in a record firm which was basically a cover operation. I never made any money at it — in fact, one record, a song from a revue Robert Gauthier had written which I brought out, did not do at all well, and cost me three thousand dollars. Being involved with the record company had one advantage; I never had to justify my lifestyle because everyone thought Danielle and I were making a lot of money.

Although Bec had promised to take care of everything in France he again phoned and asked me to come over. This was contrary to our previous arrangements and I told him again not to bother me. But he was so persistent that I agreed in the end to go.

Apparently Bec had had a few problems with our former associates and was setting up another deal with some new people. He talked about a Fiat which had been registered in Italy, had landed in Halifax and was now standing idle in Montreal. The driver of the car, who had brought it over, didn't have a U.S. visa. Could I take the car, the driver and the owner, an Italian by the name of Felix Rosso, across the U.S. border? He offered me six thousand dollars for the job and I readily accepted.

We then got together with Signoli, whom I had met before in New York in connection with the Ford job, and he asked me how I planned to handle the deal. The only solution I could see was to buy a car in Montreal identical to the Fiat, put Canadian license plates on the Italian car and take it to New York. Signoli thought that was an excellent idea and said he would introduce me to someone I would have to contact at the Laurentien Hotel in Montreal.

He and Bec then took me to the drugstore on the Champs Elysée and pointed out a gray-haired man of about forty-five, well-dressed, who looked like a minister. His name was Paul Graziani.

I found it a little strange that they didn't introduce me then and there, since we were going to meet in Montreal anyway. Signoli gave me six thousand dollars to buy the car and I took an Air France flight back to Montreal, arriving on the same day as Graziani. We arranged to meet the same afternoon in Dominion Square, near Dorchester Street, opposite the Hotel Château Champlain. I arrived in Danielle's Citroën, Graziani got in, and we drove off. He explained that he had the car, the driver and the courier.

We met the next day in front of the Laurentien Hotel and I saw a green Fiat 124, registered in Italy, parked behind mine. I met the driver, Felix Rosso, who stayed in the car without introducing himself. He was a Corsican, about thirty-two, quite slim and elegant, but going bald. He had rough features but spoke very good English and also seemed intelligent. Graziani and I left for Mont Royal where I knew we could talk without being disturbed, and Rosso followed us in the loaded Fiat.

When I again explained my idea of putting Canadian license plates on the Italian car Rosso thought it was a good idea, but added, "We'll have to hurry because I've hardly any money left and the courier is here with his wife and two children." I was sure at that time that I would have no problems finding an identical car, but although I made the rounds of all the Fiat dealers in Montreal none had that particular model. It also occurred to me that even if I found a car, the Customs people at the U.S. border might notice that the speedometer registered kilometers instead of miles.

So I dropped that scheme and found a plausible alternative. I telephoned Jean Cardon, the accordionist, and explained to him that I had a car loaded with a hundred kilos of heroin and needed his car to get the stuff into the U.S., but he would have to drive it as far as New York. I offered him six thousand dollars and he agreed.

Graziani and Felix Rosso accepted my new plan but Graziani seemed nervous and preoccupied. He told me a man had come to his hotel room that very morning to check the air conditioning, although it was working well. Also, he had noticed his case had been tampered with. "I'm sure it was the police and I think we're being followed." We looked apprehensively at each other.

The Fiat was now in the garage of the Queen Elizabeth Hotel, and we decided to proceed with extreme caution.

"Try and lose the police," I told Felix, "and Paul and I will do the same. We'll drive to Jean Cardon's house in Saint Hubert to unload it. It's on the South Shore — not far."

We arrived there without any trouble and started to dismantle the car. I could see it would take a long time so I phoned Danielle to come and spend the day with me because I missed her. I was always unhappy when she wasn't with me and didn't like to leave her alone.

There we were standing around the car: Jean Cardon, his wife Michèle, Danielle, Paul Graziani, Felix Rosso and I. We had all become mechanics, including the women. We spread out the heroin on the garage floor, millions of dollars worth of the stuff. There were ninety-six kilos in a hundred and ninety-eight sachets of ninety-six percent pure heroin wrapped in copies of *Le Provençal*, Marseilles' daily newspaper. The mechanic who had installed the caches had left his visiting card. The heroin was hidden on the back ledge, the floors, the doors and the chassis of the car. Everyone admired his handiwork.

"This man is good — the car is really well done," I said to Paul.

"It's always the same guy, he's the Uncle's mechanic."

The Uncle's mechanic? At the time I didn't understand but the "Uncle" often crept into the conversation. To me he was then just another name, but later I found out how important he was.

We then began repacking the heroin in plastic bags in Cardon's station wagon. All the doors were full and we still had thirty kilos left over. I decided to store them underneath the seats, but soon realized that they might fall out when the seats were put back in place.

Michèle Cardon and Danielle suggested making seat covers to prevent the packages from dropping out. So they became seamstresses. I didn't know that Danielle could sew. We put the seats back in place and nothing showed. Felix Rosso took the Fiat back to its owner and then left for Miami to contact the Mafia buyer.

Danielle, Graziani and I immediately returned to Montreal in the DS.

On the way Paul thought we were being followed.

"But how?" I asked naively, "It's strange that they would manage to follow us here."

The next morning, we read in the paper that the RCMP had seized a Fiat carrying fifty kilos of heroin at the port of Montreal and had arrested Edouard Batkoun, a pimp, well-known in the Paris underworld. It was June 22, 1971. Although the haul had nothing to do with us, the coincidence, nevertheless, gave us a shock. I found out later that the heroin that had been found in Batkoun's car constituted the second largest narcotics haul ever made in Canada.

It was then that I discovered the difference between French and Canadian courts. The Montreal judge gave Batkoun the benefit of the doubt when he testified that he had no knowledge of the presence of drugs in the Fiat. Once released he returned to France with the car and was arrested on arrival by the French narcotics bureau and accused of exporting heroin to Canada. The French judge didn't believe his story and convicted him.

I thought that after Batkoun's arrest the feds would find out that he had stayed in several Montreal hotels and that they could easily trace Paul Graziani who was already known as a heroin trafficker in France. The trail would then lead them to Felix Rosso and eventually to me.

The next day Rosso came back from Miami, in a panic, and told me that he hadn't been able to contact the buyer.

"What do you suggest? Throw the car into the St. Lawrence?" I asked.

The police had asked for his papers on the plane and had interrogated him on arrival at Miami airport. When they questioned him about his business he told them he was a restaurant owner interested in looking at some Florida operations. "But I knew I was being followed," he said, and even though he hadn't been taken to the police station he couldn't risk contacting the buyer. He had come straight back to Montreal to ask Paul Graziani to take his place. But Paul categorically refused to leave. "I'm being followed everywhere too; we all are," he told Rosso. I didn't want to go because I couldn't speak English, and was afraid I also might be followed.

That was when I had the idea of sending Danielle. I knew she wasn't being followed — or at least I didn't think so, because if that had been the case we would already have been arrested.

Danielle cheerfully agreed to go to Miami. She was booked into the Fontainebleau Hotel and instructed to go to a certain address, give the man there Rosso's photo and a letter, and advise him to be in New York the next evening.

Rosso, Graziani and I spent the rest of the day driving around Montreal with the police on our heels. There were lots of them, in cars and on foot. Every time we stopped we felt their presence all around us. In the evening, we bought some cokes and a pizza and went to my apartment to wait for Danielle's call. She finally phoned around ten o'clock, and went into raptures about the hotel and the beautiful weather she was having. "The only trouble is the gentleman doesn't know me and won't believe me. He definitely wants to talk to Felix," she said.

I passed the phone over to him and he arranged everything in Italian with the party at the other end.

Jean Cardon was to leave for New York that same evening, and Rosso and I arranged to meet the following day at the Holiday Inn on Fifty-seventh Street.

We spent the morning at a Montreal restaurant while waiting to hear from Cardon that he had safely crossed the border. Finally I decided to call his house and his wife answered. "Everything's fine with my husband," she said.

I waited for Danielle to return from Miami before taking off for New York. I also realized it was not safe for Felix to board a plane as he was being followed, so I called Robert Gauthier to ask him to drive Felix to New York, all expenses paid, plus two hundred dollars for his trouble. He accepted after I assured him that he was taking no chances. "You aren't carrying anything and they don't have anything on you."

Felix and I arranged to meet the next day at five o'clock in front of the Empire State Building.

"Walk around, and when I get there come up and speak to me only if the coast is clear. If not, walk away."

He and Gauthier left and as soon as Danielle was back from Miami, we too were on our way. Graziani stayed behind in Montreal.

I knew I was being watched but I wasn't afraid. I had spun a fantasy for myself. With the powerful Corvette registered in my name I felt I could outdrive anything on the road. I had so far succeeded in avoiding the RCMP and felt I didn't have to worry.

When Danielle and I arrived at the Empire State Building, Felix assured us that he hadn't been followed. Yet we still thought it would be foolish to take chances. We drove around Manhattan for a while and then I phoned Jean Cardon and told him to stay in his room and wait until he got the green light from me.

Felix suggested that we split up, he to see the buyers who had just come in from Las Vegas and I to go to the Holiday Inn to book a room in Danielle's name. We arranged to meet again at eight in a bar of the Taft Hotel.

Everything was ready by then. Danielle went back to the hotel; Jean Cardon had been instructed to park his car on Fifty-second Street near Seventh Avenue at ten o'clock and to return at one A.M. after it had been unloaded. Rosso and I went to Fifty-second Street. We drove round the block again and again, waiting, and I finally suggested we park the car and he could meet the buyer's people somewhere else.

He left and I waited an hour or so before he was back.

"The buyer's men aren't there! They aren't there!" he said. Impatiently, he left again, came back, left again, and finally told me he had seen them.

He climbed into the car and gave me directions. "I warn you," he said, "if anything happens, if the police surprise us, I'm going to run, even if they fire on us. What about you?"

"I'll do the same," I told him, "but why are you worrying about that? What's got into you?"

"Accidents can always happen," he replied.

"Did you warn them about the police?"

Just then I noticed a car on our tail and started to feel nervous. "The cops are following us," I whispered.

"No. That's the buyer's men," he said.

We drove to a house in New Jersey where I had never been before. The Italian-looking man with glasses who had been involved with the Citroën motioned us inside the garage.

As I drove down the ramp our headlights shone on four men standing inside. I looked at Felix and he nodded. When I switched off the lights the men disappeared. Felix and I were alone. He closed the door, switched on the lights and we began to dismantle the car. It didn't take us as long as before. We sorted and counted the packets. Everything checked out. "O.K. Let's go," Felix said. The man with the glasses signalled to us that the coast was clear and waved us goodbye.

We drove back to Manhattan, returned the car to Cardon and I called Danielle to let her know that I was on my way to the hotel.

Suddenly Felix told me that he had nowhere to sleep. "I didn't want to register at a hotel in case the police find me."

"But the job's finished," I said.

"No. We still have to see the buyer tomorrow to pick up your share of the money."

"Well that's no problem," I said, "Cardon has two beds in his room. We'll call him and ask if you can stay with him."

Jean Cardon was never difficult and always agreed with whatever I suggested. Felix then told me that he had been stopped at the U.S. border and that the Customs' people had searched the car and asked him a lot of questions. It now dawned on me why he had been so afraid to go to a hotel.

So the American police knew that Felix Rosso was in the U.S.! Things were hotter than I had thought. However, the fact that we had been able to unload the stuff without problems again reassured me. If the police had followed him we would be in the slammer by now.

Relieved, I joined Danielle at the hotel. We had a fantastic night. Her sensuality had developed enormously since I had first met her.

The next day Felix told me we had to pick up the money on Sixty-second Street. "Let's take the Corvette," he said.

We parked opposite an enormous building and Felix went upstairs to pick up the money.

I had waited almost an hour and a half when I suddenly

spotted three police cars parked in the next block. I was terrified! Should I stay or run? I decided to stay put. It turned out that they were only making a routine check. Lucky once again!

Felix returned, accompanied by an older man, both loaded down with two suitcases. I had never seen the other man before. He was middle-aged — about fifty — with thinning hair. Felix introduced him as The Uncle, *the* famous "Uncle."

We neatly stacked the cases in the car. I didn't dare speak in front of the Uncle. Before he left he turned to Felix and said, "Tell Jo that I held back my ten thousand dollars for the mechanic." Felix replied very courteously, as if he were a nervous student addressing his professor. I realized how very important the man was and that everyone was afraid of him. I figured the "Jo" he referred to was probably Joseph Signoli.

As we pulled away from the curb, I asked Felix, "What's in the cases? Are we taking back heroin, or what?"

"No. It's the money." Four suitcases full of cash! We had picked up the million bucks!

We drove up Fifty-seventh Street. There had been an accident and the place was swarming with police. As I slowed down a taxi bumped into the back of my car and the driver, a black, got out to apologize. He insisted on giving me his card, but I refused to accept it. But the poor man didn't understand. I got panicky; the police were only ten yards in front of us. I kept saying, "no, no," in sign language. At last the guy got the message and drove off. The police waved us on.

"What are we supposed to do with the cash?" I asked.

"We have to take it to Montreal, we can't manage to get it all back to France."

I couldn't see how we could hide four suitcases in my Corvette so Felix suggested we stash them in Cardon's stationwagon. I objected; I wasn't paid to take any further risks.

"It was an accident, Michel. You have to understand that. We wouldn't have asked you if we hadn't been stuck."

Danielle settled our hotel bill and I told her to sit in the car while Felix and I went to see Jean Cardon.

I told him that we had just picked up the money and that there was more than we'd counted on. "Pay your bill and park your car behind mine on Fifty-eighth Street. We'll transfer the cases to your wagon."

Danielle thought the scheme was crazy and she and I drove off in the Corvette leaving Cardon and Rossi to follow us in the stationwagon.

When we stopped once for gas two police cars pulled in right behind us. We looked at each other. The cops got out of their car. Danielle didn't move — she was a good actress. Finally we realized that they were simply filling up with gas too; we hadn't been tailed. A little further along we stopped by the side of the road to transfer the money. I told Felix to change places with me — he would go with Danielle in the Corvette and I would join Cardon in the stationwagon. "While he drives, I'll strip the car doors," I said.

But I couldn't pry the frame loose. So we had to keep pulling into each service area we passed and park both cars. Felix and Danielle helped us rip out the frame and stuff the money inside the doors. We hadn't planned this operation and didn't have the right tools to do the job properly. Felix helped me remove the frames while Danielle watched for other cars. Then we pulled out of the parking lot and while we were moving I worked putting the frame back in place until we were about ten kilometers away from the border. There were no more rest stops. All four doors of the stationwagon had been stuffed with dollar bills, but I was still left with one suitcase full of money.

We couldn't put it under the seats because the covers Danielle had made were torn. I had run out of ideas and was furious. Another three thousand dollars to hide — all in small denominations — and no place to put them!

In the end we decided to transfer the last case to the Corvette and let Cardon go first. We were near Plattsburg and stopped to have some coffee.

"Let's bluff our way through," said Felix. "Don't talk to the Customs' men — I'll tell them we're all Canadians. I won't even switch off the engine, and if there's a hitch I can rush them."

I said to myself that there was always the possibility that Danielle might be recognized, which would make things easier. But how I hated these last-minute plans and lack of foresight! I was worried, but Danielle and the others were absolutely fearless or, at least, they looked as if they were. We reached the border.

"I've been visiting New York. I'm going home to Montreal," I said.

"Are you Canadian?"

"Yes."

The Customs' officer asked Danielle and Felix the same question. My heart started to beat faster. Then he wanted to know if I had anything to declare.

"No. Nothing," I said. The suitcase was in full view behind us, near the rear window, but it was the only baggage, so the officer waved us on.

I suppose we could have taken apart the doors of the Corvette and buried the money inside, or we could have ripped open the seats and stuffed them with the dollar bills. But the Corvette was the first new car I had ever owned and I loved it; I didn't want to tear it apart. Of course I could have bought another one later, but we were all on tenterhooks and I wasn't thinking straight. It was another madness.

When we reached Montreal I suggested we go to my place, change cars, use the Citroën and then phone Paul Graziani at the hotel.

Today I realize how dangerous it was to call him, considering he was being watched and his telephone was probably being tapped. But at that moment we didn't think further than the ends of our noses. It would have been better to have sent someone unknown to the hotel to alert him of our arrival.

Again everything had come off well and again we thought we were supermen. The idea that we had outwitted the police went to our heads. To us they were imbeciles. They weren't, as we found out later.

I told Danielle to go home to bed while Felix and I waited for Graziani in Dominion Square. We changed cars and took the suitcase with us. As Graziani approached us, walking quickly and nervously, I looked in the rear-view mirror. Two men were immediately behind him. There was no doubt in my mind they were police officers. As Graziani passed me he said, "Michel, they're following me."

"Slow down," I said, "go down the steps. I'll wait for you there."

The policemen were on foot; we could shake them. When they spotted my car again they probably couldn't figure out why I had reappeared. I stepped on the gas and drove to the bottom of the steps and opened the car door. Graziani jumped in and we took off. We cruised around Montreal until I was convinced that no police cars were on our tail. By this time it was early Sunday morning and we decided to go to Cardon's place.

I carried the suitcase upstairs into his bedroom and then Graziani, Rossi and I went down again to get the rest of the money from the stationwagon.

Graziani stayed with Cardon for the next two nights; I felt he alone was too hot. What stupidity — we were all hot at that moment. We arranged to meet again at Cardon's the same evening to count the money.

He was supposed to get six thousand dollars, but in view of the extra risks he had run we agreed to give him ten thousand. My share was sixty thousand. There was forty thousand for Felix out of which he was supposed to pay the Italian courier.

When Felix, Danielle and I returned to Cardon's house I told his wife and Graziani that I was beat and had to get some sleep. They and Danielle could count the money by themselves. Felix also took a nap.

When I woke up everyone was smiling broadly.

"What's up?"

"There's a hundred thousand dollars too much."

"A hundred thousand? The buyer must have made a mistake — we'd better give it back," I said.

"No! Don't be stupid, Michel. We'll keep it."

I was worried what Jo Signoli and the Uncle might do if they found out.

Since becoming part of the network I had discovered new links and new members with each transaction. I had begun to understand how the hierarchy operated and how important the U.S.

buyers — the actual bosses — really were. It must have been the buyers who had made a mistake in the count. I was afraid of them and said, "You do whatever you want. Just give me the sixty thousand I have coming to me."

"But we've got to take the money over to Paris."

"The million?" I asked.

"No. The hundred thousand," replied Graziani. "Jo will take care of transferring the million, don't worry about that."

"If you like," I told them, "I'll help you transfer the money, but don't bring my name into it."

I didn't want to have any of the hundred thousand. Everyone in the drug ring was fighting everyone else at the time and even Bec, my own partner, would have gladly stabbed me in the back. Here Felix and Graziani were stealing one hundred thousand dollars, and I knew that Bec had robbed me, holding back some of the expense money he owed me.

I discussed Bec with Rosso. "You know I wasn't well paid for the previous cars."

"You don't have to tell me, I know Bec," he said. "I met him in Paris. He's disgusting and an utter fool. If you like we could have a party for him one day." He couldn't have put it more bluntly what he had in mind. "Keep your sixty thousand dollars and when you get to Paris we'll get you and Bec together. We'll act as go-betweens and spell things out to him."

I decided to send the money with Rosso and Graziani, and also suggested to Danielle that she take part in the transfer without asking for a cut. She agreed straightaway. Then I gave André his share, about fifteen thousand dollars, but kept some back for the boat. I explained to him how difficult it was to take a hundred thousand dollars to France. He decided to spend a holiday there with his wife and take some of it along. The rest would stay hidden at Jean Cardon's house until someone could give it to Jo Signoli. Felix left Montreal — the situation was too dangerous for him.

For two days we prepared to move the money and then Graziani's turn came. "I'm scared. I don't know what to do," he said. "The police are after me all the time."

I tried to explain to him that if the police had really been following us we would have been busted by now. "Pay your hotel bill and move to another hotel. I'll follow your taxi when you leave and check to see if you're being followed." Danielle and I parked near Graziani's hotel and I was about to follow his taxi when I noticed a large, blue American car with four people inside right behind him. The taxi turned and went through an amber light. The blue car went through the red light. We *were* being followed! I parked my car in front of Graziani's new hotel and told Danielle we'd have a drink at Chez Bourgetel.

At the same moment I recognized a cop. He saw me and stationed himself behind me. We casually strolled to the terrace of Chez Bourgetel, had a drink and chatted with some people we knew. I kept my eyes on the man; he was standing at the corner of Mountain Street watching us. It wasn't worth while carrying on the game and I suggested to Danielle we go back to our apartment and wait for news from Paul, who had gone for a walk at "Man and His World" and finally ended up at our place. I was livid when he arrived. "How can you be so damn stupid! With every bloody cop on our tail you show up here!"

"Calm down," he replied, "the police aren't behind me any more. I lost them at Expo. What should I do now, Michel, what if they stop me at Dorval?"

"I'll call my friend André and you can go and have a drink with him downtown. If they stop you at the airport you can say you came to see him because you're moving to Canada and you're interested in buying a club."

It was a stupid suggestion — if André was brought into the affair, the police would take a closer look at him.

When I met André the next day after he had spent the evening with Graziani he said, "The police really are following him, and us too." So I had put the police on André's track.

Graziani got through Dorval without any trouble, and I relaxed. André was supposed to carry the hundred thousand dollars to France with Danielle's help, and she decided to use the opportunity to take her parents to Italy at the beginning of July 1971. I told her we would have to go to Paris first to deliver the money, go to Marseilles to see my family, and then on to Italy. She was delighted with the plan and we started to get ready. Suddenly Bec wanted me to take *his* thirty thousand dollars but I refused. There was the matter of Daniel Guérard's car to be settled; he was still in Paris.

Danielle and I left Montreal, she carrying fifty thousand dollars in her purse and André followed two days later with the other fifty thousand. Graziani met us at Orly Airport in Paris. "Things are not good. There's a general alert out," he said. "Also the buyer knows about the extra hundred thousand." I told Graziani to return the money, but he said it wasn't possible because Jo Signoli hadn't been told about it.

But this creep was never satisfied. Now he wanted another favor. "When Jo comes to my house pretend you never bothered to count the money — you don't know about the extra cash."

"You want me to lie to him?" I asked indignantly.

When Jo arrived the three of us went down to the garage and got into Jo's BMW. Some guy was sitting in the back whom I'd never seen before.

Jo asked abruptly. "Did you bring the hundred thousand?"

"What hundred thousand?" I asked. "I got my share and yours stayed in Montreal as planned."

Then he got angry and turned on Graziani. "Listen, Paul, you were given a hundred thousand dollars too much. Where is it? If it doesn't turn up there'll be trouble." Jo had just served three months in prison. I found out later that he had made a bargain with the French police to let himself be arrested on a minor charge which would keep him out of bigger trouble later. He was very nervous. The unknown man sitting in the back of the car opened his jacket and I noticed he was armed.

"Listen Jo," I said, "I've always done as I was told. I didn't count the money, I just got my share and came to Paris on a holiday."

"O.K. Michel. But I want all of us to meet tomorrow in Marseilles. I'll be expecting you." We said goodbye and Graziani and I went back to his apartment.

The next day André arrived with the fifty thousand dollars which he handed over to Graziani.

Danielle and I flew to Marseilles, checked into a hotel and then had supper with my family.

The next day Graziani and I met Jo Signoli, Robert Lenoir and two others at Le Welcome, a Marseilles bar. Felix Rosso hadn't come but I noticed that the elite of Marseilles' traffickers were assembled there. I suggested we move to another bar. At the Lido Bar our discussion was to the point: Jo Signoli told us about the trouble he was having over the hundred thousand and that the money would have to be given back or things would get pretty rough for everyone. The Uncle was threatening to cut us off from the buyer, the mechanics and the laboratory if we didn't come across. Everyone looked shaken. Signoli continued, "We're going to Toulon to talk to the Uncle. He's expecting us."

It occurred to me that a meeting with the all-important Uncle could end in a shoot-out. I wasn't taking any chances, "If you don't mind, I've had enough; I'm leaving." He insisted that I come along to see the Uncle the next day. "I'm not going," I said stubbornly, and left them in Marseilles to make their arrangements without me.

But I still had to settle with Bec. When Jo and I met again two days later he told me his partners and he had been having trouble with Bec who had returned the car that I had sent him, the one that had been left in Biarritz. No decision to load it had been made because of the tension between Bec and me and everyone else.

"The car is still there and I need your O.K. to move it," Jo told me. But before proceeding any further I wanted to go to Paris with Jo to see Bec. When Jo and I confronted him, I told him bluntly that he had cheated me. He was scared. I had a gun on me and expected there would be a fight.

"O.K. you bastard," I said, "our agreement ends here. You stole from me, and you're damn lucky you haven't got a bullet in your brain; if you'd done this to anyone else you'd be dead by now."

"Michel, I can explain, I've got a car . . ." I really felt sorry for him, but I didn't let him finish. "No, we'll sort out the car we've got here, and that's it."

"But the boat, Michel!"

"The boat's my business."

Then Jo joined in. "It's not worthwhile for you or Michel to pay for the boat. I'll buy it and run it with Michel." Bec seemed panicky and left.

When we were alone, Signoli said, "That Bec will talk. I'm sure he'll cause us trouble. We ought to get rid of him."

"We can't kill him Jo. We'll sort the boat out between us. I'll tell Bec he can be our partner and we'll get rid of him later, bit by bit."

Bec was actually no worse than the others. Everyone stole from everyone else — a hundred here and a thousand there. When I went to see him later he told me I had misunderstood him, he had no intention of cheating me. He had been in a fix and he'd planned to pay me later.

"If you'd explained that before I'd have gladly helped you; but nobody gets away with stealing from me," I said.

I figured that he must have kept back about a hundred thousand dollars altogether. I'd made a hundred thousand for four cars and he'd received at least three times as much.

Finally he said: "Let's not end it this way Michel. After all, I got you into this game. We're good friends — those Marseillais are just a bunch of bandits."

I made peace with Bec, but promised myself I would settle with him one day.

Meanwhile, I wanted to know about the red Barracuda and Daniel Guérard, who was still waiting at the same hotel in Paris.

When I saw Jo Signoli again I questioned *him* about the Barracuda. He said it was still in Biarritz, because it had not been possible to do the work in the laboratory. "We didn't order the merchandise before we saw you because we didn't know exactly how much was involved."

Guérard had been in Paris for almost a month and had had enough. I had to tell him that the affair would likely go on for at least another month or even a month and a half and give him two thousand dollars. Somewhat reluctantly he decided to stay.

On July 14 I picked up Danielle's parents at Orly and we all left for the south. In Marseilles we met Paul Graziani who was surprised to see us. "If you like we can all go down to the beach," he suggested.

"I presume the money was finally sorted out," I said.

"Yes, it's all done. We always sort things out," Graziani replied benevolently.

"Yes, you certainly do, you steal from everyone."

We had a relaxing time, sunning ourselves. Danielle's parents didn't suspect a thing.

The four of us, Danielle, her parents and I, then left for Italy. Afterwards I returned to Marseilles, on to Paris, and along the coast. Eventually I met André who was on holiday with his parents in Cannes.

Soon we all were on our way home to Montreal.

7/
THE BARRACUDA
and the LITTLE
WHITE RABBITS

Daniel Guérard flew back to Montreal after the Barracuda had been loaded and was on its way.

When I telephoned Bec to ask him to come to Canada he said it was impossible. Edmond Taillet had been arrested in New York and also because of other complications, Jo Signoli had actually forbidden him to leave.

Signoli arrived in Montreal two days later and introduced me to Roger Preiss, a friend of Richard Berdin's, who was one of the people delegated to supervise the New York transactions. Preiss was accompanied by a German airline hostess he had met on the plane and who couldn't speak French. She wasn't in any way involved with the drug business. The next day Signoli and Roger came to my apartment at Habitat.

"We're going to sort out everything in Montreal before we get involved with the Barracuda," Jo said. "We still have a week before the car arrives so we'll go and see your friend Cardon. He's still got almost fifty thousand dollars in the suitcase — it hasn't been sent back to France yet."

We brought the suitcase to my apartment and Jo Signoli, Roger Preiss and Danielle again counted the money. It was then that Jo gave me the sixty thousand dollars that I had coming to me.

One night he asked me if he could see the boat. I described how beautiful it was and the next day we went to the Nautica shipyard, where Jo met Robert Gauthier. He liked what he saw. The boat would take another two months to finish.

The day the Barracuda arrived in Montreal, Signoli sent Roger Preiss to Miami to arrange details with the buyers. Before leaving for New York he asked me to clear it through Customs and make arrangements to get it across the border. I paid Daniel Guérard to drive it to New York and Danielle and I left separately. Two days later I met Guérard in front of the Empire State Building. I asked him to bring the car to the Air France building on Fifth Avenue where I was to meet Jo Signoli that evening.

Jo was with Meu Lastraiolli, a young man of about twenty-five who looked like a Marseilles hoodlum. Roger Preiss was there too and Jo told me the delivery had been put off until the following day. Guérard left, Danielle went back to the hotel and Lastraiolli, Preiss, Signoli and I went out to supper. During the meal Lastraiolli confessed to us one of his fantasies. "I've never slept with a black woman," he said, "and this looks like as good a time as any."

So here we were in Manhattan, looking around for a black woman for him to sleep with. Times Square seemed to be our best bet. I couldn't speak English nor could Jo, so it was hard for us to find out how much a black woman would charge. Finally he made a connection. Jo gave Lastraiolli last-minute instructions. "Watch out — the women here will steal you blind."

Our amorous friend disappeared with the girl and showed up a little later, completely happy. It had been to his liking. It was two A.M. and Daniel Guérard was bringing the car at six. We arranged an appointment on Eighth Avenue. At dawn Lastraiolli and I met Guérard and I told Guérard he could go back to Montreal. Lastraiolli took over the wheel and we circled around the block a few times before we saw Jo Signoli, an Italian and Roger Preiss in a car. We drove around Manhattan for a while longer and then headed for New Jersey. This would be the fourth time I'd been in this same garage. The Italian disappeared and Roger Preiss, Lastraiolli and I began to dismantle the Barracuda. Everything went efficiently and we were all in very good humor. Jo Signoli was singing and Lastraiolli called out, "Come on you little white rabbits," pulling the packages out of their caches. Jo even suggested we get a needle and give ourselves a fix. Some of the packages had split open and thousands of dollars worth of white powder was scattered all over the garage floor. "It's not worth picking up, just sweep it away," Jo said grandly.

One gray low-quality packet he presented as a gift to the American buyer. The rest were all neatly packed into suitcases.

We washed up and left with the American who took us back to Manhattan. The car was only good for the scrapyard so we left it in the garage.

I called Danielle and told her to join me on Fifty-second Street. When she arrived she was furious. "It's not fair," she cried. "Why didn't you phone me? I was sure you'd been arrested! I didn't know whether to go home or stay in the hotel or what!" I was calming her down, assuring her that everything had gone beautifully, when Jo cut our discussion short, suggesting that we find a place to eat — he was starving.

As we were sitting down for lunch he told us he had another problem. The buyers were going to pay him the next day and he didn't know how he'd get the money to France.

"Oh, no! Don't start that all over again! No way can we take it back to Montreal. Remember I've got the Corvette this time and no stationwagon," I cried.

"No, not you Michel," he said, "but do you think that your girlfriend . . . ?"

"If you want something from her, why don't you ask her yourself?"

He turned to Danielle, "We have five hundred thousand dollars to move tomorrow. Would you take it to Paris for us? We'll pay your plane ticket and give you ten thousand."

"Sure," Danielle replied calmly. "Why not?"

Jo suggested that Danielle stay in New York with Roger Preiss, who was going to line a suitcase with a false bottom for her to take to Paris via Brussels. But Danielle first wanted to go back to Montreal with me.

We arranged that the next day she'd return to New York and meet Roger at the Taft Hotel.

But when Danielle got back to New York she found out that her trip had been called off — it had been decided instead to make a

"Well, this is even better," I said.
bank transfer. She was back in Montreal the day after.

"Not for me. I was counting on the ten thousand dollars."

To make her feel better I gave her five thousand dollars, half of what she had been promised, out of my own funds.

I also paid Daniel Guérard the ten thousand he had coming to him. He thanked me and said, "The job suited me well. I'm pleased you thought of me. It was pretty easy. If you need me again, call me."

Meanwhile, I got busy with the boat and regularly gave Gauthier his money to cover expenses.

Shortly after the Barracuda affair I received a phone call from Jacques Bec. "Michel, what's happening over there? Where's my money? What's going on?"

"Signoli's got it. I gave him your share and he told me he was going to give it to you."

"We didn't arrange it that way," he shouted.

"No, I know we didn't, but Signoli had a chance to bring it to you and since I didn't want to deliver it myself, I gave it to him." I didn't tell him that Signoli and I had previously discussed the stand we would take with Bec, and that I had no intention of handing the money over to him.

He became hysterical and I told him to sort things out with Jo — it had nothing to do with me. Then he asked me about the boat.

"I'll carry on paying for it and call you when it's ready."

He told me he was expecting to come to Montreal, but I insisted that I had no money to give him and was looking after the finances for the boat myself. By then I'd invested about thirty thousand dollars in it.

Life was peaceful and enjoyable once again. I spent my days working on the boat with Robert Gauthier and my nights moving in glamorous circles with Danielle. I started a record company. The recording we had made with Danielle had proved to be a flop so I tried to sign up different Montreal artists.

At the beginning of September I saw Bec in Paris. He told me he still hadn't been paid and it was all my fault because I hadn't brought him the money as arranged. I told him I was going to Marseilles on holiday for a while, and would discuss the matter there with Jo Signoli.

But when I met Jo he was not too sympathetic. "Bec can go to hell," he said. "I've got the money and I'm keeping it; he can look out for himself." We left it at that and went on trips around Marseilles and to Cannes, mostly discussing the boat. He described its enormous possibilities to me. "According to Alex's calculations we can stash a ton of heroin inside it."

I was startled when I heard the name "Alex." Who was he? He was new to me. Alexandre Salles was one of Jo's partners. In fact there was a whole section of the international drug ring whose members I didn't know, largely because I lived in Canada.

Jo went on to explain, "Loading this boat won't be easy. To get at the hollow keel the works will have to be taken apart. We've thought of all that and the Uncle has agreed."

The Uncle again! I thought for a while, and then asked, "Where are you going to load it? Remember it has to cross the Atlantic first to London and then back to America."

"After London we just sail it to the Mediterranean."

But I wasn't happy with the idea. Bringing the boat to Marseilles was madness. I suggested it would be better to take it to another port. We decided on Biarritz or the Spanish coast.

We also talked about Edmond Taillet who hadn't got in touch with us since his arrest. But Jo told me Taillet had done well. "He didn't talk; the bosses are very pleased."

I stayed in Marseilles until the end of September and then returned to Canada.

Jo had forgotten to mention that Richard Berdin had also been arrested in New York. He was associated with another group after he'd split with the Signoli team and all his Marseilles friends. Apparently there had been too much dissension among them, too many underhand tricks, poor atmosphere and bad organization. Loyalty was a thing of the past.

I didn't realize then that we were running headlong into disaster. The police were on our tails and were organizing wire taps. The important people were aware of this. The net was tightening day by day, and the whole thing was going to blow up before long because everyone had thrown discretion to the wind.

I was the only one who didn't know anything. Jo and the others knew what the authorities were up to. In Marseilles some of the narks were buddies with Jo and the gang members and warned them about inquiries and imminent arrests. But no one took that into account, as was later proven; we all thought we were invulnerable.

To show how little Signoli worried about the police, I remember driving around Paris with him one day in his Porsche. I bravely asked him, "Jo, it's obvious that you live well. Can you prove to the authorities where your money comes from?"

"It's easy," he replied, "the car isn't mine; it's rented in my girlfriend's name. She works for me, and I've got some well-placed friends who keep me informed. It costs money, but it's worth it." But then he added, "In any case, I know I'm going to get twenty years sooner or later."

"That's cheerful. What about me?"

"It's different in Canada. I know things are really hot here. We've been informed that they're getting ready to make a lot of arrests."

He was right. Bit by bit, in the course of various transactions I began to realize that I was only a small cog in a huge wheel. I knew very little and progressively began to discover details about the organization and its offshoots. I could only guess the size of the network. The Uncle was the big boss on the American side as well as on the French side. His name was Jean Guidicelli and he had been known to Interpol as a trafficker for nearly twenty-five years. He had contacts with all the American buyers and he and his brother were involved in obtaining the morphine-base supplies from Turkey and the Middle East. They controlled everything, including the laboratories and employed several protection men.

When the press or the man in the street talk about bigshots in the drug business they're talking about people like the Guidicellis. They used their own chemist, sold the heroin to small teams in Marseilles and arranged for the buyers in the United States. They took ten percent from each of the teams for supplying the buyer, and also charged ten percent commission to the buyer — making money at each stage of the operation.

Organizing the courier network was a complex business too. To pass the Fiat, for example, four teams had got together to load it, each of them with a different financial interest in the car. Without naming names of Marseilles' leaders, I know a kilo or two would be put in for someone who had done another a favor, or five hundred grams or a kilo would be added for someone who had carried drugs from Marseilles to Paris out of friendship. People who had been convicted and were in prison were taken care of; their families were looked after if they had behaved well and hadn't talked.

I met the famous Uncle only by accident when Jean-Claude Kella and Laurent Fiocconi had been arrested in New York. Until then they had been thought of as the big bosses. The Uncle had been forced to personally participate in one of the operations because his assistants were in jail.

Charles-Laurent Fiocconi is the Uncle's actual nephew as well as his assistant in the narcotics business. He received a twenty-five-year sentence in New York on June 19, 1972, together with Jean-Claude Kella, another one of Guidicelli's nephews. In their bill of indictment it was stated that they had sold two hundred and ninety three million dollars worth of heroin in the United States!

In September 1974 Fiocconi was serving time in the federal pen in Atlanta, Georgia when he was transferred to New York to testify in another heroin trial. Everything was set up for his escape from the old West Street prison in Manhattan, which finally succeeded with the cooperation of one of the wardens and six other detainees, all well-known traffickers. The police never found the six or seven million dollars he had made peddling drugs.

I had completed four operations by then and was beginning to feel things closing in on me. There had been several arrests in the States and the drug problem had also become as acute in France. I had heard that the RCMP were working more closely with the French and the Americans and eventually the whole network would disintegrate. I had already decided that the boat would be my last job when Jo suggested another jaunt — a Jaguar — due shortly in New York and offered me four thousand dollars to pick it up. I refused. The car was being shipped directly to New York and I explained to him that that city really turned me off. I also had the boat to look after and felt we were all hot enough. The police had been following me and someone had been asking about me at my hotel.

"The police have absolutely nothing on you — I know that for a fact. You're completely clean," he assured me.

I still didn't want to do the Jaguar. Then he came up with another suggestion: "You know we always need an intermediary between the couriers and the buyer, and between the Uncle and the buyer. How would you like to live in the States? I'll give you ten percent on anything that moves into the country." But I insisted that I didn't like the States and wasn't going to risk arrest. "We'll do the boat, and then I'm through," I said. But I knew even then that it would be difficult to get out because he just kept coming up with more and more suggestions.

"We're going to have big problems with the boat," he said, "There's a lot of money involved. We'll have to use the boat to get the money back to Marseilles."

I had worked out everything in my head. Once "the big deal" was wrapped up I would disappear with the boat and the ten million dollars we would get from the sale. It would have been the biggest con of the century. I wanted to finish in style and the idea of the whole world searching for me and the money didn't scare me in the slightest. Not a very loyal attitude, I know, but all the traffickers fed off each other.

Danielle knew about the boat plan but she didn't know what else I had in mind. I intended to take her with me; she would have been in danger in any case. Nor did I want to doublecross Robert Gauthier.

In Montreal we found it ludicrous that the local underworld was also interested in drugs — they operated on such a small scale. To suggest a deal for one or two million dollars to someone in Canada was unthinkable; there wasn't enough money around. Although a small market for hard drugs existed in Montreal, when I worked there hashish and marijuana were primarily in demand. Heroin trafficking was more prevalent on the Vancouver coast.

The Canadian underworld didn't know that I was moving heroin, especially not in such large quantities. I knew the Montreal underworld, including the famous Frank Cotroni, one of the Mafia bosses in Canada who ended up in a U.S. pen on a cocaine charge. He was in a number of rackets and heroin hardly concerned him at all. Cotroni handled money for others and took his percentage. My dealings with him were very limited. We had originally met at Chez Clairette and I had seen him in other Montreal nightclubs. We would no more than greet each other. Later, I thought he must have known what I was doing because he started to take notice of me and one night offered to buy me a drink. His brother, Giuseppe, known as Pep, was in a Canadian prison for heroin dealing. Conrad Bouchard, a cabaret singer and a friend of his, was much more active in the business and was actually the one who controlled the heroin market in Montreal. He also ended up in jail.

All in all, there was never any tension between the Canadian underworld and us, nor was there any professional rivalry in the drug market. They didn't interfere in our affairs. Montreal was just a turn-around spot and hardly any heroin stayed there. Canadian addicts often had to get their supplies from New York. There were times when we could have satisfied all the addicts in Canada for at least ten years.

We weren't particularly discreet in Montreal and, judging by our way of life, the local hoods must have suspected that we had access to huge sums of money and it wasn't hard to imagine where it came from. They must have realized that we were directly protected by the big U.S. Mafia bosses.

8/
HABITAT 67
OCTOBER 21, 1971

Canadian girls, and Montreal girls in particular, are no more naive than any others. It was easy to recruit Danielle, Ginette, Anne-Marie, and Noella when someone had to be sent to France with a car. It wasn't a question of morality. These girls met well-dressed young men who took them out and often spent anywhere from a thousand to ten thousand dollars on them. They paid their return air fare to Europe and gave them a fantastic holiday. I know that there are lots of girls in France or in the States who would go for the same kind of proposition. We knew how to behave with women and how to treat them well, which put the odds in our favor. I personally had learned how to live in style; I drove a Corvette and a Citroën, lived in fashionable Habitat 67, and was seen with Danielle Ouimet. Jo Signoli, Richard Berdin and the others had been far from dowdy individuals. Girls found us attractive and fascinating because we looked like businessmen, with a mysterious air about us.

But my family wasn't deceived. My brother Felix told me once: "I don't have to wrack my brains to know what you're up to. Quit fooling around. Here you are a family man living with an actress. We know Danielle, what she's like and what she does. We've seen her films — *Valerie* was shown in Marseilles."

"There are two ways to become addicted to drugs," Richard Berdin once said, "the first is to take them, and the second is to deal in them." I had become addicted to the second way. We lived in constant fear, but deep down we liked it; it was a stimulant and a sickness, and when I didn't have a deal going in Montreal I became bored. Also, after getting used to earning huge sums of money, it was virtually impossible for me to go back to working for a normal salary.

I had lots of money, sixty thousand dollars from the Fiat deal and about twenty-four thousand in other liquid funds. Some of my friends in Canada had money problems and I started to make loans. When a record producer was short of cash I gave him two thousand dollars; when my cousin and his family arrived in Montreal, I had paid for their tickets to come over. Even so, I still had fifty thousand American dollars in cash at home. All I wanted to do was finish building the boat, take off for South America, and start a new life in the sun with a few million dollars in my pocket.

Towards the end of September 1971 several arrests were made in New York and in France.

One morning, Danielle and I read in the *Montreal-Matin* that the RCMP had stopped a Jaguar containing one hundred kilos of heroin. Four names were mentioned which I hadn't heard before, but I knew that the car was the one Jo Signoli had wanted me to take.

At last I began to be concerned and asked Jo whether he had read the story. He assured me it was not one of our cars and told me not to worry.

However, three or four days later I read again that a second big haul had been made in New York. This time it was a Ford carrying ninety-six kilos of heroin which had arrived by boat from Italy. The people arrested were mostly Italians, but Richard Berdin was among them. I stopped worrying — I shouldn't have.

Richard Berdin had absolute proof that his accomplices had turned him in. Someone had tipped off the police that he was in the States living under an assumed name. All the FBI had to do was keep a sharp eye on all American border points. So he decided to turn state's evidence and confessed his role in the narcotics ring. Although we'd only met once, he identified me from some photographs the U.S. agents had of Taillet and me.

Apart from Berdin, Roger Preiss had also been arrested. At that moment all those belonging to the French network who were not in jail knew of the danger, but no one warned me. They either presumed that I would never be arrested or perhaps they just didn't care.

On October 21, 1971 a friend called to tell me his car had broken down. Would I pick him up — he was on his way to look at some recording contracts.

I took my Corvette and drove him to a place on the outskirts of Montreal. He asked me to go out and eat with him afterwards, but I felt ill-at-ease and depressed; I hadn't slept well the night before. Also, Danielle was making supper for me and I preferred to go home. I drove him back to Montreal and we agreed to talk to each other in the evening.

On my way to the apartment I noticed some cars were following me. I kept saying to myself, "It's not the police — besides I haven't got anything on me so what can they do to me?" When I arrived at my apartment I knew I was going to be arrested. I slowed down and hesitated a little before driving into the garage; should I leave? I've no heroin on me, I thought, and there's nothing at the house except the fifty thousand American dollars hidden in my bar, and practically impossible to find. I had taken the bar apart and stuffed it with the money. I was carrying twenty thousand in one thousand dollar bills in my pocket.

One car followed me, left, and then appeared again. I couldn't tell if it was a police car but I was scared shitless. I decided to use the stairs to the apartment. A man was sitting in a corner of the foyer reading a newspaper. The old superintendent, who I always tipped generously, tried to signal to me. He looked at me sadly, but I didn't want to know what he was trying to tell me.

I walked into the apartment, the door was open. Danielle called from the kitchen, "Dinner will be ready soon." She was making spareribs, the only dish she really knew how to cook. I asked if anyone had called. No. I thought that was strange — we usually had lots of friends phoning us.

"Do you want to eat right now?" she asked.

"No, darling," I said, "I'm going upstairs to take a shower first." I was tired. When I adjusted the spray, I stepped into the shower and started to soap myself. The curtain parted and I saw a revolver pointing at my stomach.

"Police. You are under arrest," a voice said.

"Can I rinse myself off?"

The cop said O.K. but kept his gun pointed at me. I got out of the shower, dried myself and put a comb through my hair. I stepped out of the bathroom into the bedroom. Danielle was sitting on the bed looking terrified. I soon realized the whole building was surrounded by police; eight RCMP as well as U.S. narcotics agents were in the apartment. Escape was out of the question — anyway you're not so brave when a gun is stuck under your nose.

"What's this all about?" I asked calmly, turning to Danielle. She started to cry. "Take it easy, darling. I'm sure it's all a mistake."

"You know why we're here?" one of the officers asked.

"No I don't. But I assume you have a search warrant."

He said he had.

"O.K. Go ahead then."

I was a bit cocky. I knew there was nothing in the house that could link me to heroin trafficking apart from the fifty thousand dollars. They searched the apartment and all they could find was some French and Spanish money in small amounts — maybe one or two hundred dollars worth — and my jewelry.

"You live well," one of them said.

"Yes. Why not? I own a record company and I'm Danielle Ouimet's manager. I make a good living."

"What about heroin?"

"What's heroin?"

I kept this up with the police for an hour until Claude Savoie, one of the agents, found the twenty thousand dollars in my coat pocket. I snatched it away from him. "That's not mine, it belongs to Danielle."

I handed her the money and suggested that we go down to the livingroom. They said they were going to take me in.

"Do you have a warrant for my arrest?" I asked. I could tell from their expressions they didn't. "Then you can't take me in. I have the right to legal counsel and I'm going to call my lawyer."

They told me they didn't need a warrant and refused to let me make the phone call. One of the Americans came up to me and asked, "Do you speak English?"

"No."

I continued to talk softly to Danielle who was still sobbing. "Don't worry, it's not serious and everything will be all right, you'll see." We both sat down on the chesterfield. The police moved around the apartment, looking into closets, frisking my clothes and emptying all the pockets of my suits. They inspected every useless scrap of paper. Then they found some important ones. Danielle had a passion for collecting plane tickets and when I saw them scrutinizing them I was sure it was all over. These were my tickets and hers, including the most important one — her ticket to Miami. I suddenly remembered the fifty thousand. When one of the policemen went up to the bar Danielle and I looked at each other. I kept throwing furtive glances in that direction. If they found the money they would almost certainly confiscate it and convict us. How could we prove that the seventy thousand we had in the house had been come by honestly? Eventually they decided to take both of us to RCMP headquarters.

"Wait," I protested, "you can take me, but not her. She's not involved in any of my affairs."

But they insisted that we both come or they would get a warrant for my arrest and take Danielle along anyway.

I thought if there was a warrant the story would appear in all the newspapers. On the other hand, without a warrant things could perhaps be sorted out and I would be released on bail. So I agreed to go along.

We left in separate cars, I in the first one with four officers, and the other four with Danielle following behind. They arrived about ten minutes later. Only our old superintendent witnessed the scene.

I was especially anxious to protect Danielle, to get her out of this mess. I was also afraid she might crack up because I took it for granted I'd be beaten up, as I would have been in France. I was hungry and just about out of cigarettes. Frantically, I was trying to understand where I had slipped up. I went over every angle. There must have been one specific thing. I asked Sergeant Gilles Poissant, the head of the RCMP narcotics squad in Montreal, why I had been brought to the station. What was I accused of and who had laid charges against me?

"Do you know the meaning of the word 'narcotics'?" he asked. "You do know what heroin is?"

"What are narcotics? And what's heroin? Could you buy me some cigarettes?" I asked innocently. He went off to get some.

Then I realized that the Canadian police used methods which were completely different from those in France. Instead of being roughed up I was about to receive cigarettes from the very man who had nabbed me.

When Poissant came back he said, "You can get yourself out of this, Michel, if you sign some papers and go to the United States voluntarily — you've been indicted in New York City."

"New York City? What for?" I asked.

"What we were talking about, narcotics."

There was another man with him, Staff Sergeant Paul Sauvé, who had posed as the air-conditioning repair man in Paul Graziani's hotel room. "Who is accusing me?"

Sauvé showed me a picture of Richard Berdin, and asked, "Do you know him?" No. Then he showed me a photograph of Bec and asked if I knew *him*. I denied having ever seen him. Then he came up with a picture of Roger Preiss and I shook my head once again. When he produced one of Jo Signoli I still said, "No." So we were all implicated.

The interrogation lasted for four hours. I answered "no" to every question.

The RCMP officers kept asking me to sign papers agreeing that I would go to the U.S. voluntarily. "You can come to some arrangement with them there, all your friends are collaborating."

"What friends?" They hadn't given me too many details. In any case, I didn't really want to know.

One of the agents finally told me that he would have to arrest me. I asked where Danielle was and was told she was waiting next door. I was permitted to talk to her.

She entered the room, her face white with fear. She again started to cry. "Michel, we've never been separated for two years, and now you'll be sent away."

I tried to calm her, "Listen, it really isn't serious, don't panic. Go and see André. He'll tell you what to do."

"I'll find a lawyer . . . you're bound to get bail."

She had bought me a sandwich, but when she handed it to me I was sure it would make me ill. I couldn't eat it. I asked one of the officers if I could make a call to France. He handed me two numbers, both of my restaurants in Marseilles. "Which one do you want?"

I indicated the one I wanted and added, "You seem well informed."

"We know everything and you're just wasting your breath denying it."

Again Danielle repeated, "I'll get a lawyer, Michel. You'll be out on bail by tomorrow."

I held her close and murmured "What did you tell them?"

"Nothing, except that I was entitled to legal counsel. I sat there for four hours and I kept repeating 'I've nothing to say, I want to see my lawyer!'"

"Good girl. You and André both consult a lawyer."

Sergeant Leonard Masse and Corporal Guy David of the RCMP then took me to Police Station No. 1 in Old Montreal where I was locked in a cell. I was furious; when they'd searched me they'd taken all my cigarettes except for one or two, but had left me my own clothes.

"I'm sorry, I don't have any cigarettes," I told an officer. He offered to buy some for me. I gave him a dollar and when he came back with a pack he didn't give me any change. I thought that was strange — police officers selling cigarettes to detainees at a dollar a pack! What a nice little supplementary income for them!

The cell was very small and there was a mattress on the floor. I stretched out on it and started to relax — and think. I must have fallen asleep eventually, because the same police officer woke me a while later to tell me that my lawyer, Raymond Daoust, was on the phone. He escorted me to an office.

"Michel," Daoust said, "Danielle is with me and we are looking after things for you, so you don't have to worry. Tomorrow when you go before the judge I'll be there and we'll ask for bail. Now, pretend to carry on talking to me and I'll hand you over to Danielle."

She was in a panic. "You'll be out tomorrow, Daoust says you will."

I knew that I wouldn't be, but I tried to give her a little hope, "I'll see you tomorrow, darling."

She told me she couldn't come to court because, "it would get into the papers."

It was Wednesday evening. That night all I could think about was Danielle. I knew I was going to jail, but I still couldn't believe it. Yet they could have told me they were going to give me thirty or forty years and I wouldn't have cared as long as they didn't touch my girl.

My first big shock came when they put handcuffs on me. Even when I was arrested they hadn't done that. I was being treated like a dangerous killer! They put me in a police wagon together with all kinds of miserable types. I could see they were just as frightened as I was. We arrived at the Court House next to police headquarters and were escorted into a large room. One by one we were called up before the judge. Some people recognized me and stared, but they didn't dare come up to me to ask why I was there. I felt completely lost. My turn came and I suddenly convinced myself cheerfully that I was going to get out.

"You are accused by Mr. Richard Berdin, of the State of New York, of conspiring in the trafficking of heroin."

My heart sank. I looked around for my lawyer, Raymond Daoust, but he wasn't there to help me — a habit which he persisted in.

During these proceedings the whole scene passed before me — New York, the Mafiosi, the Cadillacs, the loaded cars. I knew the indictment was solid. They had made only one mistake, mixing up the car — a minor detail — but it certainly had been me who had transported the heroin and the number of kilos was exactly right.

Because my lawyer wasn't in court the judge remanded me for eight days, and I was taken back to my cell. I felt completely demoralized. Danielle hadn't come. I was allowed to phone her and got no reply. Then I phoned André — no reply. Finally, I received a call from Claude Archambault, another lawyer.

"Daoust is sending me over to work with him on the case," he said. "When it comes up again next week we'll try and get you bail. Danielle is in Quebec City shooting a TV show."

I was shocked. "Quebec City! That's just great!" Archambault told me Danielle *had* to work; she would come and visit me in a week's time.

So I waited a week. I was then taken by armored wagon to the Parthenais Jail together with the other detainees. One man had got twenty years, another one six. For the most part they were frightened, second-rate criminals, with narrow and restricted lives.

I knew I was going to be inside for a long time. My only real worry was Danielle. For the moment she could still come and go as she pleased, but I knew that sooner or later she could also be charged.

9/
THE
PARTHENAIS

The prison in the rue Parthenais was new, clean and ultra-modern. When I arrived there they searched me and took away absolutely everything — my watch, my rings, my wallet. The officer winced when I took the thousand dollars out of my pocket and put it on the table. He seemed edgy when I gave him my name and address: Mastantuono, Michel, Habitat 67, Montreal. Yes, that was indeed me, and it frightened him. I was ordered to undress.

Because they had been in a panic about my arrival, the prison officials were neither courteous, nor brutal, nor violent. However, they appeared ill-at-ease and their manners were brusque. The fact remains they are brutes, zoo-keepers watching gorillas in a cage.

I was issued two blankets and two sheets and sent by elevator to the seventeenth floor. Before I had time to take in what was happening to me the cell door closed. I was in jail and alone.

From my window I could see the city of Montreal stretched out below me. As it turned out, I found the Parthenais to be the worst and most demoralizing prison I had ever seen. Thoughts were going round and round in my head, as I paced back and forth in my cell.

I tried to sort things out: some people had been arrested in the States; Richard Berdin had mentioned the wrong car in his statement; he hadn't given my name and had spoken of white powder. There must be a way out. The accusation could be refuted because Berdin didn't know my name. He had only recognized me from a photograph; it could have been someone else in the picture who resembled me; it wasn't the right car, and, and, and . . .

I waited for my lawyers, for Danielle, for some news. I relived my whole life: Marseilles, my mother, my brother, the restaurant, the port, America, Danielle . . .

I met some interesting types in my new residence, including the Rose brothers, who were accused of kidnapping the Quebec labor minister, Pierre Laporte. They recognized me and asked what I was in for. When they told me they were studying the law to prepare their own defense in the Laporte murder I asked them if there was anything in the books about extradition to the United States because the Americans had accused me of conspiracy and I was supposed to be tried there.

One of the brothers went into lengthy explanations and read me a few chilling paragraphs from the Penal Code. Since the Canadians didn't have anything on me, the American authorities needed only circumstantial evidence — otherwise known as "adequate proof" — to obtain my extradition. This adequate proof of nothing at all could have been the affidavit that Richard Berdin had signed in the U.S. The words "adequate proof" scared the hell out of me.

Two days later Raymond Daoust finally appeared, affidavit in hand. I bombarded him with questions: what was going to happen to me?; how long would it take?; what was going on? He assured me in a calm manner that he would take care of me. I had been cited in Richard Berdin's affidavit which mentioned a Mustang, white powder and other details. I told him Berdin didn't know anything. Daoust questioned me about the white powder: was it sugar, flour or what?

I told him the whole truth. Yes, I had done it, but they had mistaken the car, but it certainly had been me . . . He reassured me and told me we would go to court the following Tuesday and he would get bail set for me. I asked him if Danielle had managed to change the fifty thousand U.S. dollars hidden in the house into Canadian money. Apparently a friend was looking after that.

When Daoust left I killed time until the visiting hour by pacing the floor. Then I was taken to the room where Danielle was waiting for me.

Our meeting was none too cordial. I was aggressive rather

than tender because I was afraid, and her manner was awkward because she too was frightened.

"Where were you?" I asked, "What happened? You ran out on me!"

She tried to explain about her work but I cut her off. She was close to tears. I asked her what the lawyers had said, but all she would say was, "you'll see." When I asked her about the money she told me that Frank Cotroni had come to pick it up at the house to change it into Canadian funds.

"Have you got it now?"

"No, I gave it to Daoust."

"Why in hell did you do that? That's the stupidest thing you could have done! You've just about bought me a ticket to the States! You should never have paid in advance! They'll think we're millionaires and just keep asking for more!"

Fifty thousand dollars, thrown to the wind! What with the twenty thousand taken from me when I was arrested, a total of seventy thousand dollars! I was livid, but then I calmed down and told Danielle I didn't want to stay in Canada for two reasons. First of all, the car they had accused me of using was André's and, secondly, Danielle would certainly get mixed up in this, she'd been with me every time. "You also carried money and they're bound to follow up on the plane tickets they picked up at the house. It will be better if I go to the States and plead guilty; so let's not talk about it any more."

Now she was crying bitterly. "No, Michel, no! Even if you get twenty years I'll wait for you. Please plead innocent!"

I also began to cry, just like a child. It was a grand scene, and if it hadn't been for the solid pane of glass between us and the guard standing three or four yards away from us, we would have fallen into each others' arms.

Danielle left and I was taken back to my cell. I was then transferred to a new section of the prison. There I was a celebrity, a sort of god, rubbing elbows with the cream of Montreal underworld society. It was better than pacing up and down in a cage and it helped me kill time while I waited to go before the judge for my bail.

But when the time came the judge couldn't make up his mind.

He told me that an extradition was very different from a prosecution. He almost had circumstantial evidence and normally he would be able to extradite me. However, my lawyer had presented a defense in my name and he had to study it more carefully. He remanded me for a further two weeks.

Two days after my return to the Parthenais the Clerks of the Court went on strike. Disaster! We all got very excited and there was quite an uproar. It wasn't a happy sight; the innocent and others who were awaiting bail couldn't go before the judge because the clerks weren't working. The "good guys," the ones who were there by mistake, were caught in the strike as if they were actual criminals.

Personally, I was spoilt at the Parthenais, and the treatment I received as Mastantuono, Michel, Habitat 67, was different from that given to other detainees. I was allowed more visitors, could make more telephone calls and received books and magazines — I was even allowed to read *The French Connection* — and managed to spend some time in the infirmary, though I was quite healthy, where the treatment was much better.

Danielle had used her connections with one of the prison officials to get these privileges for me and had even invited him home for a drink. I found out later that he had spent several hours with her while I cooled my heels in a prison cell!

The food in the Parthenais was atrocious and inedible — soggy cereal and cold toast for breakfast and at mid-day two sausages chased by three beans. We were literally starving.

Between meals I did no work at all. I read the stuff Danielle brought me and did some writing. Although I was bored, every day was different and I witnessed some violent scenes and scuffles. For me it was a new experience, a sort of initiation. For four hours each day I mixed with the other prisoners, types I had never come across before. There was the man who had been in prison for twenty years, had escaped and been recaptured, and wrote frequent letters to his lover: "My darling. Even though you are in Bordeaux Jail now, I will find a way to get you out of there. You will soon be free." I thought, how terrible, they are both behind bars! Then it occurred to me that Bordeaux wasn't a women's prison!

He confided to me how he had become close friends with this slender young boy he had met in jail, how he had fallen in love with him and how much they adored each other. He described him to me as you would describe a beautiful woman, down to the last detail. I found it disgusting.

From that moment on I became suspicious of him, especially when I noticed that he was looking towards the showers a bit too often, watching the young guys. One day I saw him watching me; I went over to him and told him he could do what he liked to whomever he liked, but never to try anything with me. He got the message and left me alone.

There were lots of people like him at the Parthenais, veterans, who had been in prison for ten or twenty years. For them it was normal behavior; it was all the sex they had. At night I constantly thought about Danielle and during the day I strengthened my ties with the Montreal underworld.

I think it is true to say that during my nine months at the Parthenais I met most of the people who had been involved in important Canadian trials or at least those that had taken place in Montreal.

I made friends and spent a lot of time with Marc Morin of the infamous Casa Loma nightclub killing who was responsible for shooting three men and had spent three-quarters of his life in prison. I also met Frank Cotroni's team, who had smuggled a boat with a ton and a half of hashish. To them I was someone important: a heroin trafficker and Danielle Ouimet's lover. There was a sort of glamor about me, I was a big shot. Everybody respected me because of the vast amount of heroin the newspaper had given me credit for: three hundred kilos, a boatload, a ton — they didn't know how much. They talked in astronomical figures — six hundred thousand dollars, six hundred million dollars — while I, the big boss, was waiting around in prison.

These Canadians weren't used to dealing in such large quantities of dope or in handling such enormous sums of money. Everyone wanted to know who the big boss was and asked for my advice. "Suppose I've got buyers and sellers, and couriers, how much would I make if I invested ten thousand dollars? Or ten million? Do you think it would work?" They had seen too many movies.

Conrad Bouchard, the ex-singer and well-known heroin trafficker, was impressed with me, he thought I was the narcotics king.
He told me about his business in Canada and even gave me the
name of his suppliers in France.

The clerks' strike was over, but then a hunger strike broke out
to protest the rotten food, to promote better visiting rights and
increase the number of phone calls allowed. The governor promised to obtain some of the things the prisoners had asked for and
announced over the P.A. system that we had fifteen minutes to get
back to our cells. Nobody listened. It almost came to a full-fledged
riot.

Windows were broken and the noise was deafening. The
guards, some of them wearing helmets and carrying clubs, turned
huge fire hoses on us as if we were animals. The pressure was so
strong it physically pushed us back to our cells. But the uprising
was far from over. The whole place caught fire and there was
smoke everywhere. We were screaming. Then the bastards used
clubs to get us out of our cells one by one, together with our
blankets, sheets and mattresses. They piled up the stuff in the
middle of the corridor and it all got soaked.

They clubbed anyone who protested. When they got to my
cell, I thought, "Here we go, it's my turn." But they stopped and I
heard someone say, "No, it's Michel . . ." They were strangely
gentle with me, passed me by and left me almost all my belongings.
Whereas when they came to my neighbor's cell they stripped down
everything to the bare walls. His name wasn't Michel . . .

Then one of the guards had the bright idea to open all the
windows. It was freezing outside and some people were soaked to
the skin. It was impossible to close the damn windows from the
inside and we spent the night shivering, trying to recover our
blankets which were lying in the middle of the corridor; but we
couldn't reach that far.

More scuffles followed and Paul Rose wrenched his arm.
Thirty or forty prisoners were wounded, some of them badly.

I thought that the role of the guard was to watch the prisoners,
and to open and close doors. But they are two-faced bastards. While
one of them hits you with a club, the other one takes your money to
buy protection for you.

Canadian guards are the same as some European ones. They take it out on the prisoner who can't defend himself to compensate for their own inadequacies. I don't blame them if they have a grudge against the world. I blame the government.

The hunger strike was settled, soon to be followed by another drama. This time the guards went on strike. The army was called in, our telephone and visiting privileges were cut off and no one had any cigarettes. They gave us a pack of tobacco every two days and the food was worse than ever.

Altogether the soldiers behaved decently; they were even kind. The guards would have liked to have killed us. These idiots had imagined that the prisoners would go on a hunger strike to support them. Obviously no one obliged them.

I was only slightly affected by the whole affair as I had checked in to the infirmary, one of the "little" privileges Danielle had managed to obtain for me from her friend. The guards knew this and didn't touch me. They were too afraid of the publicity: Mastantuono, Michel, Habitat 67, Danielle Ouimet's fiancé! Danielle . . .

I didn't want to believe what was happening and suffered agonies of doubt. I told myself she was doing her best for me, trying to get me out, getting me more visiting privileges. I still told myself that she loved me; I was deluding myself.

The strike ended, but nothing much was happening in my case. I decided to change lawyers and hired Nikita Tomeso. Daoust had told me that he had received the fifty thousand dollars, but had to spend ten thousand on one lawyer and a further ten thousand on another.

In order to strengthen my case I phoned my brother in France and he hopped on a plane and came to Montreal for a few days. A lawyer he met suggested a way for me to get out of prison. It involved spending sixty thousand dollars, not necessarily on bail alone but to line the pockets of some influential people. I gathered they didn't object to letting me go in exchange for sixty grand!

I told them I needed two weeks to raise the money. They agreed. As I couldn't get hold of Danielle I phoned my friend André. "Where is she?"

"We'll talk about her when you get out, Michel. She's running around all over the place," he replied evasively and quickly changed the subject.

I couldn't believe my ears. His words had about the same effect on me as a sledgehammer landing on my head. I became discouraged and demoralized. Danielle was cheating on me.

My brother Felix told me that Jo Signoli had not been arrested, that no one had been nailed in France, but that they all knew I was inside. It was to their advantage to have me released — how long would it be before I weakened and implicated them all. My freedom was theirs as well. I suggested that he ask them to lend him a hundred thousand francs, twenty thousand dollars. I would pay them back afterwards. "I can always sell the boat," I said.

My brother went back to Europe.

Danielle came to see me the next day. I confronted her. "You must think I'm a complete idiot! I've got the word that you're playing around."

At first she tried to deny it. "No, Michel, never," she said feebly. But when I told her that I had spoken to André the night before she admitted everything, adding, "This is hardly the moment to tell you about it, Michel."

Then she tried to retract her statement, telling me André was a lying bastard.

I didn't want to pursue the matter any further as Danielle was still the only person in Canada to whom I felt really close. After all, she did come to see me, she was kind to me and perhaps there was something else that drew her close to me. Illusions . . . she was merely afraid of being implicated.

Before leaving she assured me that my brother would return with the money. "You'll get bail and life will go on. We'll start all over again."

But my morale was low and I was sad, a beaten man, emotionally drained.

The following day my brother was back in Montreal. Jo Signoli had given him the hundred thousand francs but had almost immediately taken them back because he suddenly realized he was in a jam and needed money. Felix said I would have to manage without Signoli's help.

He tried to raise my spirits a little by telling me that he was working out something with André and that he would have the money by Monday. In fact he and André did get it a few hours later.

On Saturday evening I phoned Danielle. She said, "You see, it's all settled now, and you'll get your bail." I was furious with her for talking this way on the phone. One of the guards was within earshot and I was sure that my phone at Habitat 67 was being tapped.

On Sunday Felix informed me that I was due to go before the judge the next day. "They know I have the money, but I'll only pay them when you're out, not before," he said.

But it didn't turn out to be that simple. Just as the judge was about to grant bail, one of the American agents arrived with a piece of paper. It was Roger Preiss's denunciation. He, unlike Berdin, didn't confuse the cars and pointed the finger straight at me. In his statement he spoke of heroin, not of white powder.

I remember that Preiss had seen Danielle. She was certainly in up to her neck this time! When the American began to read the testimony I almost went crazy, but as he proceeded I cooled down — there was no mention of Danielle. Then the shock came. Bail was refused and I was returned to my cell at rue Parthenais.

While the lawyers bickered and passed the buck I was losing Danielle, my freedom and my money. I thought I would go mad and contemplated suicide, escape, collaboration with the police, anything!

The next morning Danielle came to tell me, "Michel, the lawyer will kill this new evidence. Everything will be O.K., you'll see."

I envied her for her optimism but I knew that the game was up. I knew I was on my way to the States. My only concern was for Danielle. "You mustn't push your luck," I said. "They've got all the trumps in their hands by now and enough on you to convict you for twenty years. Get rid of the DS, its chassis is full of holes. Arrange with Frank Cotroni or the lawyers to dispose of it, get it out of the way."

She promised to do that, but two days later she was back. "We gave two thousand dollars to Cotroni's people to get rid of the car.

But they couldn't get it started. They wrecked the transmission and couldn't move it away from where it was parked outside my parents' house. We had to give another five thousand dollars to Tomesco, and I decided to offer him the car instead of payment; he accepted it."

She had given Tomesco the famous Citroën!

Now my position was simple and complex at the same time. On the one hand I was resigned to the idea of being locked up for good; on the other hand I was still hoping that Danielle might get me out. But she was playing her own little game, trying above all else to get out of this mess comparatively unscathed. It was time to be realistic. I told her, "Neither you nor I have any money left. It's all over. I'll have to go."

But she wouldn't give in. "If you go to the States they'll torture you, and you already look sick." I reminded her that if I looked sick or if I was sick, it was mostly because of her and her little jaunts with just about everyone.

"I'm not cheating on you, Michel!" she cried, "I adore you and you know it! Down in the States everyone will talk eventually and in the position you're in, you're liable to do the same."

Roger Preiss and Richard Berdin had talked but to my knowledge they were the only ones.

She knew better. "Edmond Taillet talked too, he even mentioned my name. A friend from Washington told me. He's coming up tomorrow to bring a copy of Taillet's statement."

"Danielle, that's not true, you're telling stories. You're the one who is sick. I never said anything to Taillet and have never worked with him. Show me his statement and I'll believe you."

Meanwhile I had heard that Bec, Signoli and others had been nailed in France.

Three days later Danielle was back with Taillet's statement. He claimed that I had told him Danielle knew about the whole operation and that I had made a hundred thousand dollars on it. This was completely untrue. The paper bore Taillet's signature or what I thought was his signature; I didn't find out the truth until much later. I could have killed the bastard.

Without knowing it I had the same reason to be angry with

Richard Berdin and Roger Preiss. I was counting on my American friends to get these two out of the way. The lawyers had told me that if they would disappear one way or another, the police wouldn't have anything more against me. I had also hoped that the Mafia would have taken care of Taillet.

At the beginning of the summer Danielle came to see me, wearing one of those short transparent dresses. She had taken pains in making herself even more attractive than usual. Perhaps she did it a little out of love, but I'm more inclined to think she did it out of fear. She must have spent sleepless nights worrying that I would talk and incriminate her. It's true she always gave me moral support as the months dragged by; she phoned, visited often and showed me she really cared.

When I told her it would be better if I went voluntarily to the States without waiting to be extradited, she argued, "It's your birthday on July 2, Michel. Why not stay in Montreal until then at least. I could arrange with the governor for a special visit so that you and I can be alone."

"And maybe make love?" I added. That was Danielle all right, I knew what was on her mind. She could always find a way. I weakened and agreed to ask the lawyers to have my arraignment remanded until after my birthday.

But there was one small detail I wanted to settle with André before I left. When he came to see me I explained to him that all he had to do was say that he had lent me his car and that he didn't know what I was going to use it for. I knew he hadn't been interrogated any more than the other people I had worked with in Montreal. If he felt threatened he certainly didn't show it. Nor had they questioned Danielle again after I had been arrested. In fact, the Canadians had nothing on me — it was the Americans who wanted me.

André tried to encourage me, and again told me it would be better if I forgot about Danielle — she was sleeping around with every Tom, Dick and Harry.

For a while I tried to rationalize and told myself that Danielle was affected by my arrest and that the world was crumbling all around her. Had I been on the outside and she on the inside who is to say that I would not have done the same thing?

My birthday came and I spent it with Danielle at the Parthenais, as planned. I still have the beautiful blue dressing gown she gave me.

About two weeks later, on July 17, I again went before a judge — a self-righteous bastard whose name I soon forgot. I had intended to go to the States of my own free will because extraditions are frowned upon by the immigration people. But this judge screwed me up. He decided to have me deported because of Richard Berdin's testimony. During the hearing it was also recorded that I was leaving voluntarily following Roger Preiss's testimony. I will probably go down in Canadian history as the first man ever to be extradited and leave the country voluntarily at the same time.

The other prisoners tried to console me. "Don't get upset Michel, there are lots of Canadians in American prisons. They are a lot better than ours, the food is good and you can buy whatever you want. You'll always find someone who can speak a little French or Italian."

My fate was sealed, I was resigned, but I still needed pills to put me to sleep at night.

10/
A STRANGE
PARTNERSHIP

On the morning of July 21, four days after my final hearing, two guards came to my cell at the Parthenais and told me I was on my way to the United States. I had assumed I would be allowed to spend at least ten days in Montreal before being shipped across the border, but I was wrong. I was not even permitted to telephone Danielle or my lawyer. People who are being extradited are treated like packages and packages don't make telephone calls.

Before I knew it I was at the prison wicket collecting my watch, my rings and my thousand dollars. Someone addressed me in French: "My name is Anthony Pohl. I'm from the American Bureau of Narcotics and Dangerous Drugs. I've been instructed to escort you." With that he snapped handcuffs on my wrists. I must have looked very stupid.

Two Canadian police officers accompanied us to the airport. In the car Anthony Pohl didn't waste much time trying to make me crack. "What have you finally decided to do, Michel? Are you going to collaborate with us or not?"

"You don't leave me much choice," I replied. "What exactly do you want to know?"

Then one of the police officer fired a question at me. He wanted to know whether André was involved; I denied that. Then he wanted to know whether Danielle was implicated, and I denied that too. Robert Gauthier? — no, no, and no . . .

Pohl turned to the Canadian, "Don't waste your time talking to him."

I realized it had all started badly. At the airport they took me to a small room and to my surprise Danielle was there. Anthony Pohl removed my handcuffs and left us alone for half an hour. She started to cry. "My love, you look sick, and so downhearted . . . What will happen to you down there? You don't even speak English." She was still frightened for her own skin.

"Don't worry, I'll still cover for you," I said.

She promised to wait for me even if it took twenty years; she wanted to hear from me as soon as possible; she promised to come and see me.

"Wait until I tell you to come. Under no circumstances must you cross the border; they know enough for you to get twenty years." She trembled. It was time to say goodbye and leave.

On the plane Anthony Pohl told me if I gave him my word not to try anything funny and if I didn't make a nuisance of myself, he would remove the handcuffs. I promised. To be certain that I would keep my word, he warned me, "Remember, there are two of us, and we know how to shoot straight."

At that point I thought it might even be better if they did shoot, but then again I was glad I was traveling like an ordinary passenger, although I noticed two other police officers in the seats right behind me. A four-man escort! They weren't taking any chances.

Seated between Anthony Pohl and his colleague, I was again urged to collaborate with them. They were smart, trying to make me believe they knew everything. They told me Richard Berdin and Roger Preiss had confessed and everyone else had been arrested. More questions were fired at me in quick succession, when Pohl suddenly said, "Do you know Edmond Taillet?"

I caught my breath and didn't reply right away. My mind was working like a computer. I wondered what I could say that would be enough to cover Danielle.

Taillet. And they say they know everything. But Taillet lied, so they are lying too. They know about the two Fiats, Batkoun's and mine. I could mention the Uncle, but I said, "Taillet, he's a bastard, he's a . . ."

But Anthony Pohl wouldn't let me finish, "Do you know he

has collaborated? We know all about him. He brought over cars from Montreal together with you, and you used to phone him." He even quoted the number of kilos, but I knew he actually meant Bec. Pohl was playing games, making me think that Taillet had done the talking.

Then I confirmed what he had said, "You're right. Taillet did three cars in Montreal . . ."

He interrupted me again, "What's that? He must have forgotten to mention the other deliveries when he talked to us."

I had just put the three Montreal transactions on Taillet's shoulders. I had done it in a moment of anger and I couldn't go back on it now. Taillet had only admitted one trip in his statement and he had incriminated the American buyer.

Pohl went on: "This is all very interesting. Now, his bosses, do I know them?"

I said no, but that wasn't what he wanted to hear.

"I should tell you, Michel," he continued, "that there are two agencies in New York involved with drugs: one is the BNDD and the other the U.S. Customs. I'm from the BNDD and you are, in fact, not my prisoner. I'm just escorting you to the United States and when we get there the Customs' people will take over." I told him it was all the same to me. "Wrong," he replied, "because if you decide not to collaborate with the U.S. Customs but are willing to collaborate with me instead, certain things could be arranged. You never know what the Customs' people have up their sleeves . . . They could put pressure on your girlfriend . . ."

Was he trying to steal me from his colleagues at the Customs and keep me for himself and his agency? I quickly interrupted, "Danielle isn't involved."

He almost burst out laughing, "That's what you say! Danielle, she could get twenty years tomorrow morning if we really wanted to nail her. We've got all we need on her. We know she carried money."

"That's not true. You've been listening to too many stories."

"Well, we'll see," he concluded, as we taxied down the runway in New York.

Shortly after my arrival I met Mr. Sealy, head of the narcotics squad of the U.S. Bureau of Customs. He also tried to persuade me to collaborate. I consented, but naturally asked for some guarantees. He refused to commit himself. "We never promise anything, it's against the law. But you can expect to receive the same treatment as Richard Berdin who will be sentenced in a month's time. You'll likely get the same sentence as he gets. Will you give us names?"

I said I would. I would go before the judge that same day and he would fix bail which I would have to refuse. He lost no time explaining to me that by refusing bail I was making it possible for the U.S. Customs' agents to hold on to me. If I accepted bail it would be so high that I would never be able to pay it and would have to be detained in an ordinary prison. It was Friday and he gave me the weekend to get myself together. Interrogation would begin on Monday.

Mr. Sealy introduced me to Tony Bocchichio, who subsequently became my friend, my guardian and my confessor. I also met Arthur Viviani, the U.S. Attorney and counsel for the prosecution.

In court, the judge made a long story of it: "You transported two hundred kilos of heroin — at a thousand dollars a kilo, that makes two hundred thousand dollars. I recommend therefore that bail be set at four hundred thousand dollars." I looked at the judge; maybe he didn't know how to count? Think about it. Heroin at a thousand dollars a kilo — he must be completely mad! He went on, "We will appoint a lawyer who will try to reduce bail."

I did as I had been instructed to do — I refused bail. Then I heard a policeman say: "Take him to Nassau, but give him something to eat first, like a steak."

At the time of my arrest I weighed at least seventy-two kilos; I was now down to about sixty-five. He must have thought I needed a good meal. I hadn't eaten a steak in nine months and can still remember how delicious it was.

Afterwards, I assumed I would be taken to a house, but the car stopped in the courtyard of a large new building with grillwork gates and barred windows. A prison! No one spoke French and I began to panic again.

I was put in a cell where I could see inmates phoning. When the guard came to see me I explained in sign language that I wanted to phone Danielle. He said that was impossible because I was a federal prisoner and Nassau was a state prison. I felt sick.

I was taken down some stairs to a dismal domed room, with grillwork all around; I had to undress and leave my clothes behind. After a shower I was given a pair of pants and a jacket — my first prison uniform. Then I went back to a cell on the fourth floor, which was just big enough to turn round in, and the mattress wasn't bad either. But I was under guard in the maximum security wing.

On Monday morning I was brought to a room in the Nassau Holiday Inn. Tony Bocchichio was waiting for me. I hadn't washed and had a two-day growth of beard. The police allowed me to have a shower and to shave.

Shortly before ten A.M., just as I was coming out of the bathroom, Anthony Pohl arrived with four or five agents, a marshall and a French police officer, eight people altogether.Guns and dossiers were visible everywhere. I became terrified and confused, but the agents sensing the state I was in, tried to reassure me, telling me it was, after all, only a question of cooperating with them.

At Anthony Pohl's request I told them everything I knew about Taillet. He let me finish this time and then suddenly asked, "Tell us something about your friend, André A..."

I hesitated, "André A...? He's not a trafficker. He just lent me his car, that's all. He doesn't know anything."

Then he stuck some photos under my nose. "What about this and that and that? Take a look."

I don't know whether the expression on my face changed noticeably. The pictures, clearly and distinctly, showed André with Paul Graziani. They had been taken secretly at Dorval Airport. By then I must have looked stupified.

The French police officer showed me documents attesting to André's crossing the border and hotel registration slips from the Holiday Inn where André and his fiancée had stayed. He added, "Here's a plane ticket too. He left New York by plane but his car stayed behind. Why?" I was more than cornered.

Here is what they proposed: Tell us everything you know about André and we'll wait till he gets back to Montreal to nail him. We'll bring him back to New York and if he collaborates with us, he'll be O.K. If not, he'll be arrested in France and get twenty years.

I was in a real fix. I figured if André came to New York he would tell them everything because he would be so scared and thereby incriminate Danielle. Eight pairs of eyes were watching me. I finally broke down.

"Yes, André A... has been my partner."

Towards four o'clock Anthony Pohl ended the interrogation and told me I was going back to prison. I would have to appear the next day before the Grand Jury. He then asked me to sign an official declaration which would allow him to indict André and arrest him as soon as he returned to Montreal from France.

The next day I reluctantly stated my case against my friend before the Grand Jury. But as I was leaving the court room I had an idea and told Pohl and Bocchichio: "André is weak and he'll make the same mistake as I did. He'll play every card he's got contesting his extradition, in the same way as I did. He'll spend all his money on lawyers fully knowing he can't win in the end. Let me write and tell him not to complicate matters, and come voluntarily. That way you'll gain time and so will I."

"If you're sure he'll do it, go ahead and write," Tony agreed.

The days dragged on. Every morning they picked me up at Nassau and took me to the Holiday Inn for questioning. At first the atmosphere was cordial, almost friendly, but it didn't remain that way because I didn't always tell them what they wanted to hear. I was fighting Pohl, Bocchichio and everyone else.

I started to accuse the police, more precisely those police officers who had gone along with the traffickers and helped them. It was my interrogators' turn to feel ill-at-ease.

For example, I answered one of Anthony Pohl's questions with, "Well you know that already because one day Jo Signoli tried to sell you five kilos of heroin." When he started to say something the others got nervous, "How did you know that? Who told you?" So I had to explain at length that the French police had warned the traffickers that the Americans had set a trap for Signoli. It was the French who had then decided to arrest Jo at the airport to stop him from going to the States straight into the lion's den. I told them of Signoli's meeting with an officer from the U.S. narcotics squad whom he thought was a big buyer. "You have to remember that at that particular time Signoli was moving heaven and earth to get buyers that suited him, so much so that he got himself trapped."

Anthony Pohl and the French became agitated and insisted I tell who had informed us about the trap for Jo Signoli.

"It was someone I know vaguely. I saw him only once." I tried to describe the man.

They showed me photographs and asked me to identify him. But he wasn't in the pictures. The interrogation stopped right there, and everyone was a bit embarrassed.

The next day I was taken to a police artist in New Jersey to whom I had to more or less describe the man who had made contact with the informer. Back at the Holiday Inn the French policeman studied the sketch and then telephoned the narcotics bureau in France asking for two or three photographs of certain people to be sent over. I listened to the conversation and was able to pick up just one name: Mariani.

Anthony Pohl got a big kick out of turning the knife in one particular wound: Danielle. He tried to make me admit that she was implicated as deeply as all the others. But I held my ground and insisted she was innocent.

"Didn't she come to New York with you to collect the money?"

"Yes, she came, but she didn't know anything."

I told him I had taken her back to the hotel and she had never taken part in whatever was going on. He didn't buy it nor did he hide the fact. "You're lying."

The photos eventually arrived from France and I recognized Mariani who was an important character in France. Anthony Pohl started to swear because he hadn't been arrested.

I continued to collaborate with them as much as I could, but when I realized that they were far from knowing the whole truth, I started to invent stories and make up characters. They took notes, recorded them and analyzed my statements.

They showed me the photo of an American and asked me if I knew him. It was Jo Stassi, one of the buyers. I explained that I had

Batkoun's Fiat after it had been dismantled by RCMP agents.

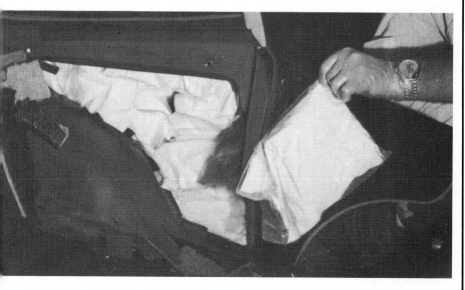

The gloved hand of an RCMP agent retrieves a heroin sachet from one of the caches in Batkoun's Fiat.

On April 27, 1971 an agent from the RCMP narcotics squad photographed Michel Mastantuono (left) and Edmont Taillet (right) opposite the Lasalle Hotel on Drummond Street in Montreal. Taillet was arrested the next day when he arrived in New York.

Danielle Ouimet emerging from a telephone booth.

Canadian drug traffickers.
Upper, Frank Cotroni
who asked Mastantuono
to introduce him to one of
his suppliers. Conrad
Bouchard, lower, and
Mastantuono met at the
Parthenais Prison in
Montreal.

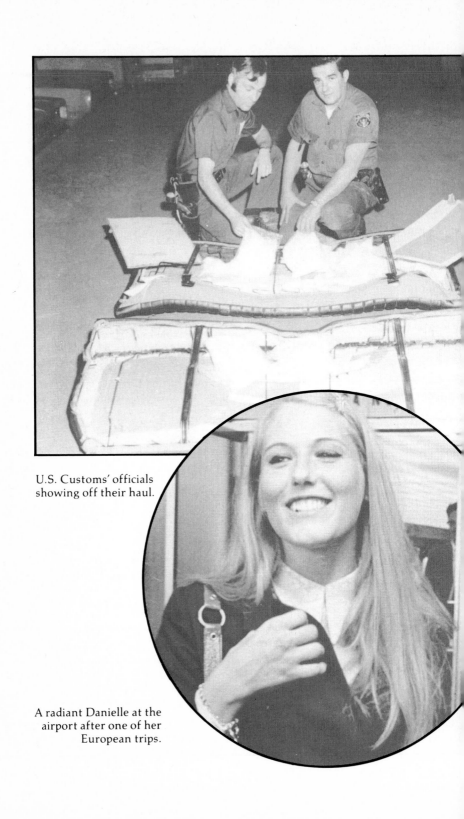

U.S. Customs' officials
showing off their haul.

A radiant Danielle at the
airport after one of her
European trips.

A fortune in drugs was seized and retrieved from a "loaded" car in New York.

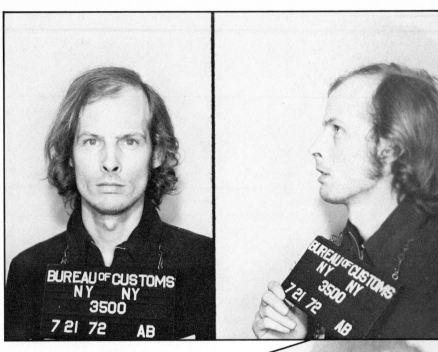

Mastantuono, Michel, on July 21,
1972, the day he arrived in New
York, after having been extradited
from Canada.

Above, William
Sorensen received a
life sentence follow-
ing Michel Mastan-
tuono's testimony.
Below, Anthony
Frank Stassi.

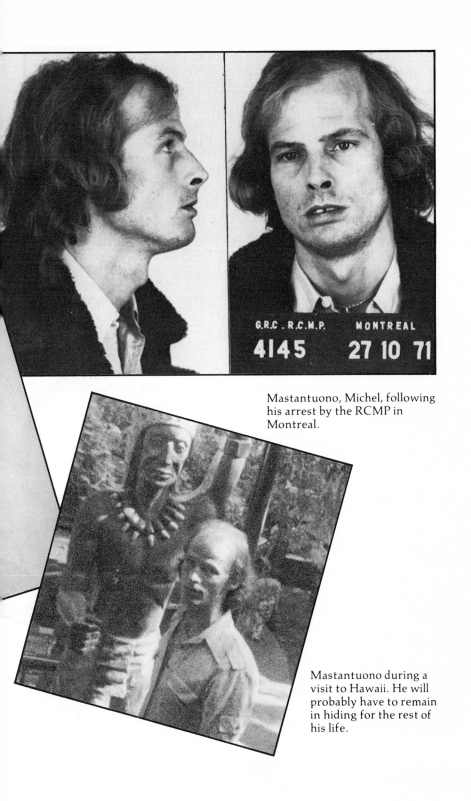

G.R.C _ R.C.M.P.   MONTREAL
4145   27 10 71

Mastantuono, Michel, following his arrest by the RCMP in Montreal.

Mastantuono during a visit to Hawaii. He will probably have to remain in hiding for the rest of his life.

Mastantuono and Berdin, who collaborated with Michel
Auger in writing this book.

seen him and that he spoke French. Bocchichio snatched the picture away and said, "No, he doesn't." Again I realized that they didn't know the whole story and took advantage of it. I guessed that they didn't have a clue who the second buyer was and continued to put them on the wrong track. I declared that the buyers belonged to the Cirillo-Astuto team; they had to, because they were the only two people I had met in New York. In this way I only half-collaborated. My goal was simple enough — my story had to be changed enough to make Danielle no longer essential to the operation of the ring and thereby no longer liable for prosecution. It was even more important to prevent Stassi, the Italian, from being arrested, because if he was, he might talk and the shit would really hit the fan.

They took me back to the prison; my interrogation was over and most of my statements had been false.

But Chamanidas, the French policeman, wasn't fooled. "Personally I don't give a damn," he said. "They've got everything on Danielle they need — they found her plane tickets to Miami, the lot . . ." He believed that the American police simply wanted to make me a gift of Danielle's freedom in return for collaborating with them so amiably. And I was reasonably happy to accept the gift despite my occasional sparring with Anthony Pohl.

In the end Bocchichio realized that I had told some phony stories, but he was not yet in a position to assess the lies I had fed them. I had denied the existence of one of the American buyers and they hadn't even suspected it.

After spending two weeks in my cell I had enough. Using sign language and by ranting and raving, I finally managed to make the guard understand that I had to speak to Tony Bocchichio. He let me make my phone call and I let Tony have it.

"You promised to put me in a better prison than the Canadian one, but this one is just as bad."

"Don't worry," he said, "we'll transfer you tomorrow."

11/
BERGEN COUNTY

Several hours later I was transferred to Bergen County prison — a fantastic place — a paradise compared with what I had seen up till then.

We lived a comparatively normal life there except that we weren't allowed to go out; the cell doors were never locked and we could walk around all day and all night if we wished. Color television, delicious food and we ate with knives and forks. I thought about the so-called model prison in the rue Parthenais.

Bergen County housed fifty-nine detainees. In fact, it was really a rehabilitation center for drug addicts. For the first time I saw close at hand the ravages caused by heroin and began to feel some compassion and remorse. My morale was at low ebb.

I made friends among the addicts and they nicknamed me "the French Connection." When they seemed to be on the way to recovery they would talk about themselves. But often those who left supposedly cured would come back a few weeks later, as addicted as before.

The situation was shocking. Their average age wasn't more than nineteen or twenty. These poor kids shivered, then sweated, then shook. I, the trafficker, lived among them for five months without receiving letters, visits or anything else to comfort me.

I found out later that during that period Danielle had been writing crazy letters to the court in the hope that they would reach me, but they were all intercepted by the censor. And what letters they were!

"My Michel, don't crack; you know they are bastards. Don't tell them anything."

I didn't see Tony Bocchichio and the promises made by the police were nothing more than hot air. Time was dragging and my nerves began to give way again. I had to do something! Through the prisoners I managed to send messages to Tony and in the end he received the one in which I begged him to tell me what was happening.

I also managed to call Danielle, telling her to try and cross the border. I had to see her and talk to her about André who was going to be extradited.

One day she arrived having used her sister's passport. I told her I had cooperated with the authorities and ordered her to stick to the story we had agreed on in case she was asked to testify. I made it clear to her the only person who could incriminate her was André. If we both stuck to the same story, and if his version were totally different from ours, he would be considered an imbecile and the police wouldn't be able to touch her.

At the time of our meeting André had already been arrested at Dorval. He had followed my advice to come to the States voluntarily without fighting the extradition order.

My final instructions to Danielle before she returned to Montreal were to wait until I told her to come and not to set foot across the border before. If I didn't corroborate André's statements they wouldn't be able to extradite her, because she was a Canadian.

A few days later I was taken to the Federal Court building. Bocchichio was there, but he seemed different from the Tony I had known before. He hardly took any notice of me and treated me like dirt. I sensed disaster and wondered whether he had seen through my gigantic double-cross.

They made me sit in a small room with American policemen and RCMP all around me. Something stunk.

"Tell us about the Fiat, Michel. You forgot to explain that in detail. Remember — you just mentioned it vaguely?"

I tried to stay calm, but I must have looked perplexed. "The Fiat," I asked, "What do you want to know about it?"

They wanted to know if Danielle had made the contact in Miami.

"No, it was Felix Rosso."

"Who sewed up the seats?"

"Just me."

"Hmm. Just you?"

They didn't look convinced. Then one of the Canadians entered into the conversation. "If we ask you one more thing will you answer?"

"If you like . . ."

"Did Danielle come here last week?"

The question had the effect of a bombshell.

I looked surly and answered abruptly, "No, she didn't come. I've nothing more to say. Nothing."

Tony understood and asked the Canadians to step outside for a few moments.

When they came back into the room, he said to me, "Michel, I warn you, if you don't tell us the truth about the Fiat we'll bring in Danielle. Understood?"

Then I made a big mistake. Tony's information could only have come from André, but I wasn't supposed to know that André had talked, nor that he had fabricated stories about Danielle. I brushed all that aside and said, "Listen Tony, André is insane, completely insane. He told you all sorts of nonsense and you fell for it."

I had written another letter to André telling him not to mention the Fiat. Now it looked as if he had made a full confession. I was livid.

Tony tried to reason with me. "We know Danielle was mixed up in this from beginning to end. We knew long ago about the contact she made in Miami."

I tried to defend her even more vehemently. "Do you think I'm crazy, Tony? Do you really believe I'd send Danielle into the arms of the American Mafia? They could have killed her. She doesn't even know what heroin is. I used her without her knowledge, leave her alone. André is crazy to get her mixed up in this. Don't believe a word he says."

Viviani, the prosecutor, suddenly came into the room. "We want to talk to Danielle," he said.

I told him there was no question of Danielle coming to the

States to be put in jail. However, if they would formally guarantee her immunity and swear not to arrest her, I would ask her to come.

Viviani proposed a deal: "O.K., ask her to come. If she tells us as much of the truth as she knows, we'll let her go back to Canada. I can't promise that the Canadian authorities won't take action against her, but as far as we're concerned we'll wait until she gets back to Montreal before we ask for her extradition."

He sounded sincere so I got on the phone to Danielle. I told her to trust me and to come down. "Tell the truth and you'll be allowed to return to Canada."

After speaking to Viviani she decided to fly down the following week. I was absolutely certain that she would tell the same story as I had told them.

On the day she arrived I was taken before the Grand Jury and Danielle was called as a witness. Her statement was more or less identical to mine. Viviani knew it was an enormous lie, but he let it pass.

After the hearing I was allowed to spend half an hour alone with her. When she left Viviani exclaimed furiously, "That damn girl — the same story! She's as big a liar as you are, Michel, telling us the same nonsense. I'm sure you arranged it all — only she's a bit sharper than you are."

That scared the hell out of me — what had she told them privately?

When she got back to Montreal I phoned her. I think she was on the verge of tears when she told me how frightened she had been and that André must have talked and told them everything, absolutely everything.

But our nightmare was far from over.

The day of my sentence was drawing closer but I still didn't know how to prepare myself for it. I was slightly encouraged by the fact that Richard Berdin had only got three years, which he could serve in fifteen months. I counted the nine months I had spent at the Parthenais in Canada and the one year's detention time in the United States and convinced myself I would be out soon. I was wrong.

I appeared in court to be sentenced. Viviani told the presiding judge that I had, up to a point, collaborated with the authorities. However, I felt he could have sounded a bit more sympathetic, and could have mentioned how I had reformed, etc. But I suppose he had his reasons for not doing so. On the other hand, he could have said that I had only pretended to collaborate, that I had told only half-truths without fully cooperating with the police, and that I had been trying to lead them astray. He must have been tempted to mention these details but he stuck to his promise, merely pointing out to the judge that I had collaborated.

My lawyer was completely useless. He was supposed to plead clemency, talk about rehabilitation and the errors of youth, or whatever. But he was as dense as they come and didn't even try to defend me.

As a result I got five years in addition to the time I had served in Canada.

I was furious and gave Viviani hell. "You fed me a lot of bullshit," I shouted. "Thanks for nothing!"

He tried to defend his actions, saying it was the judge's fault and no one could have predicted the outcome of the verdict. But he sounded hesitant, as if he were looking for excuses. Finally he said what he really had on his mind.

"O.K. Michel. Quit kidding. You'll get parole so you won't have to serve your five years. You know you fed us a pack of lies, and you're still handing them out. Do you call that cooperation? You must think we're all stupid. As for Danielle, we've handed you a present and left her out of the affair. Deep down you're two of a kind, more to be pitied than anything else. There's no need for you to snivel — five years is actually a good deal. I know people who got twenty for doing only one-tenth of what you've done. You and Danielle are lucky, two very lucky liars. Get that into your head."

I went to prison and Danielle came to see me two or three times. She had to pay her own air fare, the taxi, everything. No one picked her up at the airport as had been done in the case of wives of other prisoners who had collaborated.

Tony behaved correctly and whenever Danielle came to see me I was able to spend the whole afternoon with her. But he never left us alone. One day Danielle begged him to let us have some privacy, but he refused categorically. I learned later that Tony had earlier followed Danielle to Canada, and in the course of discreet investigations had wised up to her. He knew that a man had taken "my" Danielle to Dorval and had kissed her goodbye before she had boarded the plane. He also knew that she had slept with someone else in Manhattan.

Tony was a very understanding person. He didn't want to hurt me and felt sorry for me, but he also wanted me to break up with her. As a policeman he knew that if I saw her as she really was it would be all over between us and I would finally break down and tell the truth. He was my friend, and I can't imagine why I lied for so long to someone who was as kind and humane as he was.

Dear old Tony did give in one day and left us alone. We made love, but something had drastically changed between us.

I stayed in Bergen County Jail for twenty long months. Every three months Tony had me before the court, trying to confuse me with photographs, to make me tell the truth, but I stuck to my guns and didn't crack.

André had pleaded guilty and was condemned to three years in prison, which meant that he would be out after one year.

One day I received a letter from him full of insults and threats. "You incriminated me, you betrayed me; watch out, remember you have a son in France." When he was on the point of being released I asked to be allowed to see him. But Tony Bocchichio refused. He was probably right.

Chance plays an important part in our lives. One day when André was on his way to the prison infirmary we met face to face in the bullpen. "You miserable prick," I said, "I tried to organize things as well as I could so you would get away with as few scratches as possible. I know I implicated you, but it was to help you — you got less time than I did thanks to me. I asked you to tell them everything except what you knew about Danielle, but you involved her, you bastard."

"Michel, it was the cops who double-crossed you, not me! I swear it!"

I started to walk away in disgust, then I turned around. "Who told them that Danielle sewed in the packets? Who told them that she had carried the money? Who said she knew what was going on and that we'd waited for her at your place, that she had brought the car and had known that it carried heroin? Who told them all that? If it wasn't you, who did?"

He again denied everything, but turned green and looked frightened.

By this time I'd worked myself into a rage. "And you can stuff the threats up your ass, because when I get out of here I'll crack your skull wide open."

I wonder how well André slept that night.

12/
I'LL TELL YOU EVERYTHING TONY

To kill time inside I pressed pants and played basketball and hand-ball. I was sick to death of Bergen County Jail and the drug addicts revolted me. Then I stopped pressing pants and started making pens. With that I managed to earn a hundred dollars a week and save two thousand dollars while I was there. When Tony announced he was transferring me to another prison I made a big fuss. I wrote to him asking him to leave me where I was.

At the end of the month I was bored again, and when the order did come for me to be transferred to a Florida jail I no longer complained. This turned out to be a very special place. Situated on the Gulf of Mexico in beautiful surroundings near Elgin Airfield, it was part of a U.S. Air Force base. This was my first experience in a federal prison, and the way it was operated came as quite a shock to me. It had neither doors, nor bars, nothing. Only a notice near the entrance which read, "Federal Prison Camp" indicated it was a jail.

When I arrived I was greeted with incredible politeness. It was "Sir" this and "Sir" that and I could almost believe I was at a luxury hotel. One of the guards even offered me a chair. What a contrast to Canada!

Before going through the registration formalities — filling in forms and fingerprinting — I was offered a meal. Never before have I seen such a spread! Every imaginable dish was put in front of me and it all tasted delicious.

Then I took a trip to the barber shop. For hygienic reasons

they cut my hair shorter, and because of that I was prepared to give up a little of my vanity.

The officer in charge of clothing apologized when he gave me a pair of pants which were a little big on me. "Tomorrow, you can go to the laundry and they'll be glad to alter the whole outfit for you, or at least those things that don't fit." I couldn't believe it.

Then they asked one of the detainees to take me to my cell in one of the barrack-type buildings. I was tempted to call it my suite. These were not really cells but long, airy dormitories with beds that had thick, comfortable mattresses.

There were five hundred of us — Americans, mostly whites, some South Americans, and I — the only Frenchman.

Among the detainees were judges, federal attorneys and several people who had been implicated in the Watergate affair. I was introduced to one of the Cohen brothers who was serving five years for defrauding the U.S. treasury of fifty million dollars. I met other extraordinary people, most of them rich, respectable and cultured men who had been caught with their hands in the till or had committed grand larceny. There were government witnesses and collaborators like me. Some of the prisoners had been transferred from ordinary federal penitentiaries and were waiting to be released.

I got a job in the kitchens, which wasn't bad at all, cooking for five hundred people. The guards often dropped in to ask me what was on the menu. They and the rest of the prison staff ate with us.

These guards were extraordinary people and amazingly cultured individuals. They would talk law to the judges and politics to the Watergate people; they were very knowledgeable. They continued to address me with "Yes, sir," and "No, sir," and didn't make me feel as if I were a prisoner. They really tried to help in every way.

All the inmates did some work, even the judges and the lawyers. For example, the Watergate people were responsible for the upkeep of the lawns.

I took things easy. After work I played tennis, and if I wanted to improve my backhand I would ask one of the guards to take me to the court and give me a free lesson. My favorite tennis partners were two judges from New Orleans who were in the pen for defrauding the government. They only spoke pidgeon French, what they called Creole, but we somehow managed to communicate. In the evenings we went for long walks and carried on interesting discussions.

The inmates were a far cry from those at the Parthenais. We were in a polite world among gentlemen, not petty thieves, rapists or murderers. My morale went up considerably.

One day I was called to the administration building by a prisoner who worked in the office and had access to the files. He said he wanted to ask me some questions. My dossier was in his hand and on it was written, "Five years for carriage and distribution of one hundred kilos of pure heroin." Diagonally across the file, stamped in red ink, were the words "Not to be removed without authorization from the U.S. Department of Justice in Washington." When I realized what he had in his hand I became panicky. "How did you get these papers?" I asked. He gave me a sinister look. "You fucking rat!" I said. "Get out," and I slammed the door in his face.

When I mentioned what had happened to Juan, my Argentinian friend, another government witness, he encouraged me to see the warden.

The warden told me "an unusual and grave error has been committed." He promised to get hold of my papers and put them in his personal safe. But he was too late to stop the story from getting out and provoking a fight between the prisoners and the administration.

The director offered to transfer either me or the prisoner who had looked at my files to a prison in Atlanta. I was very upset but managed to reach Tony Bocchichio by phone. He calmed me down, and soon the other prisoner left and I stayed.

Danielle came down to see me. We spent the whole day sitting on the terrace under an umbrella and the next day I told her I had applied for a two days' leave of absence. She looked happy enough, but complained how expensive the plane ticket had been and about all the money it had cost her to come. I told her to use the money my relations had sent her that they'd been keeping for me.

She was back the following week with some civilian clothes for me. We took a room at the Holiday Inn in Walton Beach, a town about twelve miles from the prison.

It was there, in that room, that I finally realized that I no longer loved Danielle. She was confused and rambled on and on about all sorts of things that didn't make sense to me. The night we spent together was as disastrous as the whole day had been. Probably ten months had gone by since I had last made love and I found I was impotent.

The next day I didn't feel well. We went to the beach and in the evening I returned to the prison. She flew back to Montreal. I wrote a few more love letters to her so that my change of heart wouldn't come as a shock to her. But even while going through the motions of still loving her I couldn't help feeling that I was *forcing* myself to forget her. My Canadian friends had regularly sent me show business magazines and I could see with my own eyes that she was going out with a variety of men. The headlines alone said a lot: "Danielle Ouimet's perfect love affair . . ." "Danielle Ouimet accompanied by X." "New Romance." "Danielle and . . ." One day I cut out all the articles and mailed them to her with a letter saying, "Don't try to lead me on any more, my girl. I know everything, absolutely everything, even though I've pretended I didn't."

Fortunately life was more than bearable at the prison. My tennis improved steadily so that, in the end, I became the local champion.

Under normal conditions the authorities should have freed me at most after six months. So I was furious when the Parole Board informed me that I still had a minimum of eight months to serve. Once again I rushed to the phone and played hell with poor Tony Bocchichio.

"What sort of a jackass do you think I am? I got five years, which was more than anyone else, and now they've even refused parole. It's crazy!"

"There's nothing I can do about it, Michel," he replied. "However, we'll need you in New York, and you'll have to come up here as soon as possible."

I begged him not to send me to one of those rotten holes in New York State.

One morning I found myself on a jet to New York City and back in the old Bergen County Jail. Again the cell door closed on me. It was dark and the walls reverberated. It was starting all over again.

After a couple of days they took me to the Court House where I spent the day in the bullpen without being called. In the evening I was sent back to my cell without explanation.

The next day, the same thing happened, but on the third day, they walked me down to the Federal Building where I came across Tony Bocchichio.

"What's this shitty mess all about?" I asked. "Are you out of your minds or what? You brought me up here like a dog on a leash and threw me in that stinking hole. I've had enough! Let me spend the last six months in peace!"

I shouted in English; I'd learned quite a bit of it by then. Tony complimented me on my linguistic progress and on my beautiful tan. I assured him I would lose it quickly if I were left in Bergen County much longer.

He told me that there was a little problem I could help solve and that the French police wanted to have a chat with me.

"I don't give a damn about the French police and I haven't anything to say to you or to anyone else!" I shouted. "Let me take my tennis racquet and go back to Florida, thank you."

Tony changed his tone, "Michel, we know that you lied when you made your statement. We've interrogated Danielle, she's confirmed some facts which we already knew, and some other information has slipped out . . . The French have a problem on their hands — the Guidicelli brothers, Jean and Mimi. Although they've arrested them, they'll have to release them because of insufficient evidence. You know that because it was you who switched their photos."

I thought, I might as well admit it now, since they know anyway. So this time I told everything to the French policemen.

One of them suddenly shot a question at me, "Did you know that Danielle has been to France again?"

I started to say something when he interrupted me, "When she went to Cannes to collect the *Prix Citron* she had won a police officer was with her in a group of journalists. He never left her side, and believe me, Michel, while you were covering up for that girl she was cheating on you all over the place. She's not really worth bothering about." He also led me to believe that this same police-man had slept with Danielle in Nice.

Offhandedly, my French interrogator added that, of course, they could probably prosecute her in France too.

I also found out that Danielle had confessed, not completely, but almost. She hadn't admitted to the most important jobs, like the trip to Miami, but she was still trying hard to extricate herself.

To finally win me over the policeman added, "Of course you can see she's getting laid by everyone. Don't cover up for her, don't be an ass. You're handsome and young, and you've got a bit of money coming to you. You'll find all the women you want when you get out."

I had to think hard, especially since the French police knew I had met one of the laboratory chemists and a number of traf-fickers. In other words, I was very useful to them. Then the other one fired his opening shot, "It's as simple as this: A judge will fly to New York to hear your testimony. If you talk you'll get complete immunity."

They agreed to let me phone a lawyer in France, who con-firmed that the police offer was judicially sound in principle. "It's very rare for anyone to be convicted in America *and* in France. Of course, there is the case of Edmond Taillet, but that's an exception."

That was good enough for me, and I proceeded to tell the police everything I knew about the French operation, about the chemist I'd been introduced to after buying the car. I gave them his name and the location of the laboratory where the morphine base was being processed.

I supplied the facts about the Guidicelli brothers and this time correctly identified their photographs. Jean was "the Uncle" I had seen in New York. I also corrected a few other details and added some I hadn't given them previously.

The French were content and Tony was happy too. He still had another problem and counted on me to help him out.

Sensing that I was in a good mood, he told me that Jo Stassi, a major buyer for the American Mafia, had been arrested. During my first interrogation I had said he spoke French in order to mislead the police. As I had expected they thought I had identified him incorrectly because Stassi didn't speak French. His brother was serving twenty years in the same prison as Charlot Fioconni, who had escaped from there. "When he was captured," Tony continued, "he told us that Stassi's brother and he had organized a heroin job inside the Atlanta jail.

"From available files we tried to establish how it was done. We could tell from the dates, the data about the car and the number of kilos shipped that you were the one who had brought the stuff over from France.

"The first time we questioned you you lied and told us you couldn't recognize the houses you had delivered the dope to. You said you recognized two of them, but that there were at least two more. What I want now is for you to confess."

To be sure I wouldn't back out at the last minute he began to talk about Danielle again. "You lied to us about her too. We've interrogated her and have made all sorts of inquiries. In fact, she *did* go to Miami to meet Jo Stassi, but she didn't recognize him . . . I hope you understand that you got five years because of her. She doesn't give a damn what happens to you."

I thought quickly. If Danielle talked then there was nothing to stop me from doing the same. It was absolutely necessary for me to put some sort of defense line between me and the underworld. The only real way of leaving the past behind and of cutting off all my paths to the underworld was to put myself in a position where we could never work together again. To do that I would have to make a complete and total confession.

"O.K. Tony, I'll talk."

We jumped into a car, and went over the route again to identify the houses. We left out the first one because I had identified it before; had Tony observed my reaction in the rearview mirror he would have seen that I winced when we drove by the first time.

I had told him that there was a tower close to the second house. He drove there and I formally identified the house which belonged to a friend of Jo Stassi where we had unloaded the stuff.

Then I was shown a series of other photographs. I recognized Stassi and identified him as the buyer. I suddenly recognized four vaguely familiar faces — the chauffeurs of the famous Cadillacs which had escorted us across New York.

Tony brought out more photographs. I put him straight and told him absolutely everything Danielle had or hadn't done, reminding him all the while of his promise not to arrest her.

"We'd like to get her though," he replied, "especially since she's behaved so badly towards you."

"What do you mean by that?"

But he refused to go further; he knew he was on slippery ground. I tried to make him believe that I knew more so that he would tell me more.

He then informed me that they had tapped Danielle's phone and had tailed her in Montreal. He told me a few other things which show-biz magazines generally don't mention.

But my feelings were still stronger than my will, and I held out, defending her. Tony asked me if I intended to take up with her again.

"I expect I will, because she's going to have to take the stand against Stassi, and what will she do afterwards?"

He finished the interview, telling me: "If possible, we'll get you paroled. But I can't promise."

On March 22, 1975 I was released from Bergen County Jail.

I was out in the street once again, but still had to wait six more months before being completely free because I was at the disposition of New York State authorities to testify in the Stassi trial.

On the night of my release Tony invited me to dinner at a posh restaurant. The prosecutor was also at our table.

"Michel, in a way I think of you as my brother," Tony said, "despite the fact that we've been playing cat and mouse all this time. I always knew the truth, and how much you loved Danielle. I knew all about her flirtations but I couldn't tell you because it would have hurt you too much. Tonight I'm going to give you a piece of advice: forget her."

I had to be realistic. "Whatever happened is over now. But she still has my belongings and my car . . . Anything can happen in life; although I don't love her any more, things could work out between us, and if they do I'll go back to her. I'm a free man, but still the same Michel I was before. This might change in time but promise me not to stop me now."

As far as Tony was concerned it was all very simple. "If she tells us the absolute truth this time, and voluntarily corroborates your statements, things could be arranged. But we're pretty sick of her; she's hurt you and lied to us. That girl's a bitch. Maybe she did it because she was afraid, and because she wanted money. But the fact remains that if she hadn't behaved the way she did you would have come to the States straight away."

He took me back to my hotel in Manhattan and when we said goodbye he held on to my hand for a long time. Tony's a good man.

I gradually picked up the threads of ordinary life. I began to go out with one or two girls and spent some fabulous nights with them.

Then I decided to phone Danielle. She hadn't come to see me on the day I was released because she said she had to work. I asked her for my car and my other belongings, and the money I had left with her.

"That's impossible," she told me, "I gave three thousand dollars towards the Corvette, and I'm keeping it."

Then I got angry. "Just a minute, Danielle. You've got the furniture we both shared. If I don't get my car, things will get very messy."

When I asked for my clothes she told me they had been stolen. My jewelry? Part of that she claimed had also been stolen. I finally saw her in her true light. Under duress, she agreed to bring down my Corvette. The night we spent together was a disaster, but I at least had a chance to prepare her for what was expected of her.

"Tell the truth, because I can't promise you that they'll leave you alone afterwards. You're going to give evidence before a tribunal and your testimony will be reported in the newspapers. Who knows what may happen to your career."

I made a suggestion which might have seemed absurd under the circumstances; but which again shows the state I was in at the time. "Plead guilty. They'll bring in your parents and your sister to testify. We'll sell the boat and disappear to South America where I've got a big business deal waiting for me. We'll change our names and forget everything."

"We'll see," she replied.

Although we had talked about it at length before, she refused to give me my money claiming that to bring my car to New York she had had to pay for the gas and her plane fare back to Montreal. I had to telephone her two or three times and finally told her to keep the money for the plane ticket and the gas, but to send me the rest. All that was left in the end was one hundred and fifty dollars!

I was stunned by her meanness and told her so. "If that's the way you want it, go to hell," I screamed into the telephone. "Go to hell and sort out your own mess with the Americans. But let me give you one small piece of advice: If you're shabby enough not to return my things I'll ask the Americans to bring them back for me, and to bring you along too. I promise I'll do everything I can to get them to keep you here. And if you don't send every last piece of my stuff you'll get what you've been asking for. You're nothing but a bloody nuisance to me. I might even come to Montreal and take half of the furniture and just throw it in the Saint Lawrence River."

When I hung up I couldn't believe it had been me who had been saying these words to Danielle. What was happening? All the years I'd spend in jail, trying to protect her . . .

In the meantime my family sent me some money, and friends paid back loans I had made to them in the past. I thought I'd try to sell the boat Robert Gauthier had built. The American government paid me thirty-three dollars a day for my subsistence in New York before my trial. People who think that those who collaborate with the authorities are showered with gold when they're released from prison are mistaken.

With all that I was so short of money that I had to sell my beloved Corvette.

13/
A NEW LIFE

I was anxious for the Stassi trial to begin so that I could wipe the slate clean and start a new life.

When I told the truth at the trial I burned all my bridges behind me. Even if I wanted to go back into the drug business, I couldn't. The gulf that lies between me and the underworld is too wide to cross.

Yet I wasn't frightened. As a volunteer witness against the top men in the Mafia I told myself that if they killed me it would simply show that they were afraid of the truth.

But I feared for my family. About two weeks before the trial some people told my brother that they held me responsible for all their problems with the police. My brother told them that if they had any complaints they should come and see me in New York and sort things out with me. But they went further and warned him they were determined to get revenge on him, and on me and my son.

My brother was scared. "I had to tell them that you talked because you were forced to," he said. But I reassured him that if anything happened to any member of my family and if my son was in danger I would come to France and settle the score. "If they know I'm there the threats will stop." I was ready to go back to Marseilles, if necessary, either to surrender or to deny everything I had said.

I didn't care if they killed me, but my family had not been involved in what I had done. They had lived decent lives, had worked hard, and didn't have to pay off any of my debts. My son hadn't done anything — he's a fine young man today and my brothers had looked after him well. They weren't like me. Yet they had been prepared to make sacrifices for me, because deep down we are a close and loyal family.

I began to realize that I was going to testify against madmen who defy justice and are extremely dangerous. They act like beasts rather than like human beings.

A month before the trial Carmine Consalvo, one of the defendants, fell from the twenty-fifth floor of a building in New Jersey. I had implicated him in the transactions. Stassi and his companions were frightened that Consalvo would denounce them, so they simply threw him out of the window. A few people said it was suicide but I'm certain he was killed.

I stayed in contact with the police from the day I was set free until the trial. I wasn't really prepared to be a witness. Before the trial started the U.S. attorney asked me a lot of questions. I was taken to court but treated coldly. I was under constant police protection, living in a hotel, surrounded by security agents.

At the courthouse a huge security system was in operation. We went up and down in special elevators to a room reserved for witnesses. Police agents escorted me all the way and I couldn't move an inch without them. My amazing bodyguard, Duke, followed me like a shadow.

Besides Joseph Stassi, the three other defendants were his brother Anthony and the American buyers Charly Alaimo and William Sorensen, who had both been active in the Fiat and Citroën affairs.

For three weeks other witnesses were in the stand, for the most part, former associates of the accused. Some of them had turned against their partners when they found out that their wives had been directly threatened. In a sense I was one of the most respectable witnesses because most of the others had done fifteen or twenty years and some were even convicted murderers.

The defense attorney asked Palmer, one of the witnesses, how he could tell whether the heroin was good, and he replied, "I'd go and get a junkie and give him a fix. If he didn't die, the drug was O.K." Would I eventually have become a killer, an animal, like them? I really didn't know we had been working with a team of brutes, and had no idea that American traffickers could be so vile. It had never occurred to me that the buyers would go as far as killing people. You see it in the movies, but you don't imagine it could happen in real life.

Orsini was another witness who had been brought from the prison in Atlanta where he was serving a twenty-five year sentence. He was trying to take all the blame for the affair in order to protect the other defendants. He tried to tell the court that a conspiracy had been mounted against the accused.

The defendants had brought at least five or six other prisoners from Atlanta to testify on their behalf. One of them was a homosexual and his testimony turned into a farce because he tried to say that everyone had become a homosexual in prison; by using this ploy he hoped to implicate all the government witnesses. They asked him if he had known Mr. Stassi. Yes. And had he also known Mr. Sorensen and one of these witnesses, Mr. Palmer? It wasn't a comforting prospect to be a government witness at this trial.

I had been in contact with Anthony Stassi, who was a boss in Don Carlo Gambino's ring, one of the biggest Mafia families in New York. Don Carlo was the chief of chiefs in the American Cosa Nostra. Joseph Stassi was in prison serving twenty years for another heroin deal. From his cell he had made contact with certain Frenchmen he had sent to his brother who was acting as a New York buyer. There were several accomplices, among them William Sorensen, another buyer. The system was exactly the same as that used in France. A group of people would get together to "buy" a car, loaded with drugs. Each person received a share in the car. Stassi took a percentage and in addition a few kilos of heroin for himself.

The most important among the accused was Charly Alaimo, one of the biggest and most dangerous drug traffickers in the United States.

I hadn't talked about any of them for almost four years because I was protecting Danielle, but later, when I had to tell the whole truth about her, Jean Cardon and the others, they entered into the picture.

On the first day of my appearance as a witness, James E. Nesland, who was the prosecuting attorney, the lawyers for the accused, the judge, Whitman Knapp, and the interpreter were in the room. There was no jury as it was only a preliminary inquiry.

I was told to walk through the rows of spectators to see if I recognized anyone. If I didn't, I was to tell them. I looked around but didn't see a familiar face. I thought perhaps I had gone mad and started to get scared. "It's not possible. If they aren't here, where are they?"

I was immediately taken out of the room; Duke, my body-guard, was with me. I asked him what was happening and why was no one there. He didn't know. They told me absolutely nothing. I was recalled minutes later, and there I saw the defendants and recognized several friends of the Stassi brothers sitting among the spectators.

Prosecutor Nesland began to question me; he asked me my name and made me take the oath. I first had to identify the accused from photographs. I then had to walk over to them and touch them. That gave me a hell of a fright. I didn't know whether to step forward or run for the exit. At last I got up enough nerve to go over and touch them. I identified Anthony Stassi first, then Sorensen sitting among the spectators and finally Charly Alaimo.

I was told after the trial that William Sorensen had advised the president of the tribunal that he didn't want to sit with the other accused and the lawyers because it would make it much easier for me to identify him. If I could pick him out from among the thirty or so spectators, it would be O.K. His request must have been granted for he had chosen to sit in the same row as my friend Richard Berdin.*

Stassi and Sorensen hadn't changed that much when I saw them again, but when I recognized the notorious Alaimo, he looked surprised. I quickly saw why. He had lost at least thirty pounds, his hair was very short, and he hardly looked like the same man.

Yet he still looked quite impressive, the spitting image of a successful gangster. He was then about forty, handsome, despite his scarred face and hard features. He seemed full of energy and I knew if he could have killed me at that moment he would have done so. They told me afterwards that he was the most dangerous of them all, having been accused of murder two or three times.

---

* After Michel Mastantuono came out of prison he and Richard Berdin became friends. Berdin collaborated in the writing of this story.

Stassi on the other hand fell asleep from time to time, and at one particular moment James Nesland even asked the judge if he could wake him. The judge replied, citing the American Constitution, that there was no law forbidding the accused to sleep during the trial; all that he was required to do was be present. Nesland responded sarcastically, "He is present; let us proceed." Then he turned to Stassi's lawyer and asked if he would kindly request his client not to snore. Stassi couldn't have cared less, he was sixty-five years old and knew that this time he didn't stand the slightest chance of getting off.

Sorensen accused me of being a bastard and even uttered some threats against me. Throughout the trial there was a lot of tension in the courtroom and the attitude of the accused seemed to be one of bravado and arrogance.

Once again I undertook to tell my story, step by step, reconstructing all my dealings in the business. The trial lasted eight days, eight interminable days.

Nesland went into the minutest details, but I felt at ease with him. Things were not as simple during the cross-examination by the defense lawyers. They treated me as if I were a liar, but I remained calm; I was used to the games Daoust had played with me, and Stassi's lawyers were trying to do the same.

They went so far as to bring one of my friends, Michel Hattendorf, from Israel to testify against me. The defense had paid for his airline ticket and all his expenses to try to get him to break down my story.

The point they tried to get me on was why I had lied to the Grand Juries. For a start I said, "Yes, I lied." I explained my reasons, which were simple. On September 8, 1972 I had gone before a Grand Jury. In order to protect Danielle I had said absolutely nothing. However, I had mentioned Stassi's name by mistake in connection with the famous Citroën transaction, adding that I couldn't remember what I had said to the Grand Jury at the time. All I knew was that I lied to them.

The lawyers attacked again. "In 1973 you went before another Grand Jury."

"I believe so."

"And you said something different then."

"Yes, I went before the Grand Jury twice, and I lied both times. So what?"

They kept pounding away at me but I insisted, "I'm telling the truth now. Whatever I said before was a lie."

After the hearing we went down to Nesland's office. He advised me to keep calm, think back carefully and again explain my reasons for wanting to protect Danielle Ouimet and Michèle Cardon, the accordionist's wife.

The next day I had to demean myself explaining why I had lied. I knew Danielle would appear after me to confirm what I had said. She had made small confessions over a period of three years, revealing a little here and a little there, finally telling all sorts of stories without actually admitting the truth. Each time she had become a little more honest and each time I had thought I was done for. However, another government witness before me had also mentioned one or two names, implicating Stassi in the Fiat operation. I had completely whitewashed Stassi and had only brought him into one transaction.

Now I was telling the whole truth for the first time and they realized it. James Nesland questioned me later. He reread all my past statements and said, "You'll now tell me where you lied, and why you lied; exactly what is true, and what is not true."

As fast as he could read the documents, I gave him the answers. These hearings took place in front of a jury. I told them everything straight, because if I hadn't done so the defense lawyers would have called me a liar.

On Sunday, right in the middle of the trial, I had to go to John F. Kennedy Airport and found myself face to face with Stassi who was out on bail. I felt panicky. He saw me, and I was scared but I realized it would have been difficult for him to do anything. The agents had also been frightened because they didn't happen to be right beside me at the time. I then drove around for an hour to make sure I wasn't being followed before going home. Although I was scared of Stassi it would have been much more serious if I had met Alaimo. He was known for handling grudges himself. Alaimo never sent anyone in his place.

I had to go back on the witness stand once more. The defense was trying to prove I had used narcotics — they were trying every angle.

Danielle was waiting to testify after me. It was more than six months since I had seen her; she looked sad, harrassed and bewildered. The police had made her an offer she couldn't refuse: Plead guilty of having used the telephone to aid in trafficking. It couldn't have been easy for Danielle, but I was sure she would not have to go to jail. I was the one who had asked the police to be indulgent with her. I had told her to tell the truth and not to worry.

She told them everything. She described how she had telephoned Miami, had sewn up the bags of heroin, and that she had gone to Florida to meet one of the buyers. She doesn't have a good memory, but in this instance she told the truth as she remembered it. Perhaps she had known from the start that one day I would tell it too. She absolutely corroborated everything I had said.

In spite of it the judge recalled her the next day and said he had low regard for people who collaborated. That was when she got even more frightened and came to talk to me. I told her, "Judges always like to pontificate. Don't torment yourself. I'm sure you'll get a suspended sentence."

The trial marked the end of the Ouimet-Mastantuono affair in the sense that it was the last time Danielle and I collaborated, unless more traffickers are arrested or the American authorities extradite suspects who are still outside the country. This, however, is unlikely.

When I look at everything that has happened to me in my life and all that I've been through in the last four years, I have no regrets over the decisions I have made. At certain times I felt persecuted, or like a man condemned to die on death row. But not any more. I am relieved to have told the truth. As for Danielle, I feel sorry for her, and am ready to help her financially if I can; from a moral point of view there is nothing I can do for her, she is the only one who can help herself. She earned as much money as I did while we were in business together. I made fifty-five thousand dollars and so did she. I don't care what she says today, I know we shared everything.

Thanks to my testimony and that of Richard Berdin, Edmond Taillet, Roger Preiss and others, the police were able to seize enormous quantities of heroin, the laboratories were closed, and all the higher ups in the drug world were arrested.

What happened to drug trafficking after the Stassi trial? Was it paralyzed? I doubt it. The "French Connection" altered its methods, the underworld learned from its experiences and reorganized and adopted better methods to suite the new circumstances. The traffic began again as before.

The Uncle, one of the big wheels in the heroin business, is still outside at the time of writing, always under suspicion. His political connections with French espionage services helped to keep him out of prison. The same applied to gangsters such as Maurice "La Tête Cassée" and others who took part in operations. Some members of these French secret service agencies were connected with underworld personalities and received certain, let's say, fringe benefits.

After discussing the matter with the American and French police, in my view the Uncle collaborated with intelligence agencies after the war to fill their coffers by delivering heroin to America. But those are things you often hear in the underworld. Certain agencies look after their own financial needs, independent of the national budget, having amassed huge sums of money by trafficking.

The notorious Uncle had been moving heroin for twenty-five years with complete control over the French operations. His work consisted of getting the poppy heads from the Middle East and shipping them to the French laboratories he controlled. He then sold the processed heroin to small-time dealers in Marseilles where he again got a cut. In addition, he had American buyers under his thumb, making ten percent on all the heroin going into the United States.

You would think that he'd be too fearful to resume operations after everyone had given such damning evidence, but he is so sure of his immunity that he could well build a new team, establish new connections and build more laboratories, not necessarily in Marseilles. They might be in Italy, in Germany, in Spain, or anywhere.

The problems remain, in spite of temporary interruptions.

If the Marseilles underworld hadn't forbidden young people to deal in prostitution, they would not have got into heroin. The Uncle, Mémé Guérini and their kind saw this and sold to different groups. They provided the buyers in America who in turn selected their own men as intermediaries and paid them so well that it was a cinch for these small-time crooks to earn a fortune. The big guys paid twenty-eight hundred dollars for a kilo of heroin which they sold in the United States for ten thousand five hundred. Today heroin prices are even higher, and that kind of money will always attract greedy people. The drama of heroin is that there is so much money to be made in trafficking that those who think they can get away with it will try.

For me the past has passed: what counts is that I am still alive and free.

EPILOGUE

I have just exposed my true self. I am not searching for excuses for I didn't realize how much harm I had done; by now I have paid my dues.

I came to understand that laws are made with a specific goal in mind: to temper a person's egotism. Today I am less egotistic than I was before I went to jail. By stealing you injure someone and deprive that person of his or her right of ownership. By dealing in heroin you deprive millions of unfortunate people of their right to life. Although I could never have shot a man, I peddled death by the kilo. Was I not worse than a man who kills out of passion or vengeance?

Throughout my prison term I met superb and intelligent people who taught me that ordinary life wasn't so dreadful. I began to see the possibility of doing something constructive and of helping others. I also realized that I had existed in a fabricated, artificial and imaginary world. I had not lived at all, I had whirled around.

I still miss Canada. I adored living there and it hurts me to think that I can probably never go back except for brief visits. Nor can I return to France for the time being, as I may be arrested there for my previous wrongdoings. But I don't miss France.

I received immunity from prosecution in the United States, and I decided to settle here under an assumed name. My first job was in a restaurant on Fifth Avenue in New York City where a lot of mobsters were going in and out. Although the police protected me constantly against certain people who, I know, will never give up trying to get me, I left "The Big Apple" and moved to a place where I feel safe and at peace and no longer require a bodyguard all the time. However, I do have the privilege of contacting security agents day and night, should I require them.

I am still working in the restaurant business which I know best. I married a wonderful French girl I met in the United States. This is my fourth marriage and we are very happy. My son, who is now a student, and other members of my family have visited us from time to time. I had great problems getting rid of my Marseilles accent when I spoke French, but I am pleased to say that my English has improved considerably.

I have promised myself to keep out of harm's way and to lead "the good life" as I now know it. I think I am succeeding.

APPENDIX

In order that the reader may form an objective opinion, we have appended to Michel Mastantuono's story the transcripts of the testimony and the sentence of Danielle Ouimet.

Prosecutor Mr. Robert B. Fiske, Jr., United States Attorney for the Southern District of New York, is represented by Assistant United States Attorney, Mr. James Nesland. Mr. John Gross is defending Danielle Ouimet. Messrs. Naden, Garland, Newman and Kadish represent the interests of the accused, Charly Alaimo, Joseph Stassi, Anthony Stassi, and William Sorensen.

TESTIMONY OF DANIELLE OUIMET

UNITED STATES OF AMERICA

vs.

JOSEPH STASSI, et al
New York, November 11, 1975

(In open court, jury present.)

The Court: Ladies and gentlemen, greetings. I told you Friday is off, didn't I? I am trying to remember what I told you and what I haven't told you. It seems to me about time I ask you again: Have any of you seen any articles or heard anything about heroin or anything? Someone told me there was some sort of an article about heroin. Did any of you see it? If you didn't see it, don't look for it.

Juror No. 3: I saw a headline on it, but I didn't read it.

The Court: Did anybody else see the headline? Nobody did. If anybody sees the headline, don't read the article. You will learn all you need to learn right here.

Mr. Nesland: The Government calls Danielle Ouimet.

Danielle Ouimet, called as a witness by the Government, being first duly sworn, testified as follows:

Direct Examination by Mr. Nesland:

Q: Miss Ouimet, you will have to speak up so that the jury and the people back here can hear you. How old are you?

A: 28.

Q: Are you married or single?

A: Single.

Q: What is your present occupation?

A: I am a TV and radio announcer.

Q: Where is that?

A: In Montreal.

Q: Canada?

A: Canada.

Q: Do you know a man by the name of Michel Mastantuono?

A: Yes.

Q: When did you first meet Mr. Mastantuono?

A: I met him in the month of March or April 1970.

Q: Where did you meet him at that time?

A: In a place by the name of Clairette, where I was singing at the time.

Q: What was Michel Mastantuono doing at that time?

A: He was maitre d', at the door, he was serving, everything.

Q: At the Chez Clairette?

A: At the Chez Clairette.

Q: After you met him in March or April of 1970, did you begin to live with him?

A: Pardon me?

Q: After you met him in March or April of 1970, did you begin to live with him?

A: Yes.

Q: And where did you live with him?

A: In Montreal, on St. Matthews Street.

Q: In whose apartment was that?

A: Mine.

Q: After you began living with Mastantuono, did there come a time when you went to the Cannes Film Festival?

A: Yes.

Q: Approximately when did you go to the Cannes Film Festival?

A: In May of 1970.

Q: Why did you go to the Cannes Film Festival?

A: I had done one film in that year by the name of "Initiation." I was going down to promote two films, a former one by the name of "Valerie," and "Initiation."

Q: And did you go with Michel Mastantuono to Cannes?

A: Yes.

Q: Did you go together?

A: Yes.

Q: How long were you in Cannes promoting the film "Valerie" and the film "Initiation"?

A: A week.

Q: What happened after you were through promoting the film at Cannes?

A: We went to meet the parents of Michel in Marseilles.

Q: And you went with Michel?

A: Yes.

Q: And what did you do after you had gone to Marseilles?

A: We went to Paris.

Q: Approximately what month were you in Paris?

A: June.

Q: And where did you stay in Paris on that trip?

A: We stayed in various hotels, because there were various conventions over there. We started to live — to go in a hotel in Versailles first. I remember a place by the name of Elysee Palace and another one by the name of Shweirzeroff.

Q: I show you what has been marked Government's Exhibit 67 in evidence and ask you if you recognize that.

A: Yes. It is a billing from the Elysee Palace Hotel, with my signature on top.

Q: And does that reflect when you stayed at the Elysee Palace on this trip?

A: Yes. I can read the date right there, 1970, the 29th of the fifth month and the 30th of the fifth month.

Q: Meaning May, is that correct?

A: Yes.

Q: Would you please tell the Court and jury what happened while you were staying at the Elysee Palace?

A: One morning that we had, anyway, to change hotels, because we didn't have a reservation for the next day, Michel decided with me to go shopping at a certain time in the morning. So we got up very early and we decided to go in the Champs-Elysees, where usually we go and shop.

At that time, while walking, Michel stopped me in front of a car dealer by the name of Citroen and asked me to go and see the cars inside. When I was inside, he showed me various kinds of cars . . .

Q: Did you go any place before you went to the Citroen agency?

A: Oh, yes, yes. First of all, we went to have breakfast not too far from there, a little bar not too far from there, from the Elysee Palace, and I remember, while having breakfast on the terrace in front, that Michel suddenly disappeared. And it happened at the same time as a guy happened to arrive by taxi, looked at Michel, went inside without talking to him, then Michel got up, went inside, probably talked to the guy, I didn't see them talk, and after 15 minutes he came back to me, sat down . . .

Mr. Kadish: I ask your Honor to caution the witness not to testify as to what probably happened.

The Court: It is perfectly clear. She doesn't know what happened.

Q: Continue.

A: And then Michel came back, sat down, finished the breakfast, and at that time the guy that I saw coming in came out, took a taxi and went away.

Q: Now, there came a later time that you were introduced to that individual, is that correct?

A: Yes.

Q: And who was it?

A: Jacques Bec.

Q: And you didn't know him at that time?

A: No, I didn't.

Q: All right. What happened after Michel came back to the table and Bec left the little restaurant?

A: That's when we decided to go shopping and that's when we arrived on the Champs-Elysees, and that's when Michel asked me to go and see the Citroen dealer. Inside of the dealing place Michel showed me a car and he said that it would be a good idea for me to buy one, first because I had one in Montreal, but it was a publicity car that was given to me only for a year and I had to give it back shortly thereafter; secondly because I had to come back to Belgium to do a film and it would be convenient to have a car in France because I would take a vacation with him; and after that that it would make me have the car in Montreal tax free.

The Court: A car in Montreal — what?

The Witness: Tax free.

The Court: Tax free. All right.

A: (*Continuing*) Then I decided to buy the car. I bought it under my name, and Michel gave a deposit on it and we were told that the car would come at a later date.

Q: After you ordered the Citroen, what happened?

A: We went back to Canada.

Q: Now, did there come a time after you had gone to Canada that you went to Brussels?

A: Yes.

Q: And when did you go to Brussels and why?

A: In July, to make a film.

Q: And what was the name of that film that you were doing?

A: In English it is "Daughters of Darkness." But in French it is "Rouge Aux Levres."

Q: How long were you in Brussels on that occasion making the film?

A: Altogether, one month and a half.

Q: That was in July and August?

A: Yes.

Q: Where did you stay while you were there?

A: At the Astoria Hotel.

Q: Did you see Mr. Mastantuono during the period of time that you were making the film?

A: Yes. Sometimes he was coming for a few days and sometimes he was staying for a week.

Q: Where was he, if you know, when he was not with you in Brussels?

A: Well, he used to tell me that he was going back to his family in Marseilles and sometimes staying in Paris.

Q: Now, on any of these visits that Michel Mastantuono made in Brussels, did he ever bring the Citroen with him?

A: Yes. One time he came to show me the car, when he was released from France.

Q: Describe the car.

A: It was a Pallas. It was a white car, black leather inside, with a gray top.

Q: What happened when he brought the Citroen on that occasion?
A: Pardon me?
Q: What happened when he brought the Citroen on that occasion?
A: It broke down at one time.
Q: Did it break down then or later?
A: Later.
Q: How did you learn that?
A: Well, one day Michel came to Brussels and he told me that the car had broken down and he had rented another one meanwhile and that it was in repair.
Q: All right. Did there come a time that you learned where the car was?
A: Yes.
Q: Where was it?
A: In Biarritz.
Q: Did there come a time that you went to Biarritz?
A: Yes.
Q: Who did you go with?
A: Michel.
Q: And how did you go?
A: By train.
Q: All right. Would you please tell the Court and jury what happened on that trip to Biarritz?
A: We left Marseilles one day, at midnight, and arrived very early in the morning in Biarritz. Michel then gave me some money, told me to go and make some shopping while he was going to look after the car, and he met me about two hours after on a corner street and we went back to Paris.
Q: Did you take the Citroen with you?
A: Yes.
Q: Now, approximately when was this, if you recall?
A: The end of July, August.
Q: Now, when you went to Paris, how long did you stay in Paris on that occasion?
A: Oh, a few days.
Q: Did you do anything with the Citroen when you went to Paris?
A: Well, we drove with it, of course. But we gave it to a company to ship it to Montreal.
Q: Do you remember the name of the shipping company?
A: I think it was Transport Mon Diaux.
Q: Under whose name was it shipped?
A: My name.
Q: Who delivered it and where?

A: In Montreal?

Q: No. Who delivered it in Paris?

A: The Transport Mon Diaux, the company.

Q: Did you take it there or did Michel Mastantuono take it to the Transport Mon Diaux?

A: Both of us.

Q: What did you do after the car was given over to the shipping agency in Paris?

A: We stayed one day, I think, in Paris and we went back to Montreal.

Q: Did there come a time that you learned that the Citroen had arrived in Montreal?

A: Yes.

Q: And approximately when did you learn that?

A: About a month, three weeks to a month later.

Q: And what month, if you recall?

A: August. August, September.

Q: What happened at that time that you learned that the Citroen had arrived in Montreal?

A: Michel told me that he couldn't come with me to — I don't know how to say the word — the bar, the harbor, to pick it up. So he asked me to go and pick it up and to reach him after at a friend's place.

Q: At whose place?

A: Andre Arioli's place.

Q: What happened?

A: I went to the harbor and signed all the papers for the release and had the car. But there was a problem. The fenders were destroyed, or had been destroyed by the transportation, and I made a report on that.

Q: What did you do after you reported the car was dented?

A: Michel told me at the time to bring it — since I didn't know very much how to drive the semi-automatic car, he asked me to drive it to the closest parking spot and leave it there and call him so he would pick it up. But, since it was broken already, so I drove the car near Andre Arioli's place and I went to see Michel.

Q: Did there come a time after you delivered the car to Michel at Arioli's house that he told you that he wanted to take the Citroen to New York?

A: Yes.

Q: Approximately when was this after it had been delivered?

A: At the end of August, September. September, I would say.

Q: And would you please tell the Court and jury what happened at that time?

A: Yes. Michel wanted me, him and Andre Arioli to go to New York. But then he said to me that there was a problem with Andre Arioli because he was French, and he had problems crossing borders.

So he said that he would go with him in another car with a French-Canadian man by the name of Lucien Longpre, that I would have to cross the border, go to a restaurant near the border, and to call them and meet them there.

What happened is that they crossed the border, but there was a problem. The French guy could pass, but the Canadian one was arrested at the border. So Andre Arioli had to go back with the car of Lucien Longpre.

Q: Where did they meet you after they crossed the border?

A: At a place by the name of Plattsburg.

Q: And what happened when you met with them at Plattsburg?

A: Well, I was left with Michel. Andre Arioli went back and we went — he went to Montreal and we went to New York.

Q: Who went to New York?

A: Michel and I.

Q: Where did you stay on that occasion when you came to New York?

A: The name of the place is the — it is a two-letter hotel.

Q: Do you recall approximately when you stayed there?

A: In September.

Q: I show you Government's Exhibit 77 in evidence and ask you if you recognize that.

A: Yes. The Abbey Victoria.

Q: Please look at that and tell the Court and jury if that's what you were referring to when you came down with the Citroen.

A: Yes, that's it.

Q: Would you please read it? Is it your name there, Danielle Ouimet?

A: Yes.

Q: Do you recall whether or not you registered in the hotel when you came down on that occasion with Michel?

A: Yes, I did. You can see my signature right there.

Q: And what days did you stay here, by looking at that?

A: Does it show?

Q: Yes (indicating).

A: Oh, yes. Excuse me. All the slips, the phone calls. September 27th until September 29th.

Q: 1970. What did you do with the car when you came to the Abbey Victoria?

A: First we arrived in New York and then we parked it in a parking building.

Q: Was that parking building part of the hotel?

A: No. It was on a road near there, a street near there.

Q: And you stayed there the 27th, the 28th and the 29th.

A: Yes.

Q: Do you recall seeing anybody while you were in New York with Michel?

A: Yes.

Q: Who?

A: At the bar of the Abbey Victoria, Jacques Bec.

Mr. Kadish: She said at the bar at the Victoria?

Mr. Nesland: The bar at the Abbey Victoria.

The Court: At the bar at the Abbey Victoria.

Mr. Nesland: Yes.

Q: Did Michel do anything while you were in New York with the Citroen?

A: Yes. One night he asked me to stay in the hotel, in my room, and that he would go for a while. He took my car and he disappeared for the night.

Q: At that time did you know what was in the Citroen?

A: I didn't know exactly what was in it, but I knew perfectly well it was not something quite legit, probably, he was doing.

Mr. Kadish: I didn't hear her answer.

The Court: Would you read that answer?

(*Answer read.*)

Q: By "legit" you mean legitimate?

A: Yes.

Q: Did there come a time that you learned what was in the Citroen?

A: Yes.

Q: When did you learn that?

A: Well, I cannot put an exact date, but I remember one event that brought me to know this whole story:

My brother used to go out with a girl friend, and this girl — it is complicated — had, I think, a brother or a cousin, or something like that, in the RCMP of Montreal.

The Court: In the what in Montreal?

The Witness: The RCMP of Montreal.

Q: The Royal Canadian Mounted Police.

A: Yes. So he came to me one day and he said that his girl friend had told him that she didn't want to go out with him any more because I would have shortly problems because of Michel, because he was looked over.

So I turned to Michel and I asked him question and then he answered me.

Q: What was your conversation with him at that time?

A: Well, I asked him very frankly what he was doing and if it was very dangerous and if he really could have problems. And he said yes, that he was dealing with drugs and that, well, he couldn't get out of it anyway.

Q: Did there ever come a time that he told you about an incident while he was in New York with the Citroen?

A: Yes.

Q: Do you recall approximately when that was?

A: Well, probably in between the end of September and February, in between — after, you know, me knowing that he was doing that kind of business he talked to me about his trip, while I was waiting in the hotel.

    He said that very early in the morning he was driving on a highway with my car and he was suddenly surrounded by Cadillacs, two or three of them, and he found — he made the remark that it was quite a little bit stupid because it was a very good way of attracting the attention, to have a car surrounded by Cadillacs so early in the morning.

    And he said to me that these cars were there to lead him the way.

Q: Did he say anything else if you recall, about that incident?

A: Yes. He mentioned that the guys inside had probably — they had guns to protect him . . .

Mr. Kadish: They had what?

The Witness: Guns.

The Court: They probably had guns?

The Witness: Well, yes, to protect him and to shoot at the wheels of the policemen, at the cars, if there was one to come closer to the Cadillacs.

Q: What happened after you made the trip to New York with the Citroen?

A: We came back to Montreal, and then I was asked at that time to bring money back for someone.

Q: Who was that?

A: To Jacques Bec.

Q: And what happened at that time?

A: Well, Jacques Bec came home at my apartment and asked me if I could bring some money for him to France, it was cash money in a . . .

Q: Approximately how much?

A: About $15,000, in a suitcase, and I did it.

Q: Did you do that?

A: Yes, I did it.

Q: And who did you go with?

A: With him.

Q: With Jacques Bec?

A: Yes.

Q: And were you paid for that?

A: Yes, I was paid.

Q: How much were you paid, if you recall now?

A: I would say approximately from two to three thousand dollars.

The Court: I take it at this point you knew you were dealing in heroin.

The Witness: At that time, yes. Well, yes and no. It is tough to say, you know. I don't know exactly when Michel was asked — told me about the thing. I cannot really put a date on that.

Q: You knew it was heroin after you had had the conversation prompted by your brother.

A: Yes, that's it. So I don't know . . .

Q: That came after the Citroen.

A: Well, I know . . .

The Court: So at this point you just knew it was something illegitimate or heroin.

The Witness: Yes.

Q: Did there come a time about June of 1971 that you met a man named Paul Graziani?

A: Yes.

Q: Would you please describe to the jury the circumstances under which you first met Paul Graziani?

A: Well, one day Michel came to me and he said that we had to follow a guy that was followed by the RCMP of Montreal. He said, "Would you please come with me in the car? We are going to stay in front of the hotel, look at him go down his room" — well, "Come out of the hotel. He is going to take a taxi and we are going to check if he is followed."

And he left his hotel. We followed him, and we saw that he was followed.

Q: Where did you see him when you first saw him?

A: I would guess it would be in a hotel by the name of the Queen Elizabeth or the Laurentiens. I remember that because it was on Dorchester Street, and right in the middle of those two hotels there is a park with cannons over there.

And then we went to a hotel — the Ritz Carlton, a hotel on Sherbrooke Street.

Q: Did you have any conversation with Michel about that time in which he told you why he was seeing Paul Graziani?

A: Yes. He told me that Mr. Graziani had a job to do and he had trouble with a car that was supposed to come in.

Q: Did he tell you what kind of car?

A: At the time he told me it was a Fiat.

Q: Now, what did you do with respect to that Fiat yourself?

A: Well, on that Fiat, nothing, because I never saw the car. But I know that Michel after was asked to join the group because he thought he was not followed, that it would be more secure for him to do the deal than the others.

Q: All right. What was done?

A: Well, I recall Michel doing the deal, but on the first day I was not close to them properly.

Q: Did he tell you what he had done the first day?

A: He told me — no, he didn't tell me immediately. The first day I was kept home with his nephew — well, yes, I knew that he was going to do a car, actually, but I didn't know which one or exactly what car. I knew it had to do with the Fiat, but I didn't know if it was the Fiat itself. I saw it was different after.

On that day Michel left very early in the morning, left me at home with his nephew that was living with us, he was on his honeymoon in Canada, and he said that he would be back by midday. But he didn't, and I was nervous about that.

So, when he saw that I was nervous, he said that I would go back with him on the next day because they were not finished.

On the next day he brought me to a house that was Jean Cardon's house, and he asked me to stay in the living room and to check if no one was coming near the house.

After a while, when I was upstairs, they came and asked me to come and help them doing a job because they were late, on I don't know what; anyway, they were late on their work, and I was asked to help the lady of the house to sew a blanket or a sheet under a seat.

Q: All right. Who was the lady that you were helping?

A: Jean Cardon's wife.

Q: Do you know her name?

A: Michelle, I think.

Q: Would you please tell the Court and jury exactly what you were doing when you were sewing the sheet over the bottom of the chair?

A: We were covering what was — had been placed inside.

Q: What was that?

A: Heroin.

Q: And that was you and Michelle Cardon?

A: Yes.

Q: All right. Would you please tell the Court and jury what happened after you finished sewing the sheet over the seat full of heroin?

A: Since I was finished, I wanted to know if I had to stay there or to go back up. So there was an attendant's room that was the garage. So I went there where Michel was, to ask him what to do.

So, when I arrived in the room, I saw a car that was a station wagon that they were loading, like they were taking parts off from the doors and everything, and they were putting little bags of white powder in it.

Q: And who was doing this when you came in?

A: There was Jean Cardon, there was Michel, there was Paul Graziani, and there was Felix (Rosso).

Q: After you had seen that did there come a time that you were asked to make a trip?

A: Yes.

Q: Who asked you to make a trip?

A: Felix and Michel.

Q: All right, would you please tell the court and jury what you recall of the conversation you had with Felix and Michel?

A: Yes. One day Felix came home and he said that he had — he had to reach someone in Miami, and he had problems crossing the border. He went to Miami, but he was afraid of being followed, so he left — he said that at the border he left his luggage on the turn — the revolving thing, and he came back to Canada immediately. So he was — he was afraid and he asked me to reach the guy he was supposed to meet, and give him a letter, which I did.

Q: All right. Did he tell you what — what did he give you before you went to Miami?

A: He gave me a letter and a little picture of him.

Q: Of who?

A: Felix.

Q: Of the Felix who had asked you to go to Miami?

A: Yes.

Q: What did you do after he gave you the letter and the picture of himself?

A: I took a plane and I went to Miami, arriving in Miami I went directly to a hotel by the name of the Fountainebleu. Immediately I took the letter, went down in the lobby and asked where that street — there was an address on the envelope — where that street was. The guy downstairs, the clerk, guy, I don't know, gave me a map of the city and himself marked exactly where was the street I was supposed to go to. So I took a taxi and I first went there.

It was a little hotel-motel — well, attached rooms together — and I looked for the place for the address . . .

Q: Was there a name on the letter besides the address?

A: Yes, there was one by the name of Felix.

Q: Was there any name other than just Felix?

A: I really don't remember.

Q: What did you do then?

A: I knocked on the door and there was no answer, so I looked closely, because it was dark, and I saw a little piece of paper. On that piece of paper there was another address saying that the man had moved to another place.

So, I took the address and started to walk, because it was another avenue, and the avenue for me didn't look too far so I started to walk and I found out it was really farther, so I took another taxi, went to the second place, and at that time it was a hotel, not too high leveled hotel, and over there I went to the desk and asked for Mr. Felix. They had trouble because they didn't — you know, Felix is a French name, you don't find that often. They finally located the guy, rang at his room, and asked for him. Then I talked on the phone and I talked first to an English lady that asked me who I was, and why I wanted Felix, and when I told them I was coming for Felix from Montreal she passed to me the man that talked to me in French.

Q: What was said between the two of you in that time?

A: Mr. Felix and I? He came down in the lobby and then I showed him the picture, and I gave him the letter saying that it was sent by Felix Rosso from Montreal. He read the letter and then he asked me if I could reach Felix Rosso, and I said yes, he is staying at my place, you can reach him immediately. So, we went to the counter and we asked — he asked for some rolls of 25 cents. We took his car and we went to a telephone booth where I made the call — I dialed for him, and then Michel answered . . .

Q: What number did you dial?

A: My phone number in Montreal.

Q: Did you get an answer?

A: Yes.

Q: Who answered?

A: Michel answered. I asked — I said I made the connection and if Felix was there, and then I put the two Felixes together, and he closed the door of the telephone booth, and I was in the car and didn't hear anything.

Q: What language were you speaking with him at that time?

A: French.

Q: Did you have any conversation with him?

A: Well, yes. We talked, because I was quite surprised that — he was saying that he had been in the U.S.A. for a while.

Q: Did he tell you approximately how long was a while?

A: I guess it was about six months. I was quite surprised because for me I thought he couldn't talk any English, which is quite rare to have a guy stay there such a long time without talking the language. And he had a little accent so I asked him if he was from France and he said yes.

Q: What kind of accent did he have?

A: It is in between the Marseilles accent and the Corsican accent.

Q: What did you do after you put this man in touch with Felix in Montreal?

A: I came back to Montreal.

Q: Now, when you got back to Montreal, what happened?

A: We did the trip, Michel and I, to New York.

Q: And would you tell the court and jury the circumstances of that trip, approximately when was it after you got back from Miami?

A: 4th of July, around.

Q: Do you recall where you stayed?

A: In New York.

Mr. Kadish: I'm sorry, I didn't hear the last answer.

　　　(*Answer read.*)

Q: Do you recall where you stayed on that trip to New York?

Mr. Kadish: Wait. That isn't clear.

The Witness: Excuse me, I don't really remember the date.

The Court: You don't remember whether it was the 4th?

A: It was not the 4th for sure. I don't recall the date, how can I remember the date?

Q: Do you recall where you stayed when you came to New York?

A: Yes. The Holiday Inn.

Q: I will show you Government Exhibit 79 in evidence and ask you if you recognize it.

A: Yes. Yes, that's it. I remember it because it was near the water, and it is written June 21st to June 23rd — '71.

Q: Is that where you stayed on the trip you made with Michel?

A: Yes.

Q: What had Michel told you had occurred while you were in Miami and before you had come to New York?

A: Excuse me?

Q: Had Michel told you what had happened while you were in Miami and before you and he went to New York?

A: Well, no.

Q: Did he tell you what had happened to the station wagon that you had seen filled with heroin?

A: Well, he said that it was ready to go, to go to New York.

Q: Did he tell you whether or not it had gone to New York?

A: Yes. Well, he said we left about a day after the station wagon left for New York.

Q: Did he tell you who took the station wagon to New York?

A: John Cardon did.

Q: How did you go to New York and who with?

A: I went with Michel to New York in his Corvette.

Q: Now, what happened while you were in New York on that occasion?

A: Well, again I was put into the hotel and left there for the night. And Michel went . . .

Q: Did there come a time that Michel told you you were leaving New York?

A: Yes.

Q: What happened at that time?

A: Well, he arrived about maybe midday and he said that he would have to do a quick job before leaving — he went back again and came back and then he said, "We are leaving. I left the car in a towaway parking zone, please go in the car and wait for me there while I am paying the bill." I went there and there was two to three suitcases plus it was, it looked like a box, and it was something inside wrapped with paper, brown paper, it was square, it was taking the whole place of where my feet were, and Michel told me after it was some money.

Q: And what happened?

Mr. Naden: I didn't hear the last part of that.

The Court: Michel told you what?

The Witness: It was some money.

Q: What happened after Michel returned to the Corvette?

A: Well, we both left for Montreal and then along the way, going back to Montreal, we met John Cardon and Felix Rosso in a curb service, you know, those little places where you stop along the road to eat or to have . . .

Q: Coffee shops?

A: Coffee shops. And we stopped to a lot of them because at the same time both cars were parked, one beside the other one, and we were putting the money in Michel's car into the station wagon, hiding it.

Q: Where was it being placed in the station wagon?

A: It was hidden in the side doors.

Q: And how many times did you stop and put money from the Corvette into the station wagon?

A: From four to five times.

Q: And who was doing this?

A: Michel, Felix and John Cardon.

Q: What happened when you arrived at the border, Canadian border?

A: John Cardon passed first, and we passed the border with Felix Rosso, me and Michel.

Q: What happened after you had passed the border?

A: Well, Michel dropped me at the house and he went to see Cardon. Well, that's what he told me.

Q: Did there come a time that you went to Cardon's house?

A: Yes.

Q: Approximately when was that after you returned from . . .

A: The day after.

Q: The next day?

A: Yes.

Q: What happened at that time?

A: When I arrived there, I was put in a room and I was asked to count the money. There was open suitcases with piles of money around, and I was just asked to make sure that in a pile — because they were — there were piles of ten dollar bills, piles of one hundred dollar bills and they were put together with a wrapper and on the wrapper there was a number written down. I had to make sure that the money that was on the pile was the same as the amount on the tag.

Q: Who was counting the money besides you?

A: Everyone.

Q: Who was that?

A: Michel, John Cardon, the wife of Cardon, Felix Rosso, and Graziani.

Q: What was done after the money was counted, if you recall?

A: It was put in suitcases and left at Cardon's place.

Q: Did you ever hear anything about what had happened with that money?

A: Later I heard that there was some missing, and that that money had to go to France and it had to be taken by different girls coming from France.

Q: Now, after you had counted this money did there come a time that you and Mr. Mastantuono went to France again?

A: Yes.

Q: Approximately when was this after you returned from New York?

A: July or August.

Q: And did you carry anything with you at that time on that trip?

A: Yes, I carried some money.
Q: Approximately how much?
A: About 20,000, around $20,000.
Mr. Kadish: How much?
The Witness: Around $20,000.
Q: And what happened to that money when you arrived in Paris?
A: I gave it to Paul Graziani.
Q: Now, did there come a time — now, you were also involved, were you not, in a Barracuda which was brought in in 1971?
A: Yes.
Q: And you were also involved, were you not, with a Ford Galaxie?
A: Yes.
Q: Which was referred to as Arioli's car?
A: Yes.
Q: Did there come a time that Michel Mastantuono was arrested?
A: Yes.
Q: Approximately when was that?
A: August, the 28th.
Q: That he was arrested?
A: Yes.
The Court: What year?
The Witness: Oh, '71.
Q: August or October?
A: October, 28th of October, excuse me.
Q: Did you do anything after Michel was arrested with respect to the Citroen?
A: Yes. I was asked to hide evidence and have the car stolen, my car.
Q: And did you try to get it stolen?
A: Yes.
Q: And did you succeed?
A: No.
Q: Now, did there come a time that you learned that Michel Mastantuono was cooperating with the U.S. Government?
A: Yes.
Q: Did you have conversations with him during a period of time?
A: Yes.
Q: Did there come a time that you made a statement to the United States Government with respect to what had gone on before?
A: Yes.
Q: Do you recall approximately when that was, the first time you ever made a statement?
A: That probably was — I wouldn't know on that.
Q: Did you tell the truth in that statement?
A: Well, not exactly, no. I hid some evidence and I didn't complete . . .

Mr. Kadish: Hid what?

The Court: Hid from them evidence.

The Witness: And didn't complete things that could lead to help the government.

Mr. Naden: I didn't hear the end of that either.

The Court: Would you read back the last answer.

(*Read.*)

Q: Now, had you had discussions with Michel Mastantuono about making these statements?

A: Yes.

Q: Did you have any conversation with him about any particular matter which you should not tell the government about?

A: Oh, yes. Actually Michel was almost always telling me what to say or not to say. But there was one case he didn't want me to talk about was the Cardon's car.

Mr. Newman: The what?

The Witness: Cardon's car.

Mr. Newman: Thank you.

Q: Now, have you recently pled guilty to violating the federal narcotics law by making a telephone call, the telephone call from Miami . . .

A: Yes.

Q: — to make a connection?

A: Yes, sir.

Q: And what do you face on that charge?

A: I can have four years and up to $30,000 fine.

Q: And other than that charge, you have not been charged with your activities during the period 1970 and '71, is that correct?

A: No. I was told I wouldn't be.

Q: And have you also been told that the government will bring to the judge's attention at the time you are sentenced that you have cooperated with the government and testified here?

A: I was told so.

Mr. Nesland: I don't remember, your Honor, if I passed these exhibits among the jury. I believe I have. But I will just go over them. These are the exhibits Mr. Mastantuono had testified about. I believe I showed them to the jury.

Q: I will show you Government Exhibit 68 in evidence and ask you if you recognize what that is.

A: Yes, this is the buying slip of my car.

Q: The Citroen?

A: Yes, I guess this is a thousand francs, that's what probably Michel gave, the down payment I guess.

Q: Did he pay the down payment or did you?

A: He did.

Q: All right, I show you Government Exhibit 69 and 70 and ask you if you recognize those.

A: Yes. These are papers that I had to give them because I couldn't pick up the car myself, so to give them the permission to pass the border, you had to need — since the car was not under his name, he had to need permission coming from me to pass the border with my car.

Q: And is that your handwriting?

A: My handwriting.

Q: All right, would you please read Government Exhibit 69 to the jury, since it is written in French.

The Court: Translate it you mean.

Q: Translate it.

A: To whom it might belong, I, Danielle Ouimet, sign and declare, allow by his letter to give the authorization to Mr. Michel Mastantuono to take delivery of a car DS21 Pallas bought by me at the SA Citroen 42 Champs Elysees, Paris, 8, on the 29th of May, 1970, giving him all the rights on the car. Paris, 30 of May, 1970. Plus my number of passport and Michel's passport number.

Q: I show you Government Exhibit 71. Do you recognize it?

A: Yes. That's an authorization to drive the car out of the — abroad.

Q: I show you Government Exhibit 72, 73 and 74. Would you please tell the jury what they are.

A: Yes. That's a description of the slips for the delivery of the car, including — well, it is saying exactly from where it was supposed to arrive, when, I guess, somewhere around there, plus the description of what I was supposed to receive.

Q: Those are the shipping documents?

A: Yes.

Q: And do you recognize Government Exhibit 75?

A: Yes, that's the Customs declaration of incoming — of the car.

Q: That's when it arrived in Montreal?

A: Yes.

Q: Dated September 21, 1970?

A: Yes.

Q: Government Exhibit 76?

A: That's the slip of the damages on the car and the name of the boat on which it arrived.

Q: And Government Exhibit 78, do you recognize it?

A: Yes, it is a parking slip where we deposited the car in New York.

Q: Which car, do you recall?

A: The Citroen.

Q: Now, did you keep those documents?

A: Yes, both of them. The slip I don't recall though. Probably Michel had it or — I don't know.

Q: I show you Government's Exhibit 90. Do you recognize the individual in that photograph?

A: Oh, yes, Andre Arioli.

Q: I show you a photograph Government Exhibit 94. Do you recognize the individual in that photograph?

A: Paul Graziani.

Q: I show you the individual in Government Exhibit 88. Do you recognize that individual?

A: Jacques Bec.

Q: I show you the individual in Government Exhibit 91 and ask you if you recognize that individual.

A: Jean Cardon.

Q: I show you Government Exhibit 93. Do you recognize the individual in that photograph?

A: Felix Rosso.

Q: And I show you the individual in Government Exhibit 92 and ask you if you recognize him.

A: Jo Signoli.

Q: When did you meet Jo Signoli?

A: In Montreal — first we met him a long time ago in Marseilles, but it was only on a trip and we had only lunch, like a dinner.

Q: When did you meet him that you were involved in anything, that he was involved in anything?

A: When he came in Montreal for the car of John Cardon.

Q: That's the Cardon station wagon, is that correct?

A: Yes.

Mr. Nesland: I have no further questions.

The Court: We might as well take a short recess. Ladies and gentlemen, see you in about ten minutes.

(*Recess*)

Cross Examination By Mr. Kadish:

Q: Miss Ouimet, I am Mark Kadish and I represent one of the defendants over there. Would you please tell us what your educational background is, just a little bit about your schooling?

A: I had classic — basic classical studies in Montreal, and it was a — how do you say that — they were not religious people who were teaching to me.

Q: Not religious people?

The Court: Were they lay teachers?

The Witness: Laic, we say in French.

Q: Did you have a high school education?

A: Yes. I don't know how — in French it is called "college."

Q: It is called college?

A: Yes. You know "college."

Q: And did you go beyond that? How many years of study is that to get through college in Canada?

A: 12 years.

Q: 12 years?

A: Yes.

The Court: What age did you finish your education?

The Witness: I was 18.

Q: And after completing college, did you go on to any further studies?

A: Oh, yes. Well, I studied all the time. I was taking ballet jazz, beaux-arts, just name it, a little genius.

Q: When was the last time you studied?

A: I am still studying, ballet jazz dancing.

Q: Now?

A: Yes and singing class, and — just name it, when there is a class — judo I am starting shortly.

Q: Now, when you first met Michel Mastantuono I think you describe him as a sort of a maitre d' of the Chez Clairette.

A: Yes.

Q: Did he pretty much run the place?

A: Yes, and no, because Clairette was alone, and he was from Marseilles and she is from Marseilles and he was not running but he was aware of everything that was going there.

Q: You wouldn't describe him just as a simple barman, would you?

A: Probably not.

Q: Now, when you went to Cannes for the Film Festival did you say you were involved with one film?

A: No. I did a film before that by the name of "Valerie." I went to the Cannes festival on the year before, and it was my second time in Cannes then, but at that time with "Valerie" I didn't know Michel then.

Q: When you went the second time you didn't have a film showing?

A: Yes. I had "Initiation."

Q: What kind of film is "Valerie?"

A: The story of a young girl — a very melodramatic story of a young girl who gets kidnapped, kidnapped in a school and she tries to make money, she raised money by selling newspapers and then she become a go-go dancer and she becomes — she falls in love with someone, she becomes suddenly a prostitute but she at the same time falls in love with a guy that is a widow — a widow? Well, someone who has no wife but he has a kid.

Q: Widower.

A: Widower, and he has a kid, so she falls in love and finally the moral goes over, she goes with him, and she becomes the mother of a kid.

Q: She becomes what?

A: The mother of the kid.

Q: Were you Valerie?

A: Yes, I was Valerie.

Q: So you were the star of that particular movie?

A: I was mainly — well, I was so well known under that title that they still call me Valerie sometimes.

Q. And was that movie ever brought to the United States?

A: I guess that now it is going around, but the one that really made it here was the one "Daughters of Darkness," that stayed on Broadway for seven weeks.

Q: And when was that film produced?

A: In '70.

Q: In 1970?

A: '70 — '70, yes.

Q: Was that the film that you went to see at Cannes that year with Michel?

A: No, no, that's not the film I went to see. There was "Valerie," "Initiation," and the "Rouge aux Levres" that I did in Brussels that was titled in English "Daughters of Darkness."

The Court: The one you did in Brussels is the one that made it on Broadway?

The Witness: Yes, that's it.

Q: Do these films involve a lot of memorization, did you have to learn the script?

A: Of course.

Q: A lot of lines?

A: Well, yes.

Q: Are you good at that?

A: Not specially. No — well, when you do a film, in the morning — first of all they give you the text, the full text.

Q: The question simply was, Miss Ouimet, are you good at memorizing scripts?

The Court: She is trying to explain the answer. It is not a question that can be answered yes or no.

A: And it is by every day they give you two or three pages, it's easy to remember, but to learn it all at one time, no, you cannot do that.

Q: But you can remember your script for two or three days sometimes?

A: Well, you know if I give you a page and I ask you to say about two hours later you probably know it, yes.

Q: Have you done other acting too?

A: Oh, yes.

Q: Drama?

A: Stage, yes.

Q: Now, prior to the involvement with Michel Mastantuono, did you have any kind of arrest record in Canada, for instance?

A: No.

Q: Are you Canadian by the way?

A: I am Canadian.

Q: You were not born in Europe?

A: No, I am French Canadian.

Q: What kind of money were you earning in 1969, how much money did you earn in that year?

A: I — you know there is a lot of things that you can do in Montreal. First, commercials, you work on a basics of . . .

Mr. Kadish: Judge, can I get an answer to that question?

The Court: Yes, just a figure. An amount.

The Witness: An amount?

The Court: Yes.

The Witness: It could be around fifteen to twenty five thousand.

Q: How much did you report on your income tax?

A: I had a lot of problems like that because I wasn't making any income tax report, but I was asked after to do a report and someone took care of that for me, like an accountant took care of that for me.

Q: He took care of your income tax?

A: Yes.

Q: And he reported all your income?

A: Yes.

Q: About $25,000?

A: Well, not at that time, but it could be around fifteen at that time, from fifteen to twenty thousand dollars.

Q: How about your 1968? How much in 1968 did you earn?

A: About the same, like my films were not paying me a lot. Basically what was paying me was my appearances on TV and radio and commercials.

Q: And so maybe about $15,000 in '68.

A: Yes.

Q: $15,000 in '69.

A: Yes.

Q: $15,000 in '69. How much would you say you earned in 1970?

A: I really cannot say it. You know, you have to see my accountant for that because I keep no tracks. I don't know how much. Sometimes I make some TV appearances and I don't even know how much I'm paid.

Q: Well, in 1970, did you have more income than in '69 or less?

A: Of course I had more. It was increasing every year.

Q: So it is fair to say that in 1970 that your accountant . . .

A: I didn't have the accountant then. I have the accountant — I had the accountant for the last year, and he took care of my income reports from the papers I could give him, from the T-4, we call that in Montreal.

The Court: The C-4?

The Witness: The T-4.

Q: You have an income tax there, a graduated income tax like we have in the United States? You have to pay the Government so much money on money that you earn?

A: Yes.

Q: So is it your testimony — I'm not sure I understand, correct me if I am wrong — that for a certain number of years there, '68, '69 and '70, you weren't reporting your income at that time and you only recently got an accountant to straighten out your problems?

A: Well, sometimes, when I do a film, you don't have any money taken from the film, you know, you don't pay the Government on that, you are supposed to pay them yourself. And when I got on TV, they take it from the base, you know, they take the income from the base.

Q: They withhold it.

A: They withhold from the base. So I was paying at the time as much as 40 per cent of income tax.

Q: I understand that. But are you required in Canada to fill out a form?

A: Yes.

Q: And file it with the Government, stating what your income was?

A: Yes.

Q: For the year 1968 you were required to do that.

A: Yes.

Q: Did you do that in the year '69?

A: No.

Q: So you probably committed a crime in Canada for not doing that, didn't you?

A: Well, they asked me after. They came to me and asked me to do — to go back five years and to do my report, and my accountant did it.

Q: And when you say "they", you mean some agents?

A: From the Government.

Q: Revenue agents?

A: Yes.

Q: Or whatever they call them in Canada.

A: Yes.

Q: Did that come as a surprise to you?

A: Oh, no. I was waiting for that, for sure.

Q: So it is fair to say that even with all that education you knew you had done something wrong by not filling those little forms out and sending them in to the Government.

A: I thought basically that I didn't have to make any reports since the money was taken from the source.

Q: Your testimony then is that you believed that you didn't have to fill the forms out because the money was withheld.

A: Yes.

Q: Did you have any other income in the years '68, '69 or '70 and maybe back in '67 and '66 — did you have any other income that you received where the money was not withheld?

A: No.

Q: It was always withheld?

A: Yes, always.

The Court: She said the film money wasn't withheld.

The Witness: Well, I didn't do any films. I did a film in '67, '67 or '66.

The Court: The first film was in '67.

Mr. Kadish: Okay.

Q: Now, your accountant has finally straightened this mess out, is that the case?

A: Yes. He took care of that.

Q: And what year was it that you filed all of these returns that had been past due?

A: Well, when did I gave that?

Q: Yes. When did your accountant have you sign all those things and mail them?

A: Oh, last year.

Q: Last year?

A: Last year or a year and a half ago.

Q: '74, late '73?

A: Well . . .

Q: Did you have to send any money in with that?

A: Yes, sir.

Q: Okay. How much money did you have to send in?

A: I remember that there is one or two years when I didn't have to send any because I was . . .

Q: Withheld.

A: — withheld.

Q: But there were other years when you were not quite withheld enough.

A: I guess, yes.

The Court: How much in total, is that what you want to know?
Mr. Kadish: Yes.
Q: So you had to pay more money because it wasn't withheld, but how much?
A: I don't know. It was my accountant who made that.
Q: He manages your affairs.
A: Yes.
Q: He gets all your income?
A: Yes. Except that he pays me every week a certain amount of money and he receives every check, pays everything, every bill.
Q: So you don't have any idea what your past due taxes were.
A: No, sir. No.
Q: By the way, you got a tip, didn't you, from Jacques Bec when you brought over the money?
A: Yes.
Q: How many times did Jacques Bec or any of the Frenchmen that you were involved with give you a tip for bringing money, smuggling it?
A: Two to three times.
Q: Okay. And how much money in tips did you get at that?
A: I would guess around three to four thousand dollars.
The Court: Each time or all together?
The Witness: No. All together.
Q: And did your accountant include that $4000?
A: No. He didn't know about that.
Q: He doesn't know about it until today.
A: No. He still doesn't know about it.
Q: Obviously there was nothing withheld on that, was there?
A: No.
Q: Do you feel an obligation to report that now to the Canadian authorities and pay your taxes on it?
A: Well, you know, I've admitted that I haven't done something legitimate, so you don't go and say to the Government "I have done something illegitimate and I am going to pay you on that."
Q: You say you have admitted that you have done some things . . .
A: Right now, yes.
Q: But you haven't admitted that to the Canadian authorities, have you?
A: No.
Q: Only to the American authorities, right?
A: Yes.
Q: But you know that you've committed a crime in Canada and you haven't admitted that to anybody in Canada, have you?

A: I had some money, yes, over there, and you call it a crime, yes.

The Court: The question is, have you told anybody in Canada about it?

The Witness: No.

Q: No. Do you call it a crime?

A: Now I call it a crime, yes.

Q: Now, if the Canadian revenue agent comes out next week when you go home, after you are finished here, and if the revenue agent comes out and says to you, "Miss Ouimet, what about this three or four thousand dollars you testified to in Judge Knapp's court in New York, this four grand that you got from Jacques Bec and some other Frenchmen for smuggling money overseas?" are you going to admit to it?

A: I guess I will have to.

Q: You guess? Or you are going to do it?

A: Well, I am not going to run there and tell them, that's for sure.

Q: I understand that. But my question is, if they come out and ask you about it . . .

A: Yes, if . . .

The Court: The answer was that she guessed she would give it.

Mr. Kadish: I want to know if she is guessing or not.

The Court: She told you she was guessing. So that's not for sure.

Q: You might lie about it.

A: You know, there is a big difference in lying and not saying it.

Q: That's for sure.

A: That's for sure.

The Court: His question is, when the agent knocks on your door and says, "Mademoiselle, I heard about this $3000. What are you going to do about it?" are you going to lie about it or not?

The Witness: No, I cannot lie about it any more.

Q: That's right. You don't want to be deported to the United States, do you?

A: Of course not. I like it here, but not that much.

Q: Let's go back to some of the events that you talked about on Mr. Nesland's direct testimony.

By the way, since you have been here again in New York in the last few days, have you had an opportunity to see Michel Mastantuono?

A: Lately? No.

Q: In the last week or two weeks.

A: No. I saw him at the Court House, but we were always with agents or . . .

Q: You never had any conversations with him?

A: No. Well, conversations, yes, on the weather or things like that.

Q: But not about the case.
A: No.
Q: When was the last time that you saw him, as you can recall, when you had some conversation about the facts of this case?
A: It was when I was first coming to the U.S.A. to Mr. Viviani's office. When I was asked questions, Michel was always there.
Q: Do you have any idea when the date of this would be?
A: No. I don't recall.
Q: Does . . .
A: I've been collaborating for four years, you know. I wouldn't know exactly the date.
Q: You've been collaborating for four years?
A: Well, talking, meeting the agent and answering the questions be- fore the agent.
Q: Since 1971?
A: '71 or '72, something like that.
Q: Give us the date, if you can, or the month, if you can remember, in 1971 when you first collaborated with an American agent.
A: I cannot give you that. I don't remember.
Q: Who was the agent?
A: There was an agent by the name of Mr. Boulad.
Q: He is American?
A: He is American.
Q: He speaks French?
A: Yes.
Q: How about Mr. Bocchichio?
A: Bocchichio? Yes. Tony Bocchichio.
Q: You saw him here today?
A: Yes.
Q: Was he one of the first agents that you met when you began col- laborating?
A: One of the first.
Q: And you say that was in . . .
A: I don't recall the dates.
Q: Could it have been '73?
A: No, no. Well, during that time I was still collaborating. But it could be . . .
The Court: That couldn't have been the first date?
The Witness: No.
Q: Do you recall the name Viviani?
A: Yes.
Q: Maybe you said it just a moment ago.
A: Yes.

Q: Who was Viviani?

A: He has the same — I don't know the exact word, but he has — like the same work as Mr. . . .

Q: A U.S. Attorney, like Mr. Nesland.

A: Yes, Mr. Nesland.

Q: He was Mr. Nesland's predecessor, or one of his predecessors, in this case.

A: Yes.

Q: By the way, there came a time after Michel Mastantuono was arrested in Canada that you were taken into custody, didn't there? Weren't you arrested when Michel was?

A: Yes, I was.

Q: And Michel exonerated you? He said, "Danielle Ouimet knows nothing about this. Let the poor girl go home?"

A: Right.

Q: So you went home.

A: Yes.

Q: And when that happened, of course you were both lying to the Canadian authorities, right?

A: Well, I didn't say a word. So I couldn't be lying there.

Q: I understand. Then he was lying. And you didn't say anything. As you say, there is a difference between lying and not saying anything.

A: Well, he was protecting me. Let's put it this way.

Q: It is a crime to possess heroin in Canada, is it not, and to transport it?

A: Yes.

Q: To cross state lines, to cross the border to the United States? It is a crime; you know that.

A: Yes.

Q: Have the Canadian authorities brought you down for an investigation since you began cooperating here with the American authorities?

A: They once asked me to sign a deposition that I've done here to send to France because they needed the paper or my declaration.

Q: Have you received any promises from the Canadians that because of this cooperation now that you would not be subject to prosecution there?

A: No, sir.

Q: Do you expect to be prosecuted in Canada?

A: I have no idea. No one has talked to me about that.

Q: Have you asked Mr. Nesland to make any inquiries for you?

A: He said he has no power of knowing what they are going to do.

Q: The question was, did you ask Mr. Nesland to make an inquiry as to whether or not you are secure in Canada, whether you will be free from prosecution?

A: Well, of course. I tried to protect myself, but he said he couldn't do anything. If they wanted to do it . . .

Q: In other words, you asked him to make calls for you and he said he couldn't.

A: Well, not calls. But I said, "Can you please check" — I asked, "Can you please check if it is possible, since the United States is collaborating with Canada, that I could be not attacked since I collaborate here, that my testimony would serve them and then I would have certain protection?"

Q: And Mr. Nesland didn't do that?

A: He couldn't promise anything.

Q: But did he do it for you? Did he make the call?

A: I don't think so, no.

Q: You are just not sure?

A: No. I don't think so, no, because I would have heard about it.

Q: Now, does it refresh your recollection at all as to the dates when you first began to collaborate, as you used that word, that it was around early January 1973 when you received a telephone call from Michel Mastantuono that a man named Viviani, Arthur Viviani, a U.S. Attorney, wanted to talk to you, he wanted you to travel from Canada to the United States, and that he would give you free passage for that trip?

A: Yes. He also said . . .

The Court: Just yes. If you can . . .

The Witness: Okay. Fine.

Q: So, as you think about it now, is it possible that you really did not begin to collaborate in 1971 or '72 until maybe as late as January of 1973?

A: Yes.

Q: Do you remember that first phone call from Michel?

A: Yes.

Q: Were you surprised to hear his voice?

A: Not specially, no, because I was talking to him every Saturday or Sunday he was allowed to make a phone call to me.

Q: And he made those phone calls to you from some American jail, right?

A: Yes.

Q: He had special permission to do that, didn't he?

A: No, no. He is allowed — every prisoner is allowed to make one phone call a week.

Q: Okay. And you spoke to him all the time.

A: Yes.

Q: Did he tell you that you could expect a phone call from him where Mr. Viviani would be . . .

A: No. Once it arrived directly, he said, "I'm calling you because someone wants to see you. Viviani wants to see you."

Q: Did you know at that time who Viviani was?

A: No. He explained it to me then.

Q: Okay. And did you agree to come?

A: Yes, I did.

Q: You had no hesitation?

A: Well, of course I was a little bit afraid, because I hadn't been bothered since then, and then suddenly out of nowhere they call me and ask me to come. You know, of course . . .

Q: You thought it was all behind you.

A: Well, no. How do you call that? What does that mean?

Q: Because of that noise I had trouble hearing you. What was that?

A: Behind you, what does that mean?

Q: That it was in your past.

A: Oh, no, no.

Q: So you still had some feelings that the evil dealings with heroin might pop up and cause you some problems.

A: Well, it had already because, without being — pushing too much, I am known in Canada and it came out on the front pages of all the newspapers. So the damage was done then anyway.

Q: Now, when you agreed to come, or before you agreed to come to the United States, did you talk to anybody, consult with anybody?

A: Oh, yes. I had many — well, I had many lawyers while Michel was in Montreal.

Q: Did you talk to any of them before you came to the United States?

A: Oh, no, no. They took — no.

Q: You just got on that Air Canada flight and came down to see . . .

A: Mr. Viviani.

Q: . . . Mr. Viviani. It is your testimony then that you didn't seek any legal advice, you didn't come to anybody like me, like a lawyer, and say, "Should I go to New York?" You just made a personal decision that it was the right thing to do?

A: Yes.

Mr. Kadish: I would like to have this document marked.

(Defendants' Exhibit W was marked for identification.)

Mr. Kadish: This is 3504. This document, for everybody's information, is a document of two files from A. J. Viviani re Michel Mastantuono.

Mr. Nesland: Are you offering it in evidence?

Mr. Kadish: No. I'm sorry. I want to read it in evidence.

The Court: Any objection?

Mr. Nesland: No objection.

The Court: Received.

(Defendant's Exhibit W for identification was received in evidence.)

The Court: Does this purport to be in her handwriting?

Mr. Kadish: No. It is Mr. Viviani's. It is handwritten. It is Mr. Viviani's though.

Q: Let me see if this refreshes your recollection, Miss Ouimet, about what I just asked you:

"At approximately 2.20 p.m. on January 25, 1973, Miss Ouimet arrived in my office with Agent Boulad. After pleasantries I asked her if she spoke to an attorney before leaving for New York. She said she had and was advised not to come since anything she said could be used against her.

"I told her the attorney was correct. I further told her that whatever she did say could be used against her in a court of law and that she had a right to talk with her lawyer before saying anything."

Does that refresh your recollection that perhaps before leaving Canada you did talk to some lawyer?

A: Michel had four lawyers, and I got like mad with the four of them because they didn't do anything good to Michel. So I don't recall calling one of them to ask him a legal advice on that. I don't recall — don't really recall if I talked to someone, but I might have said that to Mr. Viviani because — maybe it was my wish not to come and I could probably say that I've asked someone.

I knew perfectly well — Michel told me many times that whatever I could say could be retained against me, never to talk unless I had a lawyer.

Q: Fine. So then, if you did say that to Viviani, if in fact you used those words, "I talked with my lawyer before coming down here," you lied to him?

The Court: She said she might have. She said she doesn't remember whether she talked to the lawyer before.

A: You know, it is four years ago.

Mr. Kadish: I'll ask her that.

Mr.Newman: I didn't hear what she said.

The Court: I heard that. I was listening to that because I knew that was going to be your next question.

Mr. Newman: I'm sorry. Did the young lady say, "You know, it was four years ago."?

The Court: She did say that.

Mr. Newman: Okay, sir.

Q: After saying, as the Court said, that it was something that you might have said yourself in talking with Mr. Viviani, could you explain to the jury why in your mind you might have said something like that to a man like this, who you met for the first time? Why would you place a lawyer into the midst of it when in fact that might not have happened?

A: Because, first of all, I don't know if you look at TV series, but there is one rule that you hear everywhere, and that came back with my lawyers, is never to talk without a lawyer around, because you could have problems; if you want to make testimony, you need a lawyer.

At that time I couldn't count on any lawyer to come to New York and I really said that I was afraid, sure. You never know on what you can get involved if you don't have a legal lawyer near you.

So my first wish was not to come here, of course.

Q: So, when you met with Mr. Viviani, then, you were violating one of the well known rules, never talk to somebody like Mr. Viviani without a lawyer.

A: That's not violating. That's a protection for the one who is making the testimony.

Q: It was a pretty important moment in your life, wasn't it, Miss Ouimet?

A: It is still a very important thing in my life, sir.

Q: How many times have you been called down to the United States by an official of the American Government . . .

A: Many, many times.

Q: . . . to talk to him about a heroin transaction?

The Court: Prior to that, he means.

The Witness: Oh, to that? No.

Q: Never in your life?

A: Never in my life.

Q: You must have been pretty jittery about that, weren't you?

A: What is that.

Q: Scared?

A: Of course.

Q: Was it your testimony that there wasn't a lawyer around in Canada you could have called for advice, anybody?

A: No one.

Q: You said you first met Michel in March of '70, is that right?

A: Yes.

Q: In 1969 and '70 — by the way, were you having some financial problems at the time?

A: Not at all.

Q: Did Michel seem to have any financial problems at the time?

A: No.

Q: Did he dress well?

A: Normally.

Q: Was he able to treat you in the manner in which you were accustomed as a movie star?

A: You know how the film industry pays you over there.

Q: Not good?

A: Not good, no.

Q: Did you like these things, though?

A: Of course. Everyone does, I guess.

Q: Nice cars? Nice clothes?

A: No, a car I didn't care too much, except it is a facility to me to go to work.

Q: Clothing is very important, though?

A: Clothing is very important because with the clothes that I wear I have to go on TV, and they don't allow you to put two times the same dress.

Q: There ultimately came a time when you began to have some suspicion that Michel Mastantuono was not, as you put it, legit.

A: Yes.

Q: Right?

A: Yes.

Q: Think back to March of 1970, the very first week together, you two living together in your apartment.

By the way, what was the rent on your apartment?

A: $180.

Q: For what?

A: For a penthouse.

Q: For a penthouse?

A: For a penthouse.

Q: Rents are a little cheaper in Canada than in the United States.

A: At that time, yes.

Q: When you say "a penthouse," was it really a penthouse?

A: No, it was not. It was two rooms and a half.

Q: Now, think back to early 1970, March of 1970. You starting living with Michel. When is the first time you began to wonder whether this man is legit or not?

A: At that time I cannot say exactly what's wrong or not, because

Michel used to tell me that he was receiving a lot of money from the restaurants that he had in France in co-property with his — one was with his brother and the other one was with his sister.

Q: Did you ask him about that? I mean, did that come up because you would say to him, "Michel, how do you do so well?"?

A: No.

Q: Just volunteered that to you?

A: No. I didn't know him that well. I was living with him, but you don't ask how much you have in the bank before getting in the house, you know.

Q: How did you share your expenses?

A: I was paying the apartment and he was paying whatever he could, like the food once in a while. If we were going on a trip, he was paying — sometimes I was paying the room, sometimes he was paying the fare.

Q: So you had a pretty good sharing relationship on money.

A: Yes, sir, until the end.

Q: Now, do you know a fellow by the name of Richard Berdin?

A: No. Well, I think it is a guy by the name of Patrick. There is one guy I met by the name of Patrick, and I don't know the second name.

Q: You don't know whether he was involved in any way in Michel Mastantuono's arrest, that he was the one who gave him up, so to speak?

A: No. I heard that after, when he was arrested.

Q: Michel told you that, didn't he?

A: Yes. Here too, yes.

Q: When you say "here too," you mean not recently.

A: No. When Michel was arrested and he came to the U.S.A.

Q: That "Richard Berdin gave me up, turned me in, testified against me."

A: Yes.

Q: Now, when you were over in France with this Citroen, you said that Michel came here and said, "It will be a good idea if we got a car."

A: What?

Q: "Or better yet if you got a car."

A: Yes.

Q: Did he have a car?

A: He had a car in Canada, yes. But he gave it away because it was a complete wreck and it was falling down. So he gave it away.

Q: Did he give it away before you went over and bought the Citroen?

A: I think so, yes.

Q: How did you react to his telling you that you needed a Citroen?

A: Well, how do you react to that if you know that you need it? You say yes.

Q: Was that an expensive car?

A: No, because it was tax free. It was about $3800 to $4000.

Q: Did you have any money in the bank at the time you bought the Citroen?

A: Not enough to buy the car.

Q: But you had some?

A: Well, I had some, yes, of course.

Q: You said he gave a down payment. How much did he give?

A: I think he gave a thousand francs, if I recall on the slip.

Q: What does that amount to roughly in American dollars back at that time?

A: Well, 500 francs is a hundred dollars. So I guess it is $200.

Q: And where did the rest of the money come from?

A: Well, Michel told me that I would buy the car from the money that I would make on the film. That's how he said it. "You know, I'm going to pay it for you and you are going to give it back to me when you are going to be paid by the film."

Q: When did you give it back to him? When did you pay it back to him?

A: I didn't give it back to him because after that he said, "Since we live together, I give you that as a gift."

Q: Now, do you know the manner in which Michel got the money to pay for the Citroen?

A: At that time, no.

Q: Have you ever learned how?

A: Well, after. Well, I realized that it was coming from that. But he never told me, "I paid it with the money that I make from drugs."

Q: I understand. But you are saying that you never had a conversation with him at some subsequent time, where he said, "Danielle, I paid for the Citroen out of my drug transactions?"

A: No.

The Court: I take it he didn't have to because it was obvious.

The Witness: Yes, it was obvious.

Q: Now, you took a train to Biarritz, is that right?

A: Yes.

Q: And the train was from Paris to Biarritz?

A: From Marseilles.

Q: From Marseilles. How long a train ride is that?

A: We took the train, it was midnight, and we arrived there, it was about 8.30 in the morning to 9 o'clock.

Q: So it is an overnight train.

A: Yes.

Q: Now, before going from Marseilles to Biarritz you had been in Brussels?

A: Yes.

Q: And then to Paris?

A: Yes.

Q: Had you asked Michel what had happened to this new car?

A: No. He told me that it broke down.

Q: I mean, did you say, "How or what was the problem?"?

A: No, he never told me exactly what was wrong.

Q: Is it your testimony that when you were on the way to Biarritz you had no knowledge of the fact that the car might have some stuff in it?

A: No.

Q: None at all?

A: No.

Q: No suspicions?

A: Not at that time. Well, you know, he was making — he was taking much care about that car. You wonder what is going on. But I didn't really, you know, pinpoint the fact that he was dealing with something.

Q: He seemed to be making much ado about the Citroen.

A: Well, first of all, I was quite surprised that it broke down in Biarritz. But at that time he turned to me and said — at that time I was going out with him, but I was very mad because he was, I don't know, in a bad mood, I don't know, and he left me one day, yelling at me in Brussels, and then he said that he didn't know when he was going to come back.

And at a certain time he came back to Brussels and he told me that he had gone out with a girl and they went as far as Biarritz and that the car broke down there, that he had met a girl and they were off on a trip and that the car broke down there.

Q: Left you with some questions, didn't it?

A: Well, he did that often, anyway.

Q: When you got . . .

Mr. Newman: Sorry. I didn't hear that.

The Court: He did that often, anyway.

Mr. Newman: All right.

Q: Michel was not to be trusted.

A: I think so.

Q: That is obvious.

The Court: You think so? Or you think not?

The Witness: Well, at that time he was to be trusted. But right now he told me a lot of things that I'm not very proud to know.

Q: So right now he is not to be trusted, is he?

A: No. Well, he is married and he has another life.

Q: When you picked up the Citroen, you said you went shopping first.

A: Yes.

Q: All right.

A: He left me . . .

Q: Have you seen the Citroen before that, ever?

A: No. Well, yes. In Brussels. He came to Brussels to show me the car once.

Q: When you got into the Citroen and you began to drive it back to Paris?

A: Yes.

Q: Or back to where? Where did you go?

A: To Biarritz?

Q: No. You were in Biarritz. You picked up the car and you took it where?

A: To Paris.

Q: Did you notice anything different about the car?

A: Nope, not that I recall.

Q: How was Michel's demeanor? Was he nervous?

A: No.

Q: Now, is it your testimony that you both took the car to the Transport office?

A: Yes.

Q: And who made the arrangements for the actual shipment? You or he?

A: Both of us.

Q: Together?

A: Yes.

Q: At the desk?

A: Yes.

Q: Now, when the car came in to Montreal some time later, you went to pick it up, true?

A: Yes.

Q: Michel said, "I don't want to go there."?

A: He said he was busy.

Q: You now know that is probably not the case.

A: I know now.

Q: You now know that Michel Mastantuono was using you, don't you?

A: Oh, I guess so, yes.

Q: You don't guess; you know that.

A: Well, you know, it is quite obvious now. At the time, I don't recall. I was . . .

Q: You were just a little pawn in his heroin game at the time, true?

A: What is a pawn?

Q: Like a chess pawn. A pawn.

A: Yes.

Q: You were like a pawn in his little heroin game.

A: Yes.

Q: Like when you went to Miami for him.

A: Yes.

Q: Now, when you went to Miami for him in 1971 on the station wagon affair, you no longer had any doubt . . .

A: Yes.

Q: . . . about the stuff, did you?

A: Yes, I didn't.

Q: You were right in the middle of it, weren't you?

A: Yes.

Q: Was the money attractive to you at that point in time?

A: Well, it is always something — no, it is not exactly that, you know. I was mostly in love with Michel and I was afraid at that time. And of course, when Michel was putting some money on, it was to calm me down a bit.

Then, you know perfectly well for that kind of job you have to be paid. So they were paying me. Okay, I was happy to receive the money, that's for sure. But I was not, you know, asking for it. I could have done without it and be very happy.

Q: Why didn't you tell Michel, did you ever say to Michel, "Michel, you've got to stop this heroin?"

A: I said it plenty times.

Q: And what did Michel say?

A: Michel said that he couldn't stop because he was wheeler and he couldn't stop, otherwise he could get killed or have a lot of problems, that he couldn't stop, too many people knew him and he couldn't stop.

Q: And you and Michel were able to do a lot of things with this money that you were getting, right?

A: Well, we were paying ourselves little trips. Like I remember he paid me a trip to the Canary Islands with my son.

Q: How long did you go there for? Three weeks?

A: Three weeks. Oh, you know my life.

Q: And you were able to buy expensive clothes?

A: Of course.

Q: And you got a nice car, a Corvette?

A: Yes.

Q: And things were pretty good. Money was no problem at all, was it?

A: Yes, I guess so.

Q: You had made more money in heroin than you had ever made in acting . . .

A: Again, I was . . .

Q: No.

The Court: If you can answer that yes or no do so.

A: Yes.

Q: Now, you weren't a slave there; you could have walked away from it, right?

A: I guess not, sir.

Q: Well . . .

The Court: Wait a minute. I don't know what "I guess not" means. You asked two questions. Start over again.

Q: I'll ask the first question. Were you enslaved with it somehow?

A: If being deeply in love is enslaved, yes, I was.

Q: Michel had not threatened you, though, had he?

A: He never threatened me. But he always told me that if by any chance I had to, let's say, turn over to the police, that I would probably be killed.

Q: So in the back of your mind you had that little fear.

A: Well, you know, it is being caught on one side or the other: Go to the police and be caught and be killed by the others or try to wait for the police and come and pick you up and try to get out of it. You know, it is one way or the other.

Q: You got back to France in 1970 and you had this Citroen and it was basically your car.

A: Yes.

Q: And then one day Michel said, "You are going to take the Citroen and you are going to take it over to Plattsburg."

A: Yes.

Q: And what did you say to Michel about that?

A: Well, at that time I was quite sure that what he was doing was not legitimate. So I was very afraid. So I guess that my reaction would be to go over with and try to stop it after, or try to — avoid, you know, asking questions, because it could hurt me after.

Q: It would have hurt you to have asked the questions?

A: Well, you know, to know too much. I guess that if Michel wanted to tell me something, he would have done it then.

Q: Did you think there was some money in it for you at that time?

A: Oh, no.

Q: And when you got to New York and you put the car, the Citroen, in the garage and you went up to your room and then shortly thereafter Michel disappeared overnight . . .

A: Yes.

Q: Was that a little bit unusual in your relationship?

A: That's why I was the first time very much afraid.

Q: So it is fair to say that as early as September 1970 you, Miss Ouimet, had a very distinct feeling that your man was doing illegal things in the United States.

The Court: She testified to that on direct examination.

Mr. Kadish: If I might just go on into it, your Honor.

Q: And you then continued to do the Citroen transaction in 1970, right?

A: Yes.

Q: You did the Galaxy transaction, right?

A: Yes.

Q: You did the Barracuda transaction, right?

A: Yes.

Q: You did the station wagon Fiat transaction, right?

A: Yes.

Q: One after another, right?

A: Yes.

Q: And is it fair to say that you and Michel made around $130,000 from all that?

A: I wouldn't know. I was never asking Michel how much he was receiving for that.

Q: Now, did you know that in April of 1973 or thereabouts Michel Mastantuono appeared before an American grand jury here?

A: Yes, I guess so. Well, I don't know the dates, but I know that he testified in front of a grand jury.

Q: Before a grand jury. And did you have conversations with Michel prior to the time he testified?

A: Yes.

Q: Did you have times when you actually met him, I mean during that time when you saw him face-to-face, not by telephone?

A: In Montreal or in the U.S.A.?

Q: After he came into the United States.

A: Yes, I saw him.

Q: And before the grand jury did he tell you he was going to lie in that grand jury?

A: He said he wouldn't say the whole truth.

Q: Did he ever mention the name Astuto to you at all?

A: No.

Q: One other thing. When you went down to Miami in the summer of 1973 to see that man Felix, you knew . . .

Mr. Nesland: That is an improper date. The summer of '71.

Mr. Kadish: June. Okay?

Mr. Nesland: '71.

Mr. Kadish: Okay, June of '71.

Q: When you went to see that man Felix, you knew that he was a buyer for the heroin, or a proposed buyer.

A: I didn't know that the guy I was going to meet was a buyer. I knew he was someone dealing with drugs, though.

Q: Right. Okay; somebody who would be a possible or proposed recipient of the heroin from the station wagon.

A: Yes.

Q: And when you went to Florida to see that person, and you ultimately saw him, you were able to have, and you have in your mind today, some idea what the man looks like, don't you?

A: Yes, I do.

Q: And you gave that description of that man to Mr. Viviani, didn't you?

A: Yes, I did.

Q: Would it be fair to say that this is a description of the man you saw in Miami, the recipient, or the proposed recipient, of the June '71 heroin shipment?

Mr. Nesland: I object to the question. She doesn't know who she met, now.

The Court: Does she?

Mr. Kadish: You can't testify for the witness.

Mr. Nesland: Your question implies she knew he was the recipient of the heroin. She said no such thing.

The Court: All he wants to know is the description of the man she met in Miami.

Mr. Nesland: But he put in there that he is the recipient of the heroin.

Mr. Kadish: She testified she thought he was.

The Court: She testified she didn't know. No. I take it back. She did say he was the recipient, in answer to a later question.

Q: All right. Did you say he was a white male?

A: Yes.

Q: Are you sure of that?

A: Well, dark skin, but white.

Q: Caucasian. Did you say he was approximately 35 to 40 years old?

A: Yes.

Q: Did you say he was approximately five foot eleven inches tall?

A: Yes.

Q: Did you say that he had a slightly dark complexion?

A: Um-hum.

Q: Did you say he had casual dress?

A: Yes.

Q: Did you say he spoke French with an occasional Provencal accent, claimed to be from Bordeaux?

A: Yes.

Q: And did you say that he probably understood a little English?

A: Probably, yes.

The Court: Mr. Kadish, how much longer have you got to have?

Mr. Kadish: Not much longer. I am just about there.

The Court: Then we will finish with you.

Q: And you were with that man face-to-face, weren't you, in Florida?

A: Yes.

Q: How much time did you spend with him?

A: Altogether about 10 minutes. A little more than that, because he had to bring me back to the hotel.

Q: You saw him in the hotel lobby of some hotel or motel in Florida.

A: Yes.

Q: You got in his car and you rode to a pay phone.

A: Yes.

Q: You dialed a number for him and then you turned to him, looked him in the eye, and handed him the phone, right?

A: I don't know if I looked him in the eye, but I handed him the phone.

Q: You looked at his face and handed him the phone, didn't you?

A: Yes, sir.

Q: And then, after that phone call was made . . .

A: I went back to Montreal — well, to the . . .

Q: Did he drive you some place?

A: Yes, to the hotel.

Q: Now, look around this courtroom and pick out, if you can, anywhere in this courtroom the recipient of the June '71st shipment.

Mr. Nesland: I object to the question.

Mr. Garland: She testified to it.

Mr. Nesland: She did not.

The Court: Pick out the man that you talked to, if you can.

The Witness: Anywhere in this room?

Q: If you see him.

A: Anywhere in this room? These are people, I know, that are listening.

Q: If you see him in the back, pick him out. I will get out of your way.

The Court: I assume it is conceded he is not here.

Mr. Kadish: I will concede that.

The Witness: I am looking at everyone. No, he is not here. I think so. From what I recall, he is not here.

Mr. Kadish: No further questions.

The Court: All right.

        Ladies and gentlemen, see you at a quarter of two.

        (The jury left the courtroom.)

Th Court: Does anybody have any applications he wants to make on the record?

        All right. A quarter of two.

        (Luncheon recess.)

Afternoon session   1:45 P.M.

Danielle Ouimet, resumed.

Cross Examination by Mr. Nadem:

Q: Miss Ouimet, are you aware that Michel has said that he lied in his grand jury testimony in 1973 in order to protect you from involvement in this case?

A: Yes.

Q: From April of 1973, isn't it true that you had already implicated yourself in this criminal activity of bringing narcotics into the United States?

A: Previous to what? Excuse me.

Q: Before April of 1973, when Michel testified in the grand jury, is it not true that you had already implicated yourself in this action of bringing narcotics into the United States?

A: Yes.

Q: And when did you implicate yourself prior to April of 1973 when Michel was in the grand jury?

A: Well, in all those cases that were mentioned, my car, the Citroen, the Cardon's car, Daniel Gerard's car, Andrioli's car.

Q: Perhaps you didn't understand me completely. When did you first tell the American authorities that you were involved with this ring of people, including Michel?

A: Oh, the complete truth, when I told the complete truth or when did he first testify?

Q: No, the question is very specific.

The Court: This is a very simple question. She wants to know the first time she said anything or when she told the truth.

Mr. Naden: The first time she told the authorities she was involved.

The Court: She wants to know the first time she said anything on the subject or the first time she told the complete truth. Which do you want? I don't understand what you want.

Mr. Naden: I thought the question was clear. I'm sorry, Judge.

Q: The first time you told them anything in the nature of an admission of responsibility in a criminal action.

A: When I first talked to Mr. Nesland.

Q: And when was that, please?

A: About a year ago, Mr. Nesland? I couldn't recall that.

I don't recall. You know, I made about 20 to 25 trips here. On which one I did, I don't know.

The Court: If you want the date, perhaps Mr. Nesland will tell you.

Mr. Naden: What date did Mr. Nesland first meet this witness; that might be satisfactory. What was the date?

The Court: Might I make a suggestion? Words like "implicate" mean one thing to me and mean quite another thing to a layman.

Mr. Naden: That's why I changed the question, Judge.

The Court: Do you know the date, Mr. Nesland?

Mr. Nesland: I would say maybe the summer of this year.

The Court: Of this year?

Mr. Naden: 1975, Mr. Nesland?

Mr. Nesland: This year.

Q: Now, before you told Mr. Nesland that you had been — that you knew of the nature of Michel's activities and that you had assisted him in those activities . . .

A: Yes.

Q: — had you told any other American official or agent that you knew of Michel's activities and what they were and that you had participated with him?

A: No, I said that I had participated involuntarily to some trips with him, and that I didn't know at the time what I was doing.

The Court: You don't mean "involuntarily." You mean "ignorant." You weren't taken involuntarily; that means by force.

The Witness: Yes.

Q: Do you recall, Miss Ouimet, speaking to Agent Bocchichio at any time since this — since the American authorities have been involved in this matter?

A: About the case?

Q: Yes.

A: Well, yes.

Q: Do you recall speaking with Agent Bocchichio in February of 1973?

A: Probably I did.

Q: And do you recall — I'd like this exhibit, your Honor, 3504-B marked for identification. I can either move it in now if the Government consents or wait until Agent Bocchichio is called.

Mr. Nesland: I have no problem with that.

The Court: No objection?

Mr. Nesland: No.

The Court: Received. Incidentally, ladies and gentlemen, the noise that you hear outside has to do with the city's financial problems. I thought you might be interested.

(Defendants' Exhibit X received in evidence.)

Q: Do you remember telling Agent Bocchichio that you had approached Michel before the arrest and asked him about what he had been told about — about what you had been told about the Citroen, the car you brought back from France?

A: Could you put this — this isn't clear.

Mr. Nesland: I don't understand it.

Mr. Naden: I didn't finish the question.

Mr. Nesland: You better start again.

Q: I ask the witness if she recalls telling Bocchichio about the incident when you brought the Citroen back from France.

The Court: What date?

Mr. Naden: This conversation with Bocchichio, your Honor, according to this report, took place on February 25th of 1973, which was before the April date that I am trying to work around, Judge.

A: I might have done it, yes.

Q: Now, do you remember that you told Agent Bocchichio that Michel had told you that the car you brought back from France was loaded with stuff?

A: Yes.

Q: Do you remember telling Agent . . .

A: Yes.

Q: Do you remember telling him that in February of 1973?

A: I don't recall.

The Court: You might have told him?

The Witness: Yes, I might.

The Court: She might have.

Q: All right. Do you remember Agent Bocchichio asking you what "stuff" meant, and your saying to him "I thought he meant" — Michel meant — "marijuana or drugs, but not heroin."

A: Yes.

Q: Do you remember telling him that in February?

A: I remember that I made one statement that I thought it was marijuana inside the car.

Q: And this was the Citroen that you and Michel had brought back from France?

A: Yes.

The Court: I take it that was an untruth?

The Witness: That's true, that was not the truth, yes.

Q: Untrue in terms of your thinking it was marijuana?

A: Yes.

Q: But not untrue in terms of Michel having told you that the car was loaded with stuff?

A: No. At that time Michel asked me to do something and when I was asking, you know, little hints or questions, he was not answering them, he was saying, "Well, we will buy the car and we will travel a lot, and that's it. Don't ask me any questions."

Q: But also it is not untrue, meaning it is true, that you told this to the agent back in February of 1973 . . .

A: I guess I did, yes.

Q: . . . before Michel testified before the grand jury?

A: I recall making a statement like that before, but I guess it is to Mr. Bocchichio, but I cannot certify to that.

Mr. Naden: Your Honor, may I have leave of the Court to read the paragraph?

The Court: It is in evidence. This is a document to which the Government had no objection, we just admitted in evidence.

Mr. Garland: Your Honor, what did you say about the document, it is not in evidence?

The Court: It is in evidence. It has just been received.

Mr. Garland: Excuse me.

Mr. Naden: It was offered and received.

The Court: I apologize, gentlemen. Perhaps I didn't give you an opportunity to object.

Mr. Garland: I don't understand, your Honor. I have no objection.

The Court: Do you have any objection?

Mr. Newman: No.

The Court: Mr. Kadish, any objection?

Mr. Kadish: No, sir.

The Court: I just apologized to you, I didn't ask you if you had any objection. All right, it is now in evidence.

Q: "Right after her return from France, Miss Ouimet was told by her brother that he had received information that Mastantuono was engaged in some illegal activity and that she should be careful. Miss Ouimet then approached Mastantuono and asked him about what she had been told, and he told her that the car that they had brought back from France was loaded with stuff. When questioned by the writer" — and the writer is Agent Bocchichio — "when questioned by the writer, as to when he said stuff, she stated she thought he meant marijuana or other drugs, but she never thought of heroin." Now, at the time that you made this statement to Agent Bocchichio you knew that it was a crime to import marijuana into the United States and to smuggle that across the border, didn't you?

A: Yes.

Q: So you had told him that you had assisted Michel in bringing whatever it was into the United States and the agent knew this back in 1973, in February?

A: Yes.

Q: Now, did you learn that three months — two months later, in April of 1973, that Michel testified in the grand jury in the United States?

A: Again I cannot put a date on it, but I know that Michel testified once.

Q: Thank you. Now, you testified this morning that Bec gave you some money. Is that right?

A: Yes.

Q: For taking a suitcase to France with money in it?

A: Yes.

Q: And how much did you say this morning that Bec gave you?

A: I think it is around from two to three thousand dollars.

Q: Would it refresh your recollection that you told Bocchichio that Bec paid you approximately 500 to a thousand dollars?

A: When I was asked about that, I always have to refer to Michel, because he was the one who was receiving the money and giving it to me, or putting the money in a safe and I saw so much money I cannot exactly put a number on that. To my recall, which I think is, you know, approximately, would say $2,000, according to the amount of money that was implicated in the suitcase.

Q: Well, when you told Agent Bocchichio that it was 500 to a thousand dollars was that an approximation again or was that just an effort, just to put any figure that would . . .

A: Well, no, I didn't know really at the time.

Q: When you went to Miami, were you given money for that action undertaken in behalf of this narcotics conspiracy?

A: Yes.

Q: How much money were you given for that?

A: I think it was around 500. Again I cannot put a specific amount on that.

Q: Do you recall telling Agent Bocchichio back in February of 1973 that you were paid $200 for making that trip?

A: Again, you know, an amount of money, don't ask me, I saw sometimes millions in front of me, sometimes thousands. I really cannot say exactly how much money I . . .

Q: Are you aware that I am only asking these questions in order to ascertain what the definite — what your recollection is, not in order to do anything else.

The Court: She is not concerned with the purpose of your question.

Mr. Naden: May it please the Court, perhaps the witness doesn't understand and it may make sense to explain that I am trying to test her recollection based on her present statements and her former statements, and that's all.

Q: Now, you attempted, you said, to have that Citroen stolen so that the Canadian authorities would not have an opportunity to find it and examine it for drugs, isn't that so?

A: Yes.

Q: Has it come to your attention at any time that the Canadian authorities did find that automobile?

A: I guess they did, because when Michel was arrested, they took the car away from me immediately. Well, it was in repair right then and they asked me where it was and they went directly to the place and took it.

Q: They took the car?

A: They took the car.

Q: Now, when for the first time — withdrawn. Is it your testimony today that when you spoke with Mr. Nesland for the first time that that was the first occasion when you told the whole truth about your involvement?

A: Yes.

Q: You didn't tell the whole truth I take it to Mr. Viviani?

A: No.

Q: And you did not tell the whole truth, I take it, to Agent Bocchichio, even though you had told Agent Bocchichio back in February that you did some acts in furtherance of this activity of Michel's?

A: Yes.

Q: From the time that Michel was taken by the American authorities in 1971, how many times have you seen him from then until now?

A: From — in Montreal from the time he was arrested until now?

Q: From the time he was arrested, have you seen him?

A: Yes.

The Court: How many times?

Q: How many times?

A: From the moment in Montreal he was arrested until now? Oh, my God, about a hundred times.

Mr. Newman: I'm sorry, I couldn't hear the lady's answer.

The Court: About a hundred times.

Q: I take it those visits were in the United States?

A: Yes.

Q: Did you go to visit him in Florida in jail?

A: Yes.

Q: Did you ever see him prior to now in this building?

A: Yes. Well, yes.

Q: How many times?

A: When he was in jail or outside?

Q: In this building, how many times did you see him in this building?

A: In this building about 20 — 20 times.

Q: How many times did you see him in Florida when he was in Florida in jail?

A: Twice.

Q: On one of those visits in Florida, was Michel able to leave the prison and stay outside with you?

A: He had what they call a furlough.

Q: If that's what they call it.

A: (Witness shrugs)

Q: When did you learn this word "furlough"?

A: Over there, when he phoned me and said he could have a furlough, that means that for good behavior he could have two days.

Q: And when did you pay him the visit in Florida?

A: Do I know? I don't know.

Q: You don't know?

A: Well, I don't know. I cannot put a date, you know.

Q: Can you recall generally, as best you can — what year was it?

A: It was about a year and a half ago, around. I don't know. I really don't know. I am in a business where I travel a lot. That you know is included in one of my trips, like I cannot put a date on a trip.

Q: This trip is a little out of the ordinary though, isn't it?

A: Yes. Yes.

Q: The two times that you have seen Michel since 1971 are special occasions, you were in love with this man?

A: Yes.

Q: Are you still in love with him?

A: No.

Q: But you were in love with him and you saw him twice in those days?

A: Yes.

Q: I am not trying to be fresh but that seems to be a special occasion . . .

A: Yes.

Q: . . . that you might very well remember better than a TV commercial in Montreal or Toronto.

A: I guess so.

Q: But you don't remember what year it was?

A: No. I remember — I remember it was beautiful weather over there so — you know I am trying to remember if it was cold in Montreal at the time. I don't even recall that. I guess I could pretty well say that it was near the summertime, because I already — excuse me to give such personal details, because I already had a tan and I remember taking pictures on that trip where I had a tan plus, which is very rare for me, but I had — I needed a base, so probably I had before a tan.

Q: Is it your best recollection that this visit was some time in 1974?

A: Yes.

Q: When you were with Michel in that period of time, did he tell you that he was having difficulty getting a parole?

A: Yes. Many times he had to call me back and say that he couldn't have the parole.

The Court: You mean parole?

The Witness: The furlough, permission . . .

The Court: Parole means a different thing. Furlough you are talking about.

The Witness: Okay.

Mr. Naden: Let me rephrase it then, Judge, so we won't have a misunderstanding.

Q: Did Michel tell you around that period of time that he was having trouble getting to the end of his prison tenure so that — having trouble getting released?

A: Released for . . .

Q: Not for the visit with you, but for good.

A: Oh, no. Well, no, he didn't tell me that. He was, you know, he was — he was talking to me often that he wanted to end up — end his time in prison but he had to do his time and he was just happy that he could, you know, was ready to go shortly because that was almost at the end of his time.

Q: He said that in '74?

A: Yes.

Q: Do you recall either when you visited him or in a telephone conversation that you had with him, that he told you that it looked like he could not get out until October of 1975?

A: No, I don't think so, because he didn't — he never put a date on his exit, if I can say. He I think always thought that with good behavior he could do — he was told that maybe he could do one-third of his or two-thirds of his time, so he was calculating in terms of doing his full time less one-third for good behavior, so he never talked to me that he could do the whole year or whatever.

Q: I see, so he never told you that he went before a board or hearing board . . .

A: I guess that he did, yes, once, to get out — to have one-third off, not to . . .

Q: Did he tell you that he went before a hearing board?

A: Yes. Yes.

Q: Do you remember when it was that he told you this?
A: No.
Q: Do you remember if he told you that he wasn't going to get out until October, 1975?
A: That I don't remember.
Q: When you told Agent Bocchichio, getting back to that time in February of 1973, Miss Ouimet, that Michel had told you that the car was loaded with stuff, and you told Agent Bocchichio that you had helped Michel with the Citroen, and going to Florida, did Agent Bocchichio tell you at that time that you had admitted to criminal action?
A: I really don't know.
Q: Was it your understanding at that time that in admitting or in telling the agent that you thought there were drugs in the car, whether they were marijuana or any other kind of drugs — when you told the agent that there were drugs in that car that you had told him that you were involved with knowledge of a criminal activity?
Mr. Nesland: May we approach the bench, your Honor, with respect to this line of questioning.

(At the side bar.)

Mr. Nesland: I think it is very misleading whether or not she admitted that she knew it was marijuana. We couldn't prosecute her on heroin, and if she admitted it was marijuana we didn't have crime because we knew it was heroin.
The Court: What you could do has nothing to do with it, it is what was in her mind is what counts.
Mr. Nesland: That misleads the jury that she admitted a crime and we didn't prosecute her for it.
The Court: The only thing that's important is what is in her mind. That's all that's important.

(In open court.)

The Court: The question is, did you think you admitted to a crime when you admitted to bringing in what you told him was marijuana?
Mr. Naden: What she thought was stuff and what she thought was marijuana or some other stuff?
The Witness: I guess I was admitting that I did something wrong.
The Court: Did you think that the something wrong was a crime? I am not asking about the past, just asking you what you thought at the time.
The Witness: Yes, I thought it was wrong.

The Court: Did you think it was criminal, that you could go to jail for it?

The Witness: Yes.

The Court: All right, that's what he wanted to know.

Q: In that period of time, in 1973, how many times did you see Michel in that year of 1973?

A: Here in New York?

Q: Yes. Or in the United States, New Jersey, New York, Florida.

A: Every time I was asked to come to make a deposition, and sometimes to visit.

Q: How many times, if you can remember in 1973?

A: I have no idea. I would, you know, if I would have — I kept all the tickets for the fare to come. I can give something.

Q: All right, you don't remember. Around that period of time when you were speaking to the agent and to Mr. Viviani, you were continuing to speak with Michel on the telephone, weren't you, and you were visiting him from time to time?

A: Yes.

Q: And around the time — through the whole year of 1972, 19 — 1972 after he was brought to the United States, throughout 1973, 1974, you continued to communicate by telephone with Michel?

A: Yes.

Q: And you saw him on periodic occasions?

A: Yes.

Q: And he knew, because you were keeping him apprised . . .

A: What is "apprised"?

Q: You told him what you had told the agents?

A: Most of the time he was there with me.

Q: Was he there with you when you told this to Bocchichio?

A: I guess he might have been, yes.

Q: But you are not sure?

A: No, I am not sure.

Q: If you are not sure say you are not sure.

A: I am not sure. Sometimes he was, sometimes he wasn't.

Mr. Naden: Excuse me, Judge. I am not trying to interfere but I think the witness may feel that if she says that it is pejorative of something wrong.

The Court: Don't worry about why he is asking.

The Witness: No, no, no.

The Court: Just answer it.

The Witness: Fine, okay.

Q: You think he might have been there?

A: I know sometimes I saw Agent Bocchichio with Michel and some-times I was alone with him. I don't know in what conversation I had with Bocchichio when Michel was in and what kind of con-versation I had.

Q: In any event you wouldn't tell Michel what went on with Bocchichio and the other Government officials . . .

A: Oh, yes.

The Court: Either with Bocchichio he was there or after you saw Bocchichio he was there?

The Witness: Yes.

Q: In fact you didn't tell the Government of the United States any-thing that you didn't tell Michel about afterwards?

A: Or that he didn't tell me.

Mr. Newman: Sorry, Judge.

The Court: "Or that he didn't tell me." In other words — well, I am not going to testify. I withdraw it.

Q: If he told you what to say when you went to the U.S. Attorney and the agent, you went back and said, "I said what you told me?"

A: Yes.

Q: And if you said something of your own independent mind and of your own knowledge you would say "I told him this on this occasion?"

A: Yes.

The Court: I think you have established that point.

Mr. Naden: I think so, Judge. I have nothing further, Judge. I think I have established it.

Cross Examination by Mr. Newman:

Q: Is it pronounced Ouimet?

A: Ouimet.

Q: I am going to ask you an indelicate question. How old were you when you first met Michel Mastantuono?

A: It was in '70, I am 28, and we are in '75, five years.

Q: You were about 23 years of age?

A: 22 or 23.

Q: And when you started to go with Michel, was he your first steady boyfriend so to speak?

A: Yes.

Q: And you were sort of impressed and taken with him?

A: Yes.

Q: And I don't know the French word but was he sort of a charming man with an ability to talk?

A: He still is one.

Q: I beg your pardon.

The Court: He is still one.

The Witness: Still one.

Q: You mean charming and with the ability to talk?

A: Yes.

Q: Are you familiar with the American expression "con man"? Have you ever heard that?

A: Yes, but I would never use it because I don't know the proper word, the proper meaning.

Q: Well, the Judge won't permit me to give you my interpretation.

The Court: The Judge won't permit you to ask the witness' opinion of any other witness. She is not here as an expert.

Mr. Naden: She might be expert, your Honor.

Q: Did you find —

Mr. Newman: May I continue, sir, I'm sorry.

The Court: Yes.

Q: Did you find that during the course of your relationship with Mr. Mastantuono he told you what later turned out to be untrue?

A: That later were not true?

Q: Were not true, yes.

A: On that case or on different occasions?

Q: On your general relationship with him on the case.

A: Yes, sir.

Q: And he made you a lot of promises and he gave you a lot of conversations that turned out to be nothing, is that fair?

A: Not specially, that's not exactly what — on very personal things. Not — like promising me, I don't know, a ring and then not giving it to me, yes, he was always doing that. He was very tight.

Q: Did he ever tell you about building a boat to bring in heroin into the United States?

A: First the boat was supposed to be built not exactly for that purpose, it was supposed to be used first for pleasure and then he had the idea of I guess filling it up.

Q: Filling it with heroin and bringing it in?

A: Yes.

Q: Did he tell you this is something that he wanted to do, to be in business for himself?

A: I don't recall him telling me that. I don't think so though.

Q: I'm sorry.

A: I don't think so.

Q: Did he tell you he was in this boat building operation with his friend Gauthier?

A: Gauthier was first my friend and I presented him Gauthier and then he was in that business with Gauthier.

Q: Did Gauthier have some experience in building boats?

A: Not in building but he had some experience in boating. Had a little boat at the time and he was always on the water. He knows a lot about boating.

Q: Were you ever present when Michel approached this subject of building a boat with Gauthier and that he, Michel, would finance it for him?

A: Yes.

Q: And were you present when Michel gave Gauthier some sums of money?

A: Never.

Q: Did Michel ever come back and say to you, "Danielle I just gave Gauthier 5,000, 6,000, $7,000 to build a boat"?

A: Michel was very, very rarely talking about an amount of money in front of me.

Q: He kept that to himself?

A: Yes.

Q: By the way, when he was arrested in Montreal, and he was in jail for that extended period of time, did he ever have you run errands for him while he was in jail?

A: What is errands?

Q: Oh, I'm sorry. Did he ever have you do things for him like meeting people, go get money for him or things like that?

A: No, because all the money was in our possession at the time.

Q: In other words, you had it together jointly you and he?

A: Yes.

Q: Did you have it in a bank?

A: No.

Q: You had it hidden some place?

A: Yes.

Q: Are you familiar with what we call in America safe deposit box?

A: Yes, but we didn't have it.

Q: That was not the way it was done?

A: No.

Q: Did you ever have occasion when going to get some money or to do some other errand — I take back errand — do some other thing for Michel, to count the money that you and he had together?

A: I don't understand what you mean.

Q: Did you sit down ever and say let's see how much money Michel and I have together, and count it?

A: Not altogether, no. I remember when there was some kind of — like if there was $5,000 coming in, Michel was saying there is

5,000 here and we should hide it. I remember that when the police arrested Michel they found the money in one of his pockets that was hanging in a hanger — on a hanger in a wardrobe like.

Q: Would you remember as you sit here now, Miss Ouimet, how much money they found in his pocket?

A: $17,000.

Q: $17,000?

A: Yes, $17,000.

Q: And this was in October of 1971?

A: Yes, the 28th.

Q: And did they do any search of the house at that time, do you know?

A: Yes.

Q: And did they find any other money in the house?

A: No.

Q: Did they find any heroin in the house by any chance?

A: No.

The Court: Was there any other money in the house that they didn't find?

The Witness: Yes.

Mr.Newman: Thank you, your Honor.

The Witness: I knew that you were coming there.

Mr. Newman: He is making my job easy.

Q: Do you know how much money there was, the other money that they found there, that you had in the house that they did not find?

A: All together it was $23,000.

Q: With the 17 that they found?

A: Yes.

Q: And there was six additional, right?

A: Yes.

Q: Now, do you know whether the police ever obtained this station wagon from the transaction, I think it was Cardon's car? Did the police ever seize that too, do you know?

A: Never.

Q: I believe you told Mr. Naden, but I couldn't hear it too clearly, so bear with me, that there there were two visits that you made to Elgin Air Force Base; is that correct?

A: Yes.

Q: Ones on which Mr. Mastantuono had a furlough.

A: Yes.

Q: And you left the base with him then.

A: Yes.

Q: Did you then come back to the base with him?

A: No. He left me at the airport.

Q: And then you had a second visit with him?

A: No. That was the second one. I had one before that.

Q: One before. And when you visited him the first time, did you visit with him in a visiting room, the regular visiting facilities?

A: No. It is yards that were surrounded by a fence, a very high fence, and I had to stay there the whole day picnicking because I was not allowed to go out. So we had to bring the picnic bag if I wanted to stay with him the whole day.

Q: And, if you remember, I know it was a while ago, were there other inmates picnicking with their families and with their visitors?

A: Yes.

Q: And it was pretty free and open and everybody sort of mingled together; is that a sort of fair description?

A: Yes.

Q: Would you look at that gentleman over there and tell me if by chance, on the day you were there picnicking at Elgin Air Force Base you saw that gentleman visiting somebody?

A: I don't recall, no. No, I don't recall.

Q: Did you know who Mr. Mastantuono's friends were at Elgin Air Force Base?

A: Yes. I remember two guys. One was tall, very thin, talking Spanish, and he is supposed to live in South America or something. I don't remember his name. And another one that was a little shorter, with black hair. Actually, I have pictures of them from that trip. I don't have them with me, but I have them.

Q: Would you remember if the second man's name, the one you are describing as being a little shorter, was Hattendorf, and was he from Israel, Michael Hattendorf? Would that ring a bell?

A: What is the first name?

Q: Michael Hattendorf, from Israel.

A: No, it wouldn't ring a bell.

The Court: Anybody from Israel ring a bell?

The Witness: No.

Q: Would you remember if one of the gentlemen who was his friend spoke French?

A: I am trying to think, because I know that — I guess — I wouldn't be able to answer that properly. I don't know. I might say and then no. I don't know.

Q: During all of this time that you were together with Michel, did he try to make himself seem important to you? Did he try to impress you with his conversation?

A: All guys from Marseilles are a little bit pushy.

Q: Did you say "a little bit pushy?"

A: Yes.

Q: By the way, you had experience, I think you told one of my colleagues, appearing before audiences and acting in public. Did you tell us you were on the stage?

A: Yes.

Q: And now I think you told us that your job is one of a television commentator, you said? It was difficult for me to hear over there.

A: Yes, radio and TV. I do TV and radio. Just name it. I dance, I sing, I make interviews, I go for commercials, I sing on TV, dance on TV, I go on stage, plays, cinema.

Q: So you are at home in front of an audience, is that fair to say?

A: What?

Q: You are at home in front of an audience? In other words, you are not nervous performing in front of people.

A: It all depends what situation you are in.

Q: How about today?

A: I don't like that too much.

Q: We shouldn't take that personally, should we.

A: No, no, not personally, of course.

Q: Now, I think you told us in response to a question by Mr. Naden that by and large whatever you related to the different authorities, once you started to cooperate, you either were told to do this by Michel or after you did it you went back and relayed it. I think I am repeating a question, Judge, but I wasn't too sure. Is that correct?

A: Yes.

Q: Now, you told us about an incident with Cadillacs that Michel told you about.

A: Yes.

Q: And he told you, did he not, that there were three or four people in each one of these Cadillacs?

A: Yes.

Q: I beg your pardon?

A: Yes. Excuse me. Three or four people?

Q: In each of the Cadillacs.

A: No, he never told me that.

Q: Did he tell you there were three or four Cadillacs?

A: Yes.

Q: Did he tell you that there were more than one person in each Cadillac?

A: No, he never told me about that.

Q: Did he tell you how many people there were in the Cadillacs?

A: No.

Q: So what did he tell you? That there were three or four Cadillacs? Is that the idea?

A: Yes.

Q: And whatever you are telling us about the Cadillacs is information that Michel told you about, because you weren't even there, right?

A: Yes.

Q: And during the time when Michel was giving you this advice or you were reporting back to him, did he indicate to you that it was important that you tell the same story so that he doesn't get hurt or you don't get hurt in the stories that you tell, get yourself involved with the police?

A: Yes.

Q: Now, during 1970 and 1971, I think my brother Kadish asked you about this, you were asked some questions about income tax, is that right? I think you said you met Mr. Mastantuono in March of 1970, is that correct?

A: Yes.

Q: And from that point on, that you met him, you were doing a lot of traveling with him, were you not?

A: Traveling?

Q: Yes. You know, going to Europe . . .

A: Yes.

Q: Can you estimate for us, between March of 1970 and October of 1971, when Michel was arrested, how many trips you made to Europe with him?

A: I wouldn't be able to answer that unless I had my tickets and my ex-passport.

Q: With the Court's permission, could you give us an approximate idea of the total number? Ten? Twenty? Thirty?

A: Oh, no, no. Two or three, I guess. You cannot go there many times.

Q: And on this approximate three, how long would you stay each time, if you remember?

A: It could go in between two weeks to a month.

Q: And included within this three trips to Europe would be the trip you were telling us about to the Canary Islands?

A: I don't know if it was at that time. But if it is at that time, yes.

Q: In addition to that you made a number of trips to New York with him?

A: Yes.

Q: And during these trips to New York, approximately — withdrawn.

Can you tell us approximately how many trips you made to New
York?

The Court: Before she was arrested?

Mr. Newman: Of course.

A: Before I was arrested?

Q: Between March of '70 and up to October of '71, Miss Ouimet.

A: Oh, I don't know, four, five, six times.

Q: And can you tell us approximately how long you would stay on
each trip?

A: We were not very much staying long here. Three to four days
maximum.

Q: I'm sorry. Had you finished your answer?

A: Yes.

Q: And during the same period of time you also made a trip to Florida,
you told us about.

A: Yes, Miami.

Q: Did you make any trips any other places during that period of time
from March '70 to October '71?

A: To other places than . . .

Q: To other places outside of Montreal.

A: I guess not, no.

Q: Did you and Michel go away on any vacations during this period of
time other than what you've told us about?

A: There would be Marseilles. Yes, there would be Marseilles, where
we were on vacations. But I don't recall going on vacation with
him, unless that one trip that was obvious because of my son
being with us, in Canary Islands.

Q: Is it therefore fair to say that between March of '70, once you met
Michel, and October of '71, when he was arrested, most of your
time was really spent with him and traveling with him and on
behalf of his errands rather than working on your business? Is
that a fair statement?

A: Yes.

Q: So that most of your income during this period of time would be
moneys you got from Michel or moneys you got paid yourself
from these various — I use the word "errands" again, but I take
that away — from the various trips that you made or things that
you did?

A: I was making a lot of money on my work because when I was in
Montreal I was always working.

The Court: Apparently she didn't understand you.

Mr. Newman: I don't think so, Judge. I think I had better go back.

Q: Let us start here. During this period from March of '70 to approximately October of '71, okay? We are talking about a little more than — we are talking about 17 or 18 months, something like that.

A: From the moment I met Michel to the moment I was arrested.

Q: That's correct.

A: Okay.

Q: You told us about trips that you made to Europe with him lasting approximately three weeks sometimes, sometimes a month.

A: Yes.

Q: You told us about a couple of trips to New York which didn't last too long.

A: Yes.

Q: A trip to Miami; remember that?

A: Yes.

Q: What I'm trying to find out from you is, once you met him, until he got arrested, was most of your time spent with him and the things that he was doing?

A: Most of the time I was staying — well, when he was traveling, I was going with him. And when we were in Montreal, I was working here. We made a lot, of course, of trips together, but altogether I stayed more in Montreal than traveling with him.

Q: While you were in Montreal, did you do things for him in connection with his business?

A: No.

Q: So it was mainly on these trips that you did this for him.

A: Yes.

Q: Did he have you meet people for him in Montreal or pick up money or packages or things like that for him in Montreal?

A: No. Money, I don't know. Well, yes. I remember that sometimes he used to give me some money, some American money — some Canadian and have me change it in American money, I guess, or vice versa. I don't remember.

Q: Big sums?

A: A thousand dollars. He wanted to have bills of one thousand, I remember. I don't remember how many thousands, but I remember that I went to various banks because not all of the banks had that amount of money — well, that . . .

Q: Can you estimate for us how many times he had you do that for him, that work?

A: About two times, I guess.

Q: Now, if I understood you correctly, on cross examination by one of my colleagues you acknowledged that you were involved in four cars coming in to the United States?

A: Yes.

Q: Did anybody ever tell you, prior to your pleading guilty, how much time you faced in jail if you were convicted of your involvement in those four cars?

A: Well, put that in other words because I don't really understand.

Q: I think you told one of my colleagues that you pled guilty.

A: Yes.

Q: I think maybe you told it to Mr.Nesland, as a matter of fact.

A: Um-hum.

Q: Before you pled guilty, did anybody, any Government agent or prosecutor, tell you, "Miss Ouimet, you face so many years in jail if you are convicted for these four cars that you helped bring into the United States"?

A: Yes.

Q: Did they tell you a specific amount of time that you faced in jail if you are convicted?

A: They told me that every charge could face — sometimes they were telling me seven years, sometimes twenty years. What exactly, I don't know.

The Court: Do you have any recollection of the greatest total of years you ever thought?

The Witness: Well, I think that I might have stayed there a hundred years.

The Court: A long time, in other words.

Mr. Newman: In one lifetime.

A: (*Continuing*) But again they were saying, you know, sometimes you can put all the twenty years together — I don't know how it would come to that — or I could have them one after the other.

Q: Did they use words like "concurrently" or "consecutive"? Does that ring a bell?

A: That's it.

Q: While Michel was in jail, whether in the United States or in Canada, did he ever write any letters to you?

A: Sometimes.

Q: Did you save any of those letters?

A: When he was arrested?

Q: Yes.

The Court: After he was arrested?

Mr. Newman: Yes, sir.

A: Yes, I saved them.

Q: Were the letters in French or were they in English?

A: Approximately in French.

Q: And do you happen to have any of them with you?

A: No. I was not asked to bring them. Otherwise I would.

Q: Have you ever turned any of those letters over to any governmental agency, any prosecutor in the United States or in Canada?

A: No.

Mr. Newman: Would your Honor bear with me for a minute, please?

The Court: Let me ask you a question. On television and on radio in Montreal, are you in the English language or in the French language?

The Witness: French. I am not doing too well with my English?

The Court: No, no.

Q: You are doing fine, so well, we are getting an inferiority complex. Talking about this Cadillac incident, did Michel tell you that at first he thought these men in these Cadillacs were policemen?

A: No, he never referred them as policemen.

Q: Now, prior to your coming today, when is the last time you met Michel in person and talked to him? I know you saw him here in the building.

A: Yes.

Q: Before that, when is the last time that you met with him and spoke with him about the facts of these cases?

A: I know I met him a lot lately. But I was not allowed to talk to him on the case. But I would say that before his wedding — before his wedding. I remember that, yes.

Q: I don't want to rub salt in the wound, but —

The Court: Do you remember the date of that?

Mr. Newman: Sorry. I didn't hear that question.

The Court: I asked her if she remembered the date of the wedding.

The Witness; No.

Mr. Newman: That is just about what I was going to ask.

Q: Can you give me an approximate idea about when it was?

A: I guess he got married around May. When he got out. I don't know what specific day, but about a month later he was married, and that was it.

Q: We were told "about March or April."

A: Yes; right after he got out of prison.

Q: And then right after he got out, did you see him?

A: Yes.

Q: And did you discuss anything about these cases?

A: Well, we discussed that everything was over, because he had to testify and he couldn't hide anything and he was working for the Government, he said, and everything had to be — I had to tell the truth, that no one could do anything about it, that there was too many testimonies, and that was life, he did what he could and I should do the same.

Q: Did he tell you or give you any idea of how he was going to testify?

A: For the Government.

Q: No. Aside from that, did he like say, "I am going to say this, for example, about the Galaxie."?

A: No, he never.

Q: Or "I am going to say this about the Barracuda."?

A: No.

Q: At any time while he was cooperating with the Government, did he indicate to you and say to you, "Danielle, this is how I am going to testify about the Citroen. This is how I am going to testify about the station wagon."?

A: No, not after.

Q: Not after. Just before.

A: Before.

Q: Do you remember, when he told you about these Cadillacs, approximately when it was that he told you about them?

A: Not too far after I learned about his job, what he was doing.

Q: You mean the heroin trafficking that he was doing?

A: Yes.

Q: And from time to time, if you can tell us, Miss Ouimet, would he say things to you about not cooperating, not testifying, and tell you that you can get killed or he can get killed, did you get the feeling, to sort of keep you in line so you wouldn't go tell the police anything?

A: Oh, yes, many times.

Q: I beg pardon?

A: Many times.

Mr. Newman: Nothing further of this lady.

Cross Examination by Mr. Garland:

Q: When was it that you received the information that someone had been watching Michel?

A: As I told you before, probably before February '71, because I knew about the second — the second case, the case right after my car. So I couldn't put a date, a specific date on when I learned about that, but was right after my car and before the next one.

Q: So it was after your car.

A: After my car, yes.

Q: Now, when you were driving from Biarritz to Paris, how long did that trip take?

A: Thirteen hours.

Q: Biarritz is in the southeastern corner?

A: About ten minutes from the border of Spain, near the water.

Q: And during the course of that trip did you complain about any odors in the automobile?

A: I don't recall that. I know that — excuse me. I know that we've talked about that after, when I was questioned, you know, by the agents and everything. But I don't recall, myself . . .

Q: You didn't smell any glue.

A: I don't recall that, saying that then.

Q: All right. Now, the letters that were just mentioned, did they describe in any way what you should say to any of the authorities, the letters that you received from Michel? Or were they on other matters?

A: Can you rephrase that?

Q: Yes. The letters you received . . .

The Court: The letters that he wrote you from jail that you didn't bring with you, he wants to know did they have anything to do with what you were to say or were they on other matters?

The Witness: Well, no. He would never mostly talking about that, although if I go through them, sometimes I might make statements on the way — on what he said or . . .

Q: What his position was?

A: How he would protect me, saying "Don't be afraid. Everything is going to be okay. Don't forget that I'm behind you," all those kinds of things.

Q: Did he ever in those letters refer to what his position as to what your position was?

A: No, never. He knew that his letter was read. So probably he was not taking any chances.

Q: Now, at the time the Citroen came in to Montreal, you went to pick it up, did you not?

A: Yes, I did.

Q: And when you got back, you related the fact that you had had an argument with the Customs people because it was damaged.

A: Yes.

Q: And . . .

A: Fight, I have to say.

Q: Excuse me?

A: I fight, I can even say.

Q: You had a fight with Customs authorities?

A: Yes.

Q: And Michel then had a fight with you about the fact that you had had a fight with them, didn't he?

A: No. First of all, he was sore, and then he found it very funny.

Q: Maybe I used the wrong word. He was emphatic about what you had done, somewhat, wasn't he?

A: Well, as far as I can recall, when I arrived and I said, "The car is down there," he said, "What?"

I said, "Yes."

He said, "You could have had an accident."

I said, "It doesn't matter. The fenders are completely crushed. So another one . . ."

And he said, "What happened?"

I said, "Well, they told me that they have to lift the car up on the fenders, you know, by hooks, and the fenders were crushed there because probably the thing went up too fast, I don't know."

So he asked if the damages were very bad.

I said, "Come and see it. It is downstairs."

And we did.

The Court: He is not referring to that. He is referring to the fact that you told us that you had an argument with Customs.

The Witness: Oh, yes.

The Court: Did Michel say anything to you about that argument with Customs which you had?

Q: Did he say, "You're crazy"?

A: Probably used words similar to that.

Q: All right. Before you went over to Customs, did he give you some instructions?

A: No, not specially; just to take care of not having an accident with it, because I didn't know how to drive a semi-automatic. He showed me that in Brussels. When he came to Brussels to show me the car, he showed me how to maneuver it. But I never touched it after.

Q: Perhaps you didn't understand my questions. Did he give you any instructions about what you should do . . .

A: If they were asking me questions?

Q: Yes, about picking up the car.

A: No.

Q: Do you think your recollection is fairly clear on that?

A: Well, he told me to bring it to a parking lot and leave it there.

Q: Did he tell you, "If in one hour you have not called me, then just give me one or two hours time and then you can say that it was me who had that car, who had done that with the car."? Did he tell you that?

A: I don't recall.

Q: During the course of your discussions with Michel, during the period of time after he was arrested up until the last time you dis-

cussed matters with him as to what he was going to do, it had
been the position that you all had arrived at that he would always
say that you didn't know there was anything in the car when it
arrived in Montreal and when it crossed the Canadian border.

A: From the moment he was arrested?

Q: Yes, from the time he was arrested.

A: Arrested, yes.

Q: Until the time you had had your last conversation with him.

A: Yes.

Q: Up until that time, it had always been the position, in the many
discussions you all had had, that he would say you knew nothing
about heroin being in the car when it arrived in Montreal?

A: Yes.

Q: Or when it arrived across the border.

A: Yes.

Q: And that had been the position you had taken.

A: Yes.

Q: And that is the position you have still taken, isn't it?

A: Not now.

Q: Excuse me?

A: Not now. I'm not taking that position.

Q: All right. Is it your testimony now that you knew heroin was in
there when you went to pick up the car?

A: My testimony is that I knew that there was something going on
but I didn't know then exactly that there was heroin in there.

Q: All right. And you had discussed the fact that there was something
in the car before you went to the harbor.

A: Yes.

Q: Is that correct?

A: Yes.

Q: And you knew there was something in the car before it came
across the American border?

A: Yes.

Q: And when you first related your information about it, you said
you knew there was something in there but you didn't know
what it was.

A: Yes.

Q: And you recall no instructions he gave you about the harbor.

A: No.

Mr. Garland: That's all. Thank you.

Mr. Newman: Your Honor, before my redirect, may we have a short
side bar for a moment?

The Court: Yes.

(At the side bar.)

The Court: First I'd like to find out if there is going to be any redirect.

Mr. Nesland: I have one or two questions, but I would like to talk to her ahead of time.

Mr. Newman: What I wanted to know, Judge, is to ask your Honor to have this young lady send whatever letters she has from Mastantuono to Mr. Nesland, and I particularly would like her to send any of the pictures that she took at Elgin Air Force Base to Mr. Nesland.

The Court: Do you have any objection to that?

Mr. Nesland: No objection.

Mr. Kadish: I had drawn up a subpoena, while she was testifying, for that.

Mr. Newman: Not in front of the jury.

The Court: Not in front of the jury. Okay. Will you take care of that?

Mr. Nesland: Sure. I don't want another one of those subpoenas I can't read. You have to interpret them for everybody. I can't read those.

The Court: Let him do whatever he wants. Do you want a brief recess?

Mr. Kadish: One other thing. As long as you are talking about . . .

The Court: We are going to have a recess.

(In open court.)

The Court: Ladies and gentlemen, a brief recess, ten minutes.

(The jury left the courtroom.)

The Court: Do you want the witness instructed in the presence of counsel or in the absence of counsel what you want to do?

Mr. Nesland: If he wants to serve that subpoena, your Honor, he can serve it on her. I'm not going to interpret any more of those subpoenas. I can't read them.

Mr. Kadish: Fine. I'll read it into the record so there is no problem. "Letters rogatory given to either a representative of the United States or representatives of any foreign nation." That is easy enough.

The Court: I am going to have her in. Ask her to come back.

Mr. Kadish: That's easy. Just make it a matter of record what we are asking her for.

(Pause.)

The Court: Miss Ouimet, all that is involved is that the defendants' lawyers would like you to send them, not to them but to Mr. Nesland, certain documents. Just listen to the list.

The Witness: Yes. Can I have a pencil?

The Court: Sure. In the first place, all letters that you got.

The Witness: You are getting personal.

Mr. Kadish: And the pictures at Elgin, the pictures that you had mentioned that you had taken.

The Court: Anything he sent you from jail.

Mr. Newman: No, no. These pictures she took herself.

The Court: Oh, the pictures you took yourself.

The Witness: Wait a minute. I have a problem translating. From Elgin.

Mr. Kadish: Correspondence from Elgin and the pictures that you took at Elgin.

The Witness: You need the correspondence from here too, New York?

Mr. Kadish: I suppose all correspondence with him.

The Witness: Okay.

Mr. Kadish: And then I believe you mentioned in your testimony a letter rogatory, or some statement you had given for the Canadian police.

The Witness: But I don't have that. They kept it.

Mr. Kadish: All right. I make that request. If you don't have a copy, you don't have it.

The Witness: They didn't want to give me one. I have to specify that I refused to sign it because there was at the time — now it is the truth, but at the time I said that there was wrong transcription from English to French.

Mr. Kadish: Okay. And then any correspondence between you and representatives of the United States Attorney's office or any Canadian authorities relating to this case, if there is any.

The Witness: I don't think there is any. I think I wrote once a letter to Mr. Boulad, but it had only in regards to what I should bring to Michel or whatever.

Mr. Kadish: If you would just be kind enough to make a note of that.

The Witness: I don't have it. Okay.

Mr. Kadish: Letters between you and the U.S. Attorney's office or any official in Canada about any facts that might relate to this case.

The Witness: Okay. I don't know if I have them.

Mr. Kadish: And just another general category: Any other statements that you may have made to any agent or official of either Canada, France or the United States.

The Witness: I don't have that.

Mr. Newman: One other thing, if I might, Judge: If the lady has any of those tickets that she was talking about for those trips that she made with Mastantuono to Europe.

The Witness: I guess that's — I'll look for them, but I guess the RCMP has a few of them. Do you need my ex-passport, like one that was expired? So I still have it at home.

Mr. Newman: If we could. That would show the trips that you made.

The Witness: Yes. They stamp it.

Mr. Newman: If you would.

The Court: Your expired passport.

The Witness: Yes.

The Court: Okay. Fine. Your current passport wouldn't show anything relative to this case.

The Witness: No.

The Court: Your expired passport.

Mr. Kadish: And, if you'll be kind enough, when you send that material, enclose whatever copying costs you have or your postage. We are obligated to pay it.

The Witness: There is a problem. There is a strike in Canada.

Mr. Nesland: That's true. There is a mail strike.

The Court: Then you can't mail anything.

Mr. Kadish: We might be able to put it on an airplane.

The Court: How do you do that?

Mr. Kadish: Delta flies to . . .

The Witness: Maybe give it to the RCMP agent that will bring it here, if there is one coming.

Mr.Nesland: There is none coming.

The Court: There must be ways of getting . . .

Mr. Nesland: There is some airmail delivery. I don't mean postage. I mean package deliveries like we have here in the United States.

The Court: Defense counsel will find out how it will be done, tell Mr. Nesland, and Mr. Nesland will telephone the witness and she will do whatever he says.

Mr. Naden: Greyhound takes freight from Montreal.

The Court: Let's have no more discussion. Defense counsel will tell Mr. Nesland how they want it done and he will phone the witness and it will be done. Let's not have any more discussion on the record.

The Witness: Yes, because I would like to give it to someone to make sure it is going to come to him.

The Court: That's right.

Mr. Newman: One other thing. If she has any of the tickets when she traveled down to Elgin Air Force Base.

The Court: Do you have that?

The Witness: I guess I have. I will check. I keep them all, usually.

Mr. Newman: Okay. Fine.

The Court: All right. Are you ready for redirect?

Mr. Nesland: I am ready to talk to her.

The Court: I'll see you in five minutes.

(Recess.)

(Jury present.)

The Court: Proceed.

Redirect Examination by Mr. Nesland:

Q: When you went to Miami, were you told anything about the man that you were to meet?

A: No.

Q: Were you told by anyone, Michel Mastantuono, Felix Rosso, Paul Graziani, Joseph Arioli or anybody else, that he was a buyer?

A: No.

Mr. Nesland: No questions.

Mr. Kadish: May we just have a moment?

(Pause.)

Recross Examination by Mr. Kadish:

Q: Just prior to coming back into the courtroom, did you just have a brief discussion with Mr. Nesland about that subject matter we discussed?

A: He asked me those two questions and that's all.

Mr. Kadish: No further questions.

Recross Examination by Mr. Naden:

Q: This time that you went to Miami, were you aware that Michel had the station wagon and the heroin and had problems disposing of the heroin?

A: Yes.

Q: And the reason that Felix Rosso went to Miami was to find a way to dispose of the heroin in the United States? Isn't that so?

A: I didn't know about that.

Q: But you did know that in that period of time they were having a discussion about getting rid of the heroin.

A: Yes.

Mr. Naden: Nothing further.

Mr. Newman: I have no questions.

Mr. Garland: No questions.

The Court: You are excused.

(Witness excused.)

SENTENCE OF DANIELLE OUIMET

UNITED STATES DISTRICT COURT
SOUTHERN DISTRICT OF NEW YORK
UNITED STATES OF AMERICA,

vs.

DANIELLE OUIMET,
DEFENDANT

Before: Hon. Whitman Knapp,

District Judge
New York, March 18, 1976
Room 519 - 9:30 a.m.

APPEARANCES

For the Prosecution: Robert B. Fiske, Jr., Esq.,

United States Attorney for the
Southern District of New
York, represented by James
Nesland, Esq., Assistant United
States Attorney

For the Defense: John Gross, Esq.,

Attorney

The Court: Good morning, ladies and gentlemen.

Mr. Nesland: Good morning, your Honor.

The Clerk: United States of America v. Danielle Ouimet for sentence. Is the Government ready?

Mr. Nesland: Government ready.

The Clerk: Defendant ready?

Mr. Gross: John Gross appearing for the defendant, your Honor. Defendant is ready.

The Court: Does the Government have any comments?

Mr. Nesland: Yes, I do, your Honor. I have a few comments that I'd like to make. I do not intend to go through the involvement of Miss Ouimet in the transactions about what your Honor heard the testimony, and there is no reason to do that. I do want to point out to your Honor since I think it is necessary from my point of view to point out the significance of her testimony in the case she testified in.

The Court: I am pretty well aware of that too.

Mr. Nesland: I'd like to point out what I thought to be significant. I want to point out that obviously the direct impact of her testimony was of limited value. In other words, she didn't identify any of the defendants on trial, although obviously she would be available to testify against any one of the defendants that she could identify, meaning the French defendants that were involved up in Canada and coming into the United States, but, of course, the American defendants she did not know, had no contact with because of the limited involvement she had, and therefore her testimony was not directly against them.

The Court: Her testimony is most important in fortifying the credibility.

Mr. Nesland: I think in two ways, your Honor. As I was preparing for the trial it occurred to me that the strongest defense attacking the credibility of Mr. Mastantuono would be to dispute the fact that the Fiat transaction and the Citroen transaction ever occurred, and the reason that the defense could have used a tactic like that would have been that there was no other witness to those transactions, although Berdin and Preiss could have testified about the two transactions in which the Stassis were not involved, they could not testify about the two that they were involved in, and Mastantuono because Berdin and Preiss were not involved, had never been indicted for those two transactions, so it occurred to me that a significant defense or a possible defense could have been that those transactions never occurred but were made up by Mastantuono in order to serve his own ends, and for that reason I thought it was important to have Danielle's testimony with respect to those two transactions to corroborate the fact that they occurred in the first instance, and of course the second point was what your Honor pointed out, was to corroborate Mastantuono especially in light of his perjury which was admitted on the stand, and to point out that as he said it was his devotion to Danielle Ouimet that made him perjure himself on those transactions, and I think your Honor found the trial, and I think it was pretty clear to the jury, that in fact that was why he perjured himself, and her testimony gave flesh and blood to the rationale that he had for perjuring himself prior to trial and for being truthful at the trial.

The Court: And also as I recollect it she kept a lot of documentation that wouldn't have been otherwise available.

Mr. Nesland: That is correct, she had, and obviously he never would have and had he known she was keeping it, I can rest assure that he would have destroyed it. When he was arrested most of it was taken from her, and then she produced a number of documents after she began cooperating with me in 1975.

    The second thing I'd like to point out, and I do this because we did it with respect to the defendants that you have just sentenced, the two Stassis and Sorenson. I'd like to point out to your Honor the sentences of those who were involved in this transaction or in this scheme, and I am limiting it to those that cooperated with the Government, and I point out first of all Michel Mastantuono who was the prime courier got five years.

The Court: Who got five years?

Mr. Nesland: Roger Preiss who was another prime courier got three years.

The Court: Did he testify before me?

Mr. Nesland: Yes he did. He didn't testify before you. I am pointing out those in this entire French connection here.

The Court: I didn't remember.

Mr. Nesland: Richard Berdin who did not testify before your Honor received three years for cooperating with the Government. Tony Verzino, who did testify before your Honor, received three years to life in the State and no federal charges were brought against him as a result of his cooperation.

The Court: That was part of the deal, I take it?

Mr. Nesland: That was part of the deal with Tony Verzino. In addition, Tony Verzino's wife who you heard much about during the trial who actually received the narcotics with Bubbie Sorenson and distributed some of it, at least that part of the end of Verzino and Perna. Her case was entirely dismissed in the State. She has in effect been dismissed.

The Court: That was part of the deal also?

Mr. Nesland: Part of the deal with Tony Verzino, right, and although she cooperated she never did testify. Only Verzino has testified. And likewise with Mr. Perna, he has not been sentenced yet, but his wife has been dismissed as a result of his cooperation, and as your Honor remembers, she was distributing the narcotics on the Perna-Verzino end that was received through these shipments, and the case against her, the federal case against her has been dismissed, and the State does not intend to prosecute her, and, of course, that leaves Perna's and Verzino's wife. Both have been dismissed and Joseph Condello testified before your Honor. All charges against him have been dismissed, and I think I just wanted to highlight that for your Honor to take into consideration in sentencing Miss Ouimet.

The Court: Condello got no sentence?

Mr. Nesland: That is correct. All charges against him were dismissed.

The Court: Was that part of the deal?

Mr. Nesland: It was part of it with Joseph Condello.

The Court: That was the one that was made by Newark. It was subject to some discussion.

Mr. Nesland: He was cooperating at the time he began to tell about our case, and therefore no federal charges were brought against him, and therefore he has all of his charges dismissed other than a Hudson County numbers charge and I don't know — I know they are moving to dismiss that, but whether or not it's been dismissed, I don't know, and I think that your Honor should consider those sentences and those dismissals in determining what sentence to impose on Danielle Ouimet, and also to consider the significance of her testimony in the two respects that I have just outlined, and the Government would ask that you do so, and we will leave it in your hands.

The Court: What about these Frenchmen that she could have testified about? They have never been arrested?

Mr. Nesland: Some of them have not been arrested. Some of them have been arrested and pled guilty in France, and I don't know what the sentences are.

The Court: She was never called upon to testify?

Mr. Nesland: She hasn't been called upon to testify as yet that I know. She may be able to clarify if she has or not. As far as I know she has not been called upon to testify, and I think at least two or three of those are still fugitives, and no one knows where they are. Thank you.

Mr. Gross: Your Honor, Danielle Ouimet is a young woman who some six years ago had a minor involvement in an illegal activity. Her involvement occurred because she was young, and she let an overbearing, revolting boyfriend lead her into this. As a result she filed for bankruptcy. She was treated by a psychiatrist for depression. Her salary dropped from $50,000 a year to now $250 a week, and her mother had a heart attack as a result of the publicity that was received in Canada. For the last six years obviously she has had no involvement in anything illegal, immoral or anything that touched anything near that. In fact, she's been a productive Canadian citizen, and I respectfully submit, your Honor, that some six years after she made a mistake, it wouldn't serve anybody's interest to take her from Canada and now put her into an American jail. She came down here and testified voluntarily. She could have remained in Canada, your Honor, and tried to do whatever she thought she could do there, but she came down here and testified for the Government voluntarily.

She testified against some major narcotics traffickers whom she knew at the time were involved in organized crime, and she knew at the time because I told her that those people and their friends could at any time kill her for the rest of her life as a result of her testimony.

In fact, there are now fugitives still around who know that she could be a potential witness, and as a result, your Honor, she frankly has to live with the knowledge that at any time any one of these people or any one of their friends can kill her. These are the problems that she undertook by coming here voluntarily to testify in a major narcotics case.

Your Honor, she suffered tremendously. As I say, she is bankrupt. Her mother had a heart attack. Hopefully she will be able to continue making a minimum salary, but her career is absolutely destroyed, and I respectfully submit that since she assisted the government in every way that Mr. Nesland has said, and since this crime happened some six years ago at a time that she was very young, and since her involvement was minor, that no one's interest, your Honor, I respectfully would submit, would be served by now taking her from Canada, and putting her in jail. Thank you.

The Court: Mr. Nesland, under the treaties with Canada could she have been extradited?

Mr. Nesland: She could have, your Honor. I believe that Canada is one of the only countries that we have an extradition treaty which allows us to have reciprocal extradition of one's own nationals. I think it is about the only treaty that allows it. Maybe England does, too, but I am not sure. I know Canada does.

The Court: And what, if any, are your views on the danger in which Miss Ouimet now is under?

Mr. Nesland: I would submit, your Honor, that to the extent the fugitives exist, and I know that there are at least two if not more, they obviously pose a risk to Miss Ouimet because she can testify against them. As your Honor remembers in the Fiat transaction she was involved directly with each one of those French nationals who were importing the heroin in the Fiat. Felix Rosso, Paul Graziani, Joseph Signoli, and I believe that was the three that were involved in that transaction. She also has the testimony that she could give against Cardon whose car it was that was used, so you have four, and I believe one or two of those are still fugitives.

The Court: We don't know if they are alive or not?

Mr. Nesland: No.

The Court: Have we ever identified, has the Government ever identified the persons she met in Florida?

Mr. Nesland: No. Obviously.

The Court: She doesn't know who he was either, does she?

Mr. Nesland: She has identified a photograph of the person that she thinks it was, and that person so far as known is nowhere to be found, and whether or not he poses a risk, depends upon whether or not he knows that he's been identified, and it came out in a trial, the photograph, the name that was picked out by her, but other than that I don't believe it is public knowledge.

Mr. Gross: Your Honor, may I just impose on the Court for a moment. It is not only the fugitives who are still in existence who pose a threat. I as an Assistant, and I can tell you from some unfortunate experiences that people who testify were later killed even though the people against whom they testified were still in jail because their friends decided to make things right in their own venal minds.

The Court: Miss Ouimet, do you want to say anything?

The Defendant: Yes. I don't know what to say. I don't know where to start. I know it's been so long. It's been now six years.

When I met Michel I possibly have no excuse to follow except, well, no legal excuse to have knowingly that he was doing that kind of thing, to accept it, except that it looks terrible out on paper, but you have to live it to really know. You have to know that first of all I was loving that man, and secondly he was holding me by saying that I could be killed if I was talking. He was never, never asking me if I was willing to do a thing. He was saying to me, "You are coming with me," and I couldn't say yes. I couldn't say no. I just had to follow. As my lawyer was saying, you do things probably mostly because you are afraid and you don't know what to expect.

I did meet some people in New York. You never know if somebody was going to strike you in the back. I was following Michel because he was always saying I would be safe with him, and of course at that age and with that fear you follow. You don't know, but you follow, and you try to get out of it the more you can.

Michel in some way, although I don't want to protect him, but Michel in some way protected me by not letting me know some people here in New York. That's why I couldn't testify more. I did probably the best.

When Michel was arrested I realized what was to be done was to talk and to testify. I could have stayed in Montreal and asked for protection because Michel brought me in that business, but I guess I have lost it and that was it.

As a result of the arrest of Michel I would like to know, your Honor, have you received my report because I wrote a report in French and gave you the names.

The Court: My law clerk heard the whole tape, and I heard parts of it, and she told me what was in the part I didn't hear.

The Defendant: Many, many things happened to me since then, and I guess I didn't have a peaceful life since then. I received some anonymous phone calls saying that my life was in danger if I was talking.

Actually I guess Mr. Nesland doesn't know it, but I did testify for France. The RCMP received a paper of my testimony here in New York, and they asked me to read it back, to sign it, and they sent it in France so it was like a testimony.

Mr. Nesland: I didn't know that.

The Court: I suppose you don't know whether they can use that in court or not?

The Defendant: Oh, yes. They can. They can use it in court. It was to be used in court against the whole French files, the guys I met.

You have also to realize that when Michel was presenting me these people he was always presenting me these people as agents, agents for show business people. One was a decorator, and later I found out that they weren't involved in that business.

Of course, I was not going to check everyone that was coming in the house and everyone that was coming to see Michel. Some of them were friends. I was mostly aware that if I was going to the police, you don't know . . .

Actually right now in Montreal just to give you proof there has been not a trial, but we call that La Ceco Commission. I don't know if you heard about that. It's everyone in Montreal that's been involved in a certain field that are into — and most of them have been in the Mafia business, an illegal business. All of those that have talked to that Commission now are being killed.

Where is justice if you cannot be in front of the justice to try to say something, and then you don't know in the street what can happen to you, and I didn't know at the time what the police was going to make, and I had a name. I didn't want to have front page "Miss Ouimet is giving up some big people. Maybe she is involved. Maybe she is not. The car was full." All kinds of things like that, so the best thing you think of is just let things happen. If you see a way out one day, you get out of it, and if you can't you just wait for the justice to do it, and when the justice came, I just came here, and I didn't at one time try to get out of it, never, never.

I faced it for four years, I guess very toughly because a lot of things happened in my personal life. I had a lot of problems in finding back my work. Of course, it seems a little bit pretentious to say that I am very well known over there, but it is a fact, and that's why there is a lot of publicity on that.

Michel's case was not Michel's case. It was my case, and my name was on every piece of paper possible. They were always saying that I was involved. They were not talking about Michel. The result, where there was people insulting me on the street, stopping my parents. My father lost mostly all of his jobs because he was an appraiser and it involved cars, so they thought that he was in that business.

After a year of that I had to go to the psychiatrist because I couldn't take it any more. I was getting completely dizzy about the whole thing. I felt guilty because I didn't go to the police and at the same time I felt that probably I would have got killed. I really did not know what to do.

I cannot see the end of it, and to show you how much it is still on not too long ago I was in a reception, and someone jumped on me.

The Court: You mentioned that in your tape. I didn't quite understand what happened.

The Defendant: I was in a reception, at a cocktail reception for a book coming out, and someone came to me.

The Court: Your book or somebody else's?

The Defendant: Yes, my book. Someone came to me, and he said to me, "You are writing well."

I said, "Thank you, sir." I didn't know that he was going to be mad or sick or something like that. He said, "You are writing so well that I am going to jump at your neck," and he jumped at me, and he said, "You are a stool. You are a stool. I am going to choke you." I was petrified. It is really something that you — and I didn't want anyone to tell that because of my parents. My mother had a lot of problems with her heart not too long ago.

The Court: Is that book about this case?

The Defendant: Yes. I had to explain because they were really giving it to me very, very badly. They were doing the whole story as if I was the chief of the big gang, and I was doing it.

The Court: It is not a book by you, it is a book by someone else?

The Defendant: Yes, that wrote it on me.

The Court: You authorized it?

The Defendant: Yes. I didn't hide the facts. I did say what happened, but I told of my life with Michel. I told of my involvement.

The Court: The author, whoever he is, thought he would sell more books talking about you than talking about Michel?

The Defendant: Of course, and I heard Michel is doing a book too.

The Court: Do you get royalties on this book?

The Defendant: Five cents a book, which is when you consider that in Canada there are six million people and three-quarters of it is English and that don't know me, that leaves me if it is a big success, it will be about 15,000 copies. It is just to say that they give me a little something, but I had to explain it because my parents cannot face it any more.

My brother in school has to fight many times to try to protect me. I heard that one day he got violent over a guy who said that I was a stool and a smuggler. My brother mostly couldn't take it so he decided to take some studies in the U.S.A. and get out of the city. As soon as he was presenting himself somewhere and they were knowing that he was from my family, my brother, they were not exactly giving. — I cannot prove it, but it is obvious. He has a lot of talent, and he could never find a job, you know, never.

My sister Judith had a lot of problems. She tried to open a school. Now she has it, but at that time it was tough for her.

I have lost a lot of commercial credibility because the image I lost all of what can be like personal appearances on TV. I have friends that come to me and say, "Well, I know you are a good girl, that you have suffered a lot, but we cannot do anything. You have to let the time pass," but to let the time pass, I have things to pay.

Right now I am very, very low. I am probably going to lose everything because of a bankruptcy of a problem of Michel again. It's a story that we wanted to put some money on a building, and I bought the land. It was the land of my grandfather. My mother was crying on the fact that his father was losing his land, and he was brought up here, and everything, and no one had money, so I bought the land, but there was a stipulation saying that I had to build a house in two years, so everything was okay because I had a certain amount of money, cash down for the house, but then Michel got arrested, and I gave all the money to the lawyers. That's another problem. And then what happened is that I didn't have any cash down, and I still had the contract, and I couldn't sell the land all alone, so I did build a house with personal loans and a company that financed my house. What happened is that after a while since I didn't have any cash, it cost me a lot from my pocket, and I was paying and paying for the electricity, the gas, whatever, just everything because I didn't put any cash down.

On the result of that came a time where they came to me and they asked me for $5,000 for the taxes. I couldn't pay because at that time I didn't have any work. I didn't have any money left so they took away my house for the first mortgage, but I had to face two banks and $20,000 loan, personal loans. As a result of that, I tried to pay them for about five months. I went as far as five months, but now I have no strictly no work. Before I had commercials that were passing in other cities and were paying me and I was paying the apartment, the building, but now there is nothing coming on. They don't take back the commercials.

The Court: All you have now is your radio program?

The Defendant: The radio program, that's the only thing I have left, the only thing I have left, and I am not allowed to talk about anything. I have to just present records.

The Court: You have to do what?

The Defendant: I just have to present records. Before I used to talk and say things. Another thing that happened to me that was very, well, painful and still is, were the lawyers. One of them — first of all you know if you heard the tape that I had four lawyers. The first one took all the money that Michel had left in the house and I. We both put our money together. How much I had, how much he had, I don't know. We never really counted it, and all together it was about $35,000. From every transaction Michel had more money than that.

At one time Michel told me, "Now you know that you cannot talk because they are going to put you in jail," and things like that, and he was making me much afraid of the fact that if I could talk I could have more and more problems coming up, not only from the justice, but from his friends, and then he said to me, "The only way that they can attack you is that your car was filled up and there is some — you can see some joints inside," and he told me, "Well, I don't know what to do with that car, but tell your lawyer."

The Court: You testified about that at the trial.

The Defendant: Yes, and now the lawyer right now is doing a lot of problems to me. He is writing me some letters saying it is terrible how much I have been attacked lately, and that he would like to see me, but I know why he wants to see me. He's known to be something quite tough, so on that part I am quite afraid too.

I hope that what I am telling you won't go to Canada because otherwise, even the guy from the La Presse, which is the biggest newspaper in Montreal, who related the fact that my car — it was asked for my car to be stolen, didn't tell on La Presse the name of the lawyer. He was afraid himself, although he was not afraid of saying the whole thing, the whole story about me, and I think I have lost about everything.

I have kept my parents, of course, but they are very, very low right now. My mother is probably going to have a depression because my father is probably going to die within a year. He is very, very sick, and he is throwing up blood most of the time.

The family situation, the monetary situation, the personal situations are a complete catastrophe so if I can plead for mercy, I have nothing in front of me.

I would like to have right now a little bit of good time because I guess I couldn't get out of it then, and if I can't now, I don't know what to do. That's about it. Thank you.

The Court: Does the Government have any further comment?

Mr. Nesland: No, your Honor.

The Court: Miss Ouimet, this is a very difficult situation. One thing, unfortunately I can't characterize your involvement as only minor. If all that had happened was that you went with Michel wherever he went, that would be one thing, but you didn't.

The Defendant: Your Honor, I couldn't. Please try to know I couldn't do better. I don't know how to explain it to you. I couldn't do better. I couldn't stop it.

The Court: But you didn't have to go on trips to Florida.

The Defendant: They presented me — excuse me, but they presented me — the guy at the beginning, they didn't tell me that he was a salesman. I knew it. There was one guy in my apartment.

The Court: When you went to Florida and made that phone call, you certainly knew what you were doing then?

The Defendant: I was knowing at that time that I was meeting a guy that had a job to do with someone that was dealing with drugs in my apartment.

At that time when I gave the letter I didn't know it was to do with a transaction, although I was, of course, knowing that guy in my apartment was dealing with drugs, but I didn't know what was in the letter, and what was involved, what was inside the letter. I didn't know if there were to be an action then, but probably you realize that you are going to meet someone that they give a big problem, and they make a big fuss about reaching that guy, so I knew it was about drugs, but I didn't know it was really to — what kind of action it was to be in that thing, was going to be involved in that thing.

Of course, they never talked about drugs in front of me. They were talking about shirts or about furniture, business or whatever. Not always direct conversation. Never.

The Court: At the time you sewed up the . . .

The Defendant: At that time — can I explain to you how it happened? That day Michel — I was in the house and Michel told me, "I am going for the morning."

I said, "Okay."

He said, "I am going to be back for 12 o'clock," and he didn't come back at 12 o'clock. He came back at 5. At that time there was the nephew of Michel at home. They were on their honeymoon, and they were really bugging me about the fact that Michel was not in, that he might have had an accident, that he might have had a lot of problems and things like that. They didn't know that he was in that business. At that time I didn't know that Michel was going for that kind of business too, and when he came back to the house I was completely, completely to the ground. I thought first he had an accident, then he was arrested by the police. I didn't know what he was doing anyway, so Michel told me, "I am going to bring you where I was today because I have to go back tomorrow." I arrive over there, and it was a house. At the beginning I thought it was at some friends, but when I arrived, they were all talking silently, and then I realized at that time that they were making something wrong.

Michel told me at the beginning, "Don't move. Stay up here in the living room and if something happens tell us. If you see someone coming to the front door or the rear door, tell us," and nothing happened, so at one time Michel called me to go downstairs. I didn't know at the time what they were doing down there. I know it was illegal, but I didn't know there was drugs over there in that room at that time, so I came down, and I saw the whole thing, and they asked me to stay there.

So I was not going there knowing that there was going to be drugs, knowing that I was going to be asked to put the things inside, so I didn't really do it on purpose. I was brought there, and what can you do? Do you get out of the house and say, "My God, I am going to go to the police because I saw some drugs?"

Now, you don't do that. You are scared, and you just stay there, and you do whatever they ask you because there is about five guys over there, and they have seen you and they know you, and they know where to reach you if they want you. You cannot get out of it.

The Court: When was this episode in relation to your two trips?

The Defendant: I guess it was — my trip for the letter?

The Court: Yes.

The Defendant: To Miami?

The Court: Yes.

The Defendant: It was a little bit before, about a week before.

The Court: The trip was a week before?

The Defendant: Yes, about a week and a half or two.

The Court: What about your trip to Paris?

The Defendant: Bringing money there?

The Court: Yes.

The Defendant: Right after that, about a week and a half after that, but I really didn't make a relation in between the letter and the Fiat, no way.

The Court: As I said, this is a troublesome case, and it is one which has given me a great deal of concern, and although we don't have in this court as we do, as they do in Brooklyn, for example, in the Federal Court formal consultation among colleagues, this case has troubled me, and I have consulted with many of my colleagues to see what . . .

The Defendant: I understand, sir. I understand very well. I know that you base everything on the thing that has been done before. I know a part of the justice, but it is still a very — every story is different I guess. I couldn't talk to you. It is not permitted. I could have explained to you all of these things before, and a piece of paper cannot really explain it. I have looked at the sheet that was given to me of all the acts that I have been done. I almost collapsed. I couldn't believe that it was the fact cold like that. I know the involvements.

The Court: You are referring to the probation report?

The Defendant: No, to the accusations, and all my declarations. When I saw it on the paper, I couldn't believe that I have done all that. It was true.

The Court: What are you referring to, this paper?

The Defendant: Yes.

The Court: The probation report?

The Defendant: But I said to myself these are the facts, but I have reasons for that and how can I explain it. Everything is a different story. Everything is a different fear. Everything is a different non-possibility of getting out of it, and now I think I have proven that I wanted to do my best in by coming here every time, giving somebody up, although that I knew I was going to have problems anyway, but I felt if I could do something about it, it was to talk.

I was not, I was not liking what I was doing then. I couldn't get out of it. There was no way. I cannot explain that to you. That's why I am asking for mercy, because I really don't know what I would do as of that, if I go to jail, sir.

I had a depression. I probably will have my career completely finished because, of course, the radio station wouldn't keep me. I have no work that I can do after that, and no one will, no way, living in Montreal I was too much known. Of course, it doesn't continuate, if I can say the word properly, but there was a reason.

I know it was bad, but I think I really think that I have paid for it. Probably not completely, but it is not finished. My mother has no health any more. My father is not there. Probably not there any more. I have no money, no job, nothing. They are going to seize everything in my apartment. Where am I going from there, and if you put me in jail, that's the end. That's really, really the end.

I cannot see any future, and I guess that — I don't want to put a sentence in your mouth, but if there is justice somewhere, God, I need it. I really, really need it, sir.

I am much afraid of the future, and I know that my future is in your hands so, sir, I don't know what to do. It's something that I have to get out of it, otherwise I don't have anything for the future for sure.

I know that you have to give a judgment, but it is a special case, and I cannot explain exactly what you feel when you do such a thing. I cannot tell you. There is no words to explain what I have passed through, of course. There are other people that have passed through a lot of things, but I guess there is some reasons for what I have done, and the big one is that I could never, please try to believe when I tell you that I could never, never get out of that thing when I was there, never. I thought of it many times. How can you get out of it? And I was loving that guy when I should have had brains, you know. But at 23 it was the first time I was in love, the first time I was seeing things like that. I was dealing with things like that. If I would have been crooked, I would have probably been crooked myself, I would have known what to do, kill someone, hit someone, I don't know what, but I didn't know, so I went along, and I hope that I won't pay for that, please. I hope, I really hope, because I have nothing left. Thank you.

The Court: I think I will take a short recess.

(Recess.)

The Court: Mr. Nesland, Mr. Condello, he had two brothers?

Mr. Nesland: Yes, he did, your Honor.

The Court: And they were both . . .

Mr. Nesland: The charges were dismissed against his two brothers, and also against the girl friend, but that was a result of her co-operation against him, so that probably is contributable to Mr. Condello. What we had was a dismissal in the overall case of Condello, Condello's brothers, who were involved in the distribution of Condello's narcotics which he received from Perna. We had a dismissal of Perna's wife. We had the dismissal of Verzino's wife. She was dismissed last month by Judge Pecora, and I was present at that time, so you had those five dismissals as a result of the cooperation of those individuals.

The Court: Mastantuono got five years, and who got three, three and three?

Mr. Nesland: Roger Preiss and Richard Berdin both got three years. They cooperated prior to Mastantuono, and made the case against Mastantuono and Louis Cirillo.

The Court: I have three, three years here.

Mr. Nesland: And Tony Verzino who testified before your Honor. Mr. Perna who also testified has not been sentenced, but Mr. Verzino was sentenced by Judge Pecora and received a term of three years to life which is the minimum sentence that he could receive. The minimum was three to life. He had three to six on the conspiracy and one to life on the substantive which meant that the minimum term would be three to life. That's what he received.

The Court: All right, thank you. Anything further, Mr. Gross or Miss Ouimet?

Mr. Gross: I don't think so, your Honor. Thank you very much, and I don't think she should say anything more either so thank you, your Honor.

The Court: Well, as I started to say, the problem in a sentence is to try to give both the appearance of equality of justice and fact, and this seems difficult in this situation. Four of the persons who have cooperated and two of whose testimony was essential to this case have been sentenced to five and three years respectively. Of course, the five years that Mr. Mastantuono got were before his cooperation, although that must have been in contemplation of some cooperation that he got only five years.

Mr. Nesland: I don't think that's accurate, your Honor. He began cooperating in June of 1972 and was sentenced in May 1973 by Judge Weinfeld so it was prior to it. Obviously the only thing before Judge Weinfeld was the grand jury item of Mastantuono. He had not testified at the trial. The only trial he has testified in is the one before your Honor, but he had given the grand jury testimony.

Mr. Gross: Your Honor, I don't mean to impose, and I am sorry because your Honor did ask me, and I didn't say anything. I happen to know the involvement of Roger Preiss and Richard Berdin because I don't think this is improper. I was the Assistant on the Cirillo case. Roger Preiss and Richard Berdin were two of the largest narcotics smugglers that ever came into the United States, and to put her anywhere near that category, to me, your Honor, respectfully, is a little difficult.

I met with both those men, and they were two of the largest narcotics smugglers to be apprehended by the old Bureau of Narcotics and Dangerous Drugs in the last five years, and she was a 23-year old girl who was used to deliver a message. I am sorry, your Honor, to interrupt.

The Court: Is that a correct observation about them?

Mr. Nesland: Yes, your Honor. I think they are probably on a par with Mastantuono. He is correct that they are one of the biggest that have been apprehended. I think they are one of the biggest.

The Court: Well, then on the other hand we have Mrs. Verzino and Mrs. Perna and the two Condello brothers and Condello himself. When I first looked at this situation it seemed to me those persons were in a different category than Miss Ouimet because the

Court had no — was given no option in their case, and the Court had no imput into the situation, and therefore they can't be considered relevant. However, in thinking it over, I am not sure that it is a valid point of view. As far as Mrs. Verzino and Mrs. Perna and Miss Ouimet are concerned, the government is the government, and the government isn't compartmentalized between courts, prosecutors and police so the net impact of this whole prosecution is that Mrs. Verzino and Mrs. Perna — I don't remember Mrs. Perna's activities in the case.

Mr. Nesland: I can outline it for you if you want. I think it is easier if you just start with Mrs. Verzino.

The Court: I remember her.

Mr. Nesland: Mrs. Verzino received the narcotics from Bubbie Sorenson. She then diluted the narcotics, put it in safe deposit boxes, and when it was to be distributed, gave it to Mrs. Perna who then distributed it to customers on the street that she had prior to the time that she even knew Perna.

You have to understand with Perna's wife, he and her were not even known to each other at the time that she received the narcotics. She was just a street distributor, and she had customers, and Suzie Verzino sold it to Cuzzie Perna who in turn distributed it on the street. That's the relationship there.

The Court: She got her immunity as a result of the Government's bargain with Perna?

Mr. Nesland: That is correct.

The Court: As I said, when I first approached this question, and I must say in my conversations with my colleagues to which I referred earlier, it had seemed to me that Verzino and Perna's situations were not relevant for the reasons I have just stated, but I now call that judgment into question for the reason I just indicated, that the point of view of the individuals involved, the Government isn't a compartmentalized operation. The Government is the Government.

So we have the situation where these two people, as far as I know, neither Mrs. Verzino nor Mrs. Perna contributed anything of their own to the prosecution. Is that correct?

Mr. Nesland: They haven't testified at trial, no.

The Court: Have they given material to Assistants?

Mr. Nesland: They have given information, your Honor, yes, and I would say in part for tactical reasons they were not called, and I think it is clear from the trial, your Honor, why they wouldn't be.

The Court: Sure, obvious. Then we come to Miss Ouimet, and I agree with the government that her testimony was of material value.

Actually what she said on direct examination didn't amount to anything, which isn't her fault. What she testified to is what happened, and had she not been cross examined, her net impact of her testimony might have been minimal, but she was cross examined at length, and to her credit, and the impact of her testimony was due to the fact that she was obviously telling the truth, and that that rubbed off on Mastantuono, and also the conversations which were brought out between her and Mastantuono on cross-examination demonstrated the fact that his testimony in turn had been truthful.

So I can't speculate what would happen if she hadn't been called. It is certainly obvious that her testimony strengthened the government's case materially, and it might well have been the difference between a conviction and a hung jury. I doubt if there would have been an acquittal in the case even without her.

So I come back to the proposition that I don't think that her role can be regarded as minimal, but it is certainly no greater than what you have just described Mr. Verzino and Mrs. Perna's role to have been, and also although I don't say that Miss Ouimet is being untruthful to the Court today in the sense that I think she is deliberately saying anything that she doesn't now believe, it is quite clear to me that she has minimized in her own recollection the state of knowledge and awareness of what was going on, and I am not being cynical about that. That is a human reaction. However, in the light of the appearance of even-handed justice I don't think I could consider her in a different light than Mrs. Verzino and Mrs. Perna, and I don't know what the Condello brothers did. Condello himself, of course, was in a different category because his testimony was more crucial, and the case couldn't have got off the ground I imagine without him, but if I categorize with Mrs. Verzino and Mrs. Perna as I have concluded, which I must do, I have no alternative but to suspend sentence which I shall do, and place her on probation for a period of five years. That is the sentence of the Court.

Mr. Gross: Thank you, your Honor.

The Defendant: Thank you. Thank you very much.